Step by Step

Microsoft®
Visio®
Version 2002

 Microsoft® Office Family Member

Resources Online

C000193091

PUBLISHED BY
Microsoft Press
A Division of Microsoft Corporation
One Microsoft Way
Redmond, Washington 98052-6399

Library of Congress Cataloging-in-Publication Data
Microsoft Visio Version 2002 Step by Step / Resources Online.
        p. cm.
    Includes index.
    ISBN 0-7356-1302-8
    1. Computer graphics. 2. Microsoft Visio. I. Resources Online.

    T385 .M5238 2001
    650'.0285'66869--dc21   2001041067

Printed and bound in the United States of America.

1 2 3 4 5 6 7 8 9   QWT   6 5 4 3 2 1

Distributed in Canada by Penguin Books Canada Limited.

A CIP catalogue record for this book is available from the British Library.

Microsoft Press books are available through booksellers and distributors worldwide. For further information about international editions, contact your local Microsoft Corporation office or contact Microsoft Press International directly at fax (425) 706-7329. Visit our Web site at www.microsoft.com/mspress. Send comments to *mspinput@microsoft.com*.

Acquisitions Editor: Kong Cheung
Project Editor: Jenny Moss Benson

Body Part No. X08-06250

Contents

1   Creating a Diagram   1

2   Adding Shapes to Diagrams   18

3   Formatting Shapes and Diagrams   40

Contents

9 Using Visio with Office XP   164

10 Customizing Shapes and Templates   186

What's New in Microsoft Visio 2002

You'll notice some changes as soon as you start Microsoft Visio 2002. The toolbars and menu bar have a new look, and there's a new task pane on the right side of your screen when you start the program to help you find the right drawing type. But the features that are new or greatly improved in this version of Visio go beyond just changes in appearance. Some changes won't be apparent to you until you start using the program.

To help you quickly identify features that are new or enhanced with this version, this book uses the New Features icon in the margin whenever those features are discussed or shown.

The following table lists the new features that we think you'll be interested in, as well as the chapters in which those features are discussed.

To learn how to	Using this new feature	See
Create new and open existing drawings	Task pane	Chapter 1, page 7
Work with menus that remember the commands you use most	Personalized menus	Chapter 1, page 10
Save space on the screen	Window merging	Chapter 1, page 10
Find an answer to a question	Ask A Question box	Chapter 1, page 15
Locate a shape	Find Shape command	Chapter 2, page 35
Export a timeline to create a Gantt chart	Export Project Data Wizard	Chapter 5, page 92
Save and display shape data when you save a diagram as a Web page	Custom Properties pane	Chapter 6, page 124
Work with new office furniture shapes	Cubicles stencil	Chapter 7, page 137
Format a picture	Picture command	Chapter 7, page 143
Format an object with a transparent color	Transparency slider	Chapter 7, page 143
Create reports based on drawing data	Report command	Chapter 8, page 160

Some new features are beyond the scope of this book. However, you can easily find out more about them. In Visio, type the name of the feature in the Ask A Question box at the top of the Visio window, and then press [Enter].

Feature	Description
Directional Map 3D template	You can create maps with a 3-D look.
Network equipment shapes	You can use up-to-date shapes such as the **Flat screen monitor** and **Tower PC** shapes on the **Basic Network Shapes** stencil.
Curved wall shape	Office layout diagrams can now include curved and straight walls.
Scanner and digital camera interface	You can directly import pictures from digital cameras or scanners.
Microsoft Clip Organizer	If you have Office XP installed with Visio, you can directly access the Clip Organizer from within Visio.
Office XP compatibility	Visio includes the same features as other Office programs, such as built-in AutoCorrect features, Office spelling checker, keyboard shortcuts, and **Open**, **Save**, and **Save As** dialog boxes
Auto save and recovery	Visio can save your drawing files automatically at specified time intervals. If an error occurs, the recovered file is opened so that you can recover changes.
AutoCorrect (Intellisense)	You can insert, correct, and format text as you type, just as in Word.
Integration with Microsoft Project	You can import .mpx files in Visio to generate timelines and Gantt charts.
Timeline/Gantt chart interoperability	Not only can you export a timeline to create a Gantt chart, you can also export a Gantt chart to create a timeline.
Synchronize employee shapes	When you use the **Organization Chart Wizard**, you can synchronize shapes that represent the same employee on different pages.
Organization chart layout	Shapes drop into position automatically and maintain their positions when you add more shapes.
Organization chart properties	Shapes can include an unlimited number of custom properties, and you can select the properties that are displayed on shapes.
CAD conversion	You can convert individual objects created in a computer-aided design (CAD) program.

Feature	Description
Export to Database command	Database integration features are consolidated into one dialog box.
Save as XML	You can save a Visio drawing, stencil, or template in a native XML format.
Find command	You can now search within custom properties, shape names, and user-defined cells.
Smooth text	Smoother text and lines look better on the screen, but you can choose faster text display with the **Options** command on the **Tools** menu.
PowerPoint integration	Visio drawings can adopt a presentation's color scheme when you create the diagram in PowerPoint.
Auto Update	A utility on the Visio Web site can analyze your Visio installation and recommend needed updates.

For more information about the Visio product, see *http:/www.Microsoft.com/office /visio*, or in Visio, click **Visio on the Web** on the **Help** menu.

Getting Help

Every effort has been made to ensure the accuracy of this book and the contents of its CD-ROM. If you do run into problems, please contact the appropriate source for help and assistance:

Getting Help with This Book and Its CD-ROM

If your question or issue concerns the content of this book or its companion CD-ROM, please first search the online Microsoft Knowledge Base, which provides support information for known errors in or corrections to this book, at the following Web site:

http://www.microsoft.com/mspress/support/search.asp

If you do not find your answer at the online Knowledge Base, send your comments or questions to Microsoft Press Technical Support at:

mspinput@microsoft.com

Getting Help with Microsoft Visio 2002

If your question is about a Microsoft software product, including Visio, and not about the content of this Microsoft Press book, please search the Microsoft Knowledge Base at:

http://support.microsoft.com/directory

In the United States, Microsoft software product support issues not covered by the Microsoft Knowledge Base are addressed by Microsoft Product Support Services. The Microsoft software support options available from Microsoft Product Support Services are listed at:

http://support.microsoft.com/directory

Outside the United States, for support information specific to your location, please refer to the Worldwide Support menu on the Microsoft Product Support Services Web site for the site specific to your country:

http://support.microsoft.com/directory

Using the Book's CD-ROM

The CD-ROM inside the back cover of this book contains tools that you'll need to learn and work with Microsoft Visio.

- A 30-day evaluation version of Visio Standard 2002 that you can install now and use while you work through the exercises in this book.
- Multimedia demos that show you how to complete common tasks in Visio.
- Practice files that you'll use as you work through the exercises in this book.

Important

You should install the evaluation version or a full version of Visio 2002 before using this book.

System Requirements

To use this book, your computer should meet the following requirements:

Computer/Processor

Computer with a Pentium 166-megahertz (MHz) or higher processor

Memory

RAM requirements depend on the operating system used.

- Microsoft Windows 98, or Windows 98 Second Edition
  24 MB of RAM
- Microsoft Windows Millennium Edition (Windows Me), or Microsoft Windows NT 4.0
  32 MB of RAM
- Microsoft Windows 2000 Professional
  64 MB of RAM

Hard Disk

- 7 MB of hard disk space is required for installing the practice files

Operating System

Windows 98, Windows 98 Second Edition, Windows Me, Windows NT 4.0 with Service Pack 6 or later, or Windows 2000 or later. (On systems running Windows NT 4.0 with Service Pack 6, the version of Microsoft Internet Explorer must be upgraded to at least version 4.01 with Service Pack 1.)

Drive

CD-ROM drive

Display

Super VGA (800 × 600) or higher-resolution monitor with 256 colors

Peripherals

Microsoft Mouse, Microsoft IntelliMouse, or compatible pointing device

Applications

Microsoft Visio 2002

Microsoft Word 2002 recommended

Installing Visio 2002 Evaluation Software

This book's CD-ROM contains a 30-day trial version of Visio Standard 2002, which helps business professionals document and share ideas and information visually.

Tip

If you would like to order a 30-day trial of Visio Professional 2002, which helps business and technical professionals understand and communicate technical information, visit the Visio Trial Web site to order: *http://www.microsoft.com/office/visio/trial.htm*

The trial included on this CD is in English. To find information about Visio 2002 trial availability in your country or region, visit our Office Sites Worldwide page: *http://www.microsoft.com/office/worldwide.htm*

The trial version that's included on this CD has some important limitations:

- This trial is intended for evaluation purposes only.
- Each trial can be installed and activated on only one computer.
- There is no product support for this trial.

■ The first time you start Visio 2002, the Office Activation Wizard will automatically appear and walk you through the online activation process. The trial will not be fully functional until you complete this process. You'll need to activate using the Internet option; phone activation won't work for this trial.

■ If you order the Visio Professional 2002 trial, you must remove any previous version of Visio installed on your computer before installing the trial. If you want the option to reinstall that previous version after the trial has expired, you must have a copy of the installation source for it (for example, the installation CDs).

■ This trial allows only one activation on one computer. If you do a significant hardware upgrade while the trial is still active, you will be prompted to reactivate the trial but will be unable to do so.

System Requirements for the Evaluation Software

To use Microsoft Visio Standard, you need:

■ PC with Pentium 166-MHz or higher processor; Pentium III recommended

■ Microsoft Windows 98, Windows 98 Second Edition, Windows Millennium Edition, or Windows NT 4.0 with Service Pack 6 or later (requires Microsoft Internet Explorer 4.01 browser software with Service Pack 1 or later), or Windows 2000 Professional or later operating system

For Windows 98 and Windows 98 Second Edition:

■ 24 MB of RAM for the operating system plus an additional 16 MB of RAM for Visio Standard

For Windows Me, Windows NT Workstation 4.0, or Windows NT Server 4.0:

■ 32 MB of RAM for the operating system plus an additional 16 MB of RAM for Visio Standard

For Windows 2000 Professional:

■ 64 MB of RAM for the operating system plus an additional 16 MB of RAM for Visio Standard

■ 110 MB of available hard disk space (hard disk usage will vary depending on configuration; custom installation choices may require more or less hard disk space)

■ VGA (640 x 480) or higher-resolution monitor with 256 colors; Super VGA (800 x 600) recommended

■ Microsoft Mouse, Microsoft IntelliMouse, or compatible pointing device

Additional items or services required to use certain features:

- 9600-baud modem; 14,400 or higher baud recommended
- Some Internet functionality may require Internet access and payment of a separate fee to a service provider; local and/or long-distance telephone toll charges may apply
- Collaboration features compatible with Office 97 or later

Instructions for Installation

Important

To activate the trial version of Microsoft Visio Standard 2002, you will need to be connected to the Internet. You can't activate the trial using the phone option.

1 Insert the CD-ROM into the CD-ROM drive of your computer.

A starting menu appears.

Tip

If the menu screen does not appear, start Windows Explorer. In the left pane, locate the icon for your CD-ROM and click this icon. In the right pane, double-click the file **StartCD.exe**.

2 Close any Windows programs that are running.

3 Click **Install Visio Trial**.

The installation wizard will walk you through the setup.

4 You will be prompted to enter a Product Key. This number can be found on the CD sleeve bound inside this book.

5 The first time you start Visio 2002, the **Office Activation Wizard** will automatically appear and walk you through the online activation process. The trial will not be fully functional until you complete this process.

Important

There is no product support for this trial.

Installing the Practice Files

You need to install the practice files on your hard disk before you use them in the chapters' exercises. Follow these steps to prepare the CD's files for your use:

1 Insert the CD-ROM into the CD-ROM drive of your computer.

A starting menu appears.

Tip

If the starting menu does not appear, start Windows Explorer. In the left pane, locate the icon for your CD-ROM and click this icon. In the right pane, double-click the file **StartCD.exe**.

2 Click **Install Practice Files**.

3 Click **OK** in the initial message box.

4 If you want to install the practice files to a location other than the default folder (C:\SBS\Visio), click the **Change Folder** button, select the new drive and path, and then click **OK**.

Important

If you install the practice files to a location other than the default folder, the file location listed in some of the book's exercises will be incorrect.

5 Click the **Continue** button to install the selected practice files.

6 After the practice files have been installed, click **OK**.

A folder will be installed on your hard disk: C:\SBS\Visio. Within that folder are subfolders for each chapter in the book.

7 Remove the CD-ROM from the CD-ROM drive, and return it to the envelope at the back of the book.

Using the Practice Files

Each chapter's introduction lists the files that are needed for that chapter and explains any file preparation that you need to take care of before you start working through the chapter.

ExpoLayout

Each topic in the chapter explains how and when to use any practice files. The file or files that you'll need are indicated in the margin at the beginning of the procedure above the CD icon.

The following table lists each chapter's practice files.

Chapter	Folder	Files
Chapter 1: Creating a Diagram	Creating	ExpoHelp ExpoLayout
Chapter 2: Adding Shapes to Diagrams	Adding	BlockEditing BlockFinding BlockMoving BlockSaving BlockStarting
Chapter 3: Formatting Shapes and Diagrams	Formatting	FormatDecorate FormatPrint FormatScheme FormatShapes
Chapter 4: Connecting Shapes	Connecting	ConnectGroup ConnectLayout ConnectModify
Chapter 5: Creating Project Schedules	Projects	GanttChart NewGantt Timeline
Chapter 6: Creating an Organization Chart	OrgChart	OrgChart OrgChartCustom OrgChartLayout OrgChartWeb TGC Employees.xls TGC Logo.gif
Chapter 7: Laying Out Office Space	OfficeLayout	OfficeFurnished OfficeLogo OfficeWalls TGC Logo.gif
Chapter 8: Creating a Network Diagram	Networks	NetwkCP NetwkRpt Network
Chapter 9: Using Visio with Office XP	OfficeXP	PlanPhase Proposal.doc TimelinePrelim
Chapter 10: Customizing Shapes and Templates	Customizing	CreateStencil EditShapes GroupShapes Perennials

Uninstalling the Practice Files

After you finish working through this book, you should uninstall the practice files to free up hard disk space.

Tip

If you saved any files outside the SBS folder, they will not be deleted by the following uninstall process. You'll have to manually delete them. For example, you can use Windows Explorer to search your hard disk for Visio files (*.vsd, *.vss, and *.vst), and then delete them.

1 On the Windows taskbar, click the **Start** button, point to **Settings**, and then click **Control Panel**.

2 Double-click the **Add/Remove Programs** icon.

3 In the list of installed programs, click **Microsoft Visio 2002 SBS Files**, and then click **Add/Remove**. (If you're using Windows 2000 Professional, click the **Remove** or **Change/Remove** button.)

4 Click **Yes** when the confirmation dialog box appears.

Important

If you need additional help installing or uninstalling the practice files, please see the section "Getting Help" earlier in this book. Microsoft's product support does not provide support for this book or its CD-ROM.

Watching the Multimedia Demos

This book's CD-ROM contains multimedia demos that demonstrate how to create and use Visio diagrams and drawings.

To view the demos, you'll need Microsoft Windows Media Player (version 6.4 and the Windows Media Player 7 video decompressor, or Windows Media Player 7 or later). In case you need to install or upgrade Windows Media Player, this book's CD contains both version 6.4 and version 7.1. You'll also need to be connected to the Internet in case you need to install the video decompressor or Macromedia Flash Player.

To determine what version of Media Player is already installed on your computer, launch the Windows Media Player (which is usually found by clicking the **Start** button, pointing to **Programs**, pointing to **Accessories**, and then pointing to **Entertainment**). Start Media Player, and then on the **Help** menu, click **About Windows Media Player**.

- If you are using Microsoft Windows 95 or Microsoft Windows NT 4.0, you should install Microsoft Windows Media Player 6.4. Your video decompressor version will be detected by Windows Media Player, and, if necessary, an updated version will be downloaded from the Internet.

- If you are using Microsoft Windows 98, you should install Microsoft Windows Media Player 7.1.

- If you are using Microsoft Windows 2000, you already have Windows Media Player 6.4. Your video decompressor version will be detected by Windows Media Player, and, if necessary, an updated version will be downloaded from the Internet.

- If you are using Microsoft Windows Millennium Edition, you already have Windows Media Player 7, but you can upgrade to version 7.1 if you want.

To install Microsoft Windows Media Player 6.4 (for Microsoft Windows 95 and Microsoft Windows NT 4.0 only):

1 Insert the CD-ROM into the CD-ROM drive of your computer.

A starting menu appears.

2 Click **Install Media Player**.

3 On the **Install Windows Media Player** page that appears, click the link **Windows Media Player Version 6.4**

OR

Open the MPlayer folder and double-click the **MPfull.exe** file.

4 Click the **Run this program from its current location** option.

5 Follow the prompts that appear on your screen.

To install Microsoft Windows Media Player 7.1

1 Insert the CD-ROM into the CD-ROM drive of your computer.

A starting menu appears.

2 Click **Install Media Player**.

3 On the **Install Windows Media Player** page that appears, click the link **Windows Media Player version 7.1.**

OR

Open the MPlayer folder and double-click the **MP71.exe** file.

4 Click the **Run this program from its current location** option.

5 Follow the prompts that appear on your screen.

To View a Demo

To view the demonstration files, you will need to be connected to the Internet in case you need to download Windows Media Player components or Macromedia Flash Player.

1 Insert the CD-ROM into the CD-ROM drive of your computer.

A starting menu appears.

Tip

If the starting menu does not appear, start Windows Explorer. In the left pane, locate the icon for your CD-ROM and click this icon. In the right pane, double-click the file **StartCD.exe**.

2 On the starting menu, click **Visio Multimedia Demos**.

3 On the **Explore Microsoft Visio** page that appears, click the demo that you want to view.

If you're using version 7.0 or 7.1 of Windows Media Player, you'll need to change to full screen mode to view the demos correctly. On the **View** menu, click **Full Screen**.

Demo Name	Description
Introducing Microsoft Visio	Learn how Visio can help you work and communicate more effectively with this brief multimedia presentation.
Flowcharts	Drag and drop Visio shapes to create flowcharts, easily add a professional look, and share diagrams in Office documents.
Project Schedules	Generate project timelines from data stored in Microsoft Project; update diagrams after inserting them into Office documents.
Organization Charts	Create organization charts from scratch or using existing data, and then publish them as detailed Web pages.
Custom Shapes	Use Visio drawing tools to create custom shapes, and then store them with other images on stencils for easy reuse.
Network Diagrams	Document network equipment using shapes with built-in custom property fields for easy asset tracking.

Demo Name	Description
Active Directory Diagrams	Diagram proposed directory services structures, and then export the information to Active Directory to assist in Windows 2000 migration.
Network AutoDiscovery	Accurately document network topologies with AutoDiscovery technology and exact-replica Visio Network Equipment shapes.
Database Diagrams	Reverse-engineer database schema for SQL Server 2000 databases and other popular databases to document and understand their structures.
Software Diagrams	Plan software development using the Unified Modeling Language, or reverse-engineer Microsoft Visual Studio projects.
Web Site Maps	Map existing Web sites to identify broken links or to determine how a proposed change will fit into an existing site structure.
Custom Solutions	Automate tasks in Visio using built-in Visual Basic for Applications 6.3, a flexible object model, and Automation.
Space Plans	Easily create scaled space plans using intelligent shapes that represent walls, doors, windows, and furniture.
Floor Plans	Populate floor plans with data from common sources, and even color-code the diagram by any data field.
Engineering Schematics	Create a wide variety of engineering drawings and schematics using common electrical symbols and connectors.

Conventions and Features

You can save time when you use this book by understanding how the Step by Step series shows special instructions, keys to press, buttons to click, and so on.

Convention	Meaning
1 **2**	Numbered steps guide you through hands-on exercises in each topic.
●	A round bullet indicates an exercise that has only one step.
Filename (CD icon)	This icon at the beginning of a chapter lists the files that the chapter will use and explains any file preparation that needs to take place before starting the chapter. Practice files that you'll need to use in a topic's procedure are shown above the CD icon.
new for **Office**XP	This icon indicates a new or greatly improved feature in this version of Microsoft Visio.
Tip	This section provides a helpful hint or shortcut that makes working through a task easier.
Important	This section points out information that you need to know to complete the procedure.
Troubleshooting	This section shows you how to fix a common problem.
Save (button icon)	When a button is referenced in a topic, a picture of the button appears in the margin area with a label.
Alt + Tab	A plus sign (+) between two key names means that you must press those keys at the same time. For example, "Press Alt + Tab" means that you hold down the Alt key while you press Tab.
Black boldface type	Program features that you click or press are shown in black boldface type.
Blue boldface type	Terms that are explained in the glossary at the end of the book are shown in blue boldface type within the chapter.
Red boldface type	Text that you are supposed to type appears in red boldface type in the procedures.

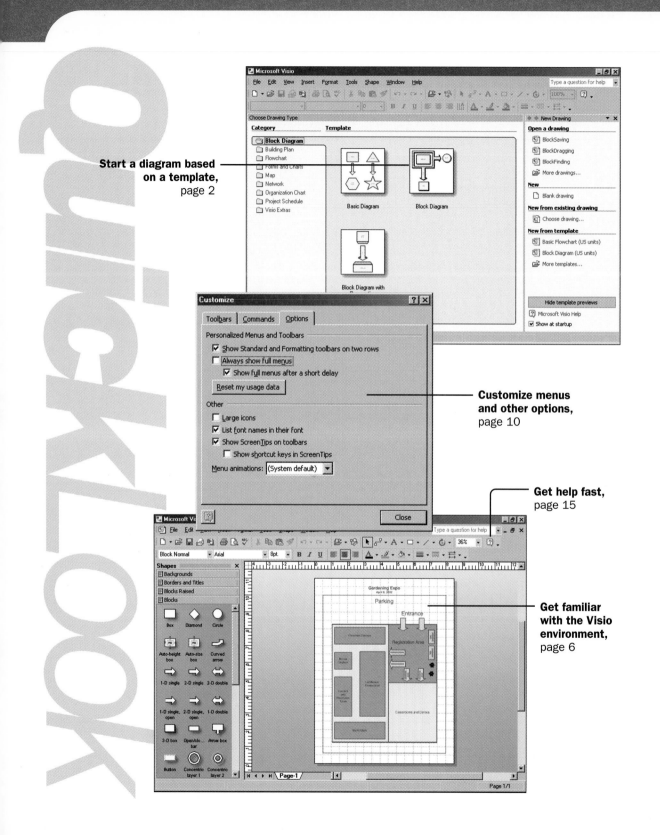

Start a diagram based on a template, page 2

Customize menus and other options, page 10

Get help fast, page 15

Get familiar with the Visio environment, page 6

Chapter 1
Creating a Diagram

After completing this chapter, you will be able to:

✔ **Start Visio.**
✔ **Identify template and stencil files.**
✔ **Open templates to create drawings.**
✔ **Identify features of the drawing environment.**
✔ **Customize the drawing environment.**
✔ **Display, reposition, and close stencils.**
✔ **Get online Help.**

Have you ever tried to explain a new team organization or inter-departmental process in an e-mail message or memo only to find that no one quite understood? Did you ever give a presentation about critical project milestones and watch your audience walk away with a puzzled expression? Each situation represents an ideal time to use Microsoft Visio 2002, the business drawing and diagramming application that helps you communicate visually. With Visio, you can *show* your audience what you mean by using clear diagrams, such as organization charts, flowcharts, and project timelines. Whether you need to convey a new business process or create a map to the company picnic, you can do it using Visio—and no particular artistic talent is required.

This book can help you clarify your message visually with Visio drawings and diagrams. This chapter will first show you the different ways to start a Visio diagram. Then you will be introduced to the types of drawings and diagrams in Visio. You will also learn how to customize the drawing tools. Finally, you will practice using online Help to answer any questions that might arise while you work.

 This chapter uses the practice files ExpoLayout and ExpoHelp that you installed from the CD-ROM. For details about installing the practice files, see "Using the Book's CD-ROM" at the beginning of this book.

Starting Visio

Regardless of your drawing abilities, Visio makes it easy for you to create all types of diagrams and drawings. **Shapes** that you **drag and drop** in a drawing are your key to quick and effective diagrams. A shape is a pre-drawn symbol. For example, in an organization chart, you might use an employee shape—a decorative box that can display a name and job title—whereas in a flowchart, you might use a decision shape—a diamond that displays text about a decision in a process. By dragging shapes onto a page, you can assemble a complete diagram.

The easiest way to start a diagram is with a **template**, which is the kit for building a particular type of drawing. It's always best to start with a template in Visio, because the template opens all the shapes you need. For example, if you want to create a flowchart, use the **Basic Flowchart** template, which includes shapes for indicating process, decision, data, and other flowchart controls. Templates also set up the drawing page and formatting styles for you. Most templates set up a letter-sized page suitable for printing on a desktop printer, and text styles that ensure your text is attractive and readable. In addition, some templates even add special-purpose commands or toolbars, such as the Organization Chart toolbar, which makes it easy to rearrange employees in a drawing you start with the **Organization Chart** template.

Visio organizes templates by category, a group of related drawing types, as the table below shows.

Template Category	Purpose
Block Diagram	Create general-purpose graphics that show relationships.
Building Plan	Arrange office space and furniture.
Flowchart	Create audit diagrams, basic flowcharts, cause and effect (fishbone) diagrams, cross-functional flowcharts, mind mapping diagrams, total quality management (TQM) charts, and workflow diagrams.
Forms and Charts	Design business forms and quick charts, graphs, and diagrams for presentations.
Map	Draw simple street maps and attractive 3-D maps.
Network	Use shapes that look like network equipment to document small or medium-sized networks.
Organization Chart	Show reporting structures in an organization. Use the Organization Chart Wizard to import employee information and create a chart for yourself.
Project Schedule	Track project details in PERT charts, Gantt charts, timelines, and calendars.

Visio stores shapes on **stencils**. You can drag a shape from a stencil onto the drawing page to create a diagram. Visio distinguishes between a **master shape**—which is the original shape that appears on a stencil—and the copy of the shape that you drag onto a drawing. You don't need to open a template first in order to open a stencil; you can open stencils at any time to add shapes to a diagram.

Tip

If a template doesn't seem to create the particular drawing you need, open a template that looks close to what you want. For example, you can use the **Basic Flowchart** template to create a data flow diagram. You can always add more shapes if the template didn't open all of the ones you need.

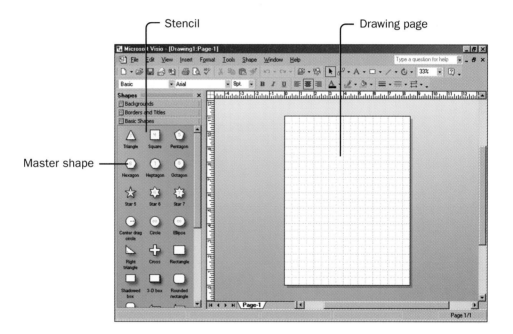

Stencil | Drawing page

Master shape

Visio Standard vs. Visio Professional

This book describes how to use Visio Standard to create common business diagrams. Visio Professional is geared toward technical business professionals. What's the difference between the two products? In a word: shapes. Visio Professional includes all the shapes that come with Visio Standard, as well as special-purpose shapes for creating detailed network diagrams, database and software models, engineering schematics, and building plans. All of the information in this book also applies to Visio Professional. Visio displays the version name when you first start it, or you can click the **About Microsoft Visio** command on the **Help** menu to determine your version.

Templates, stencils, and drawings represent the three different types of files that you can open and create in Visio. Each is associated with a different file extension. When you browse files in Windows Explorer, these file extensions are indicated in the following manner:

File Extension	File Type
.vst	Visio template file
.vss	Visio stencil file
.vsd	Visio drawing file

In this exercise, you start Visio and then browse the available templates. You start a new drawing with a template, review the stencils opened by the template, and then start with a different template.

1   On the taskbar, click **Start**, point to **Programs**, and then click **Microsoft Visio**.

Task pane

new for
OfficeXP

Visio opens with the **Choose Drawing Type** task pane on the left and the **New Drawing** task pane on the right.

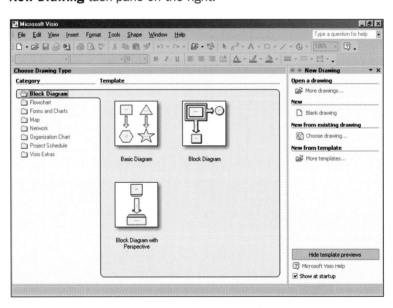

2   In the **Category** list, click **Flowchart**.

In the **Template** area, the template names are listed and sample diagrams are displayed.

3   Point to **Basic Flowchart**.

In the lower left corner, a description of the template appears.

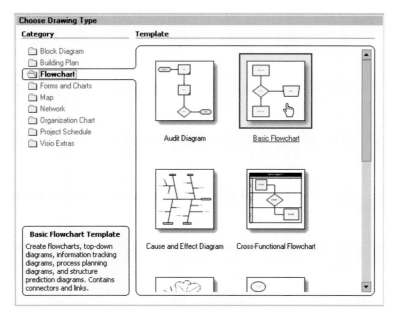

4 In the **Category** list, click **Block Diagram**.

In the **Template** area, the **Basic Diagram** template, the **Block Diagram** template, and the **Block Diagram with Perspective** template appear with sample diagrams.

5 In the **Template** area, click **Basic Diagram**.

Visio creates a new, blank diagram and opens the **Basic Shapes** stencil, the **Borders and Titles** stencil, and the **Backgrounds** stencil.

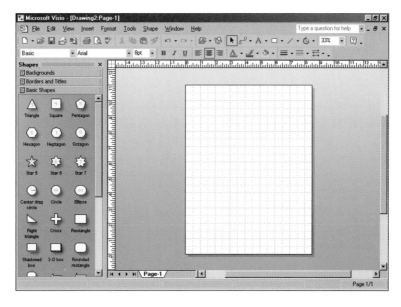

6 On the **File** menu, click **Close** to close the diagram and stencils.

7 On the **View** menu, click **Task Pane**.

The **Choose Drawing Type** and **New Drawing** task panes appear again.

8 In the **Template** area, click **Block Diagram**.

If you don't see the **Block Diagram** template, in the **Category** list, click **Block Diagram**. Visio creates a new, blank diagram and opens the following four stencils: **Blocks**, **Blocks Raised**, **Borders and Titles**, and **Backgrounds**.

Close

✖

9 In the gray area of the drawing page window, click the **Close** button.

Visio closes the new drawing without saving changes and remains open.

Troubleshooting

The **Close** button in the upper right side of the **Microsoft Visio** title bar closes the drawing *and* Visio. In step 9, make sure to click the **Close** button that is below the title bar.

10 On the **Microsoft Visio** title bar, click the **Close** button.

Visio closes.

Getting Acquainted with Visio

When you start a diagram using a template, Visio sets up the windows, menus, and tools you use to create a particular type of drawing. You can change the look of Visio to fit your needs by changing the display and arrangement of windows, the drawing page grid and rulers, and toolbars.

The **drawing page** resembles graph paper with its **grid** of criss-crossing lines that help you align and space shapes evenly. The horizontal and vertical **rulers** also help you align shapes and show you the size of the page as it will be printed. Above the drawing page are the Standard and Formatting toolbars, which contain the most commonly used commands for creating, editing, and formatting shapes. (If you use other Microsoft Office programs, many of the buttons should look familiar to you.) Below the drawing page, the page tabs help you switch among pages in multiple-page drawings, and the status bar displays information about selected shapes on the drawing page. The light blue area surrounding the drawing page is the **pasteboard**, which you can use as a temporary holding area for shapes and other drawing elements. Objects on the pasteboard aren't printed.

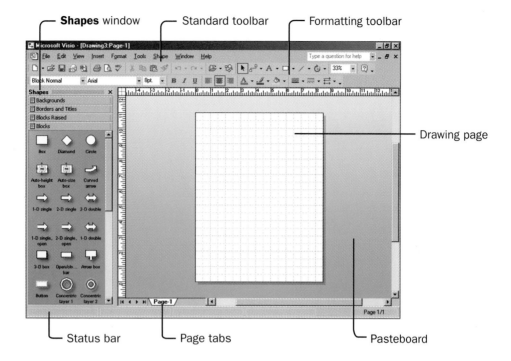

Shapes window — Standard toolbar — Formatting toolbar

Drawing page

Status bar — Page tabs — Pasteboard

When you start a new drawing using a template, the entire drawing page is the first view you see. As you assemble your diagram and add shapes, you can zoom in for a closer view of an area or back away for a broader view. Visio provides several ways to zoom in and out, including a toolbar button and keyboard shortcuts. One method isn't necessarily faster than another—you can do what works best for you. To see more of a page, especially when you're zoomed in, you can **pan** a drawing, which is like grabbing the page with your hand and moving it. Zooming and panning help you work efficiently in Visio.

In this exercise, you explore the fundamental parts of the Visio drawing window. You display stencils in the **Shapes** window and then zoom and pan the drawing page.

1 Start Visio.

Task pane

new for
OfficeXP

2 In the **New Drawing** task pane, click **Block Diagram (US units)** in the **New from template** list.

Visio creates a new, blank block diagram and opens four stencils.

3 In the **Shapes** window on the left, click **Blocks Raised**.

The **Blocks Raised** stencil is displayed on top, and the **Blocks** stencil is minimized at the bottom.

7

Troubleshooting

If a menu appears when you click **Blocks Raised**, you clicked the green icon on the stencil by mistake. Make sure to click in the gray part of the stencil's title bar or directly on the stencil name.

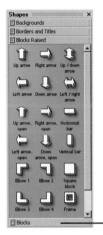

———— Minimized stencil

4 Click the **Blocks** stencil to display it on top.

5 Drag the scroll bar on the **Blocks** stencil down to the bottom, if necessary.

Visio displays the additional master shapes on the **Blocks** stencil.

Troubleshooting

Your monitor's display resolution and the size of your Visio window determine whether a scroll bar appears on the **Blocks** stencil. Because of these factors, your screen might not exactly match the illustrations in this book. If you don't see a scroll bar on the stencil, that means all the master shapes are already visible.

6 Scroll to the top of the **Blocks** stencil.

7 Point to the **Box** shape.

A ScreenTip appears that describes the shape's purpose.

8 Drag the **Box** shape onto the drawing page, and as you drag, watch the status bar at the bottom of the Visio window.

Visio displays the shape's position on the page as measured from the horizontal and vertical rulers.

| Left = 1 in. | Right = 2.5 in. | Bottom = 7.5 in. | Top = 8.5 in. |

9 Release the mouse.

The shape remains selected, and the status bar displays its width, height, and angle of rotation.

Zoom

| 33% | ▼ |

10 On the Standard toolbar, click the **Zoom** down arrow to display a list of magnification levels, and then click **100%**.

Visio zooms in, with the selected shape at the center of the magnified area.

11 Hold down the [Shift] and [Ctrl] keys while you right-click.

Visio zooms out, and the **Zoom** box displays the current level of zoom.

12 Hold down [Shift] and [Ctrl] while you left-click.

Visio zooms in again to 100%.

Tip

When you press [Shift] and [Ctrl], the pointer changes to a magnifying glass icon to indicate that clicking will zoom your view in or out.

13 Hold down [Shift] and [Ctrl] while you drag with the right mouse button.

The pointer changes to a hand icon as Visio pans the drawing page.

Close

✖

14 In the **Microsoft Visio** title bar, click the **Close** button.

Visio displays a message asking if you want to save your changes.

15 Click **No** to close Visio without saving the diagram.

Tip

New

📄

For quick access to Visio templates, click the **New** down arrow on the Standard toolbar.

Customizing the Visio Environment

Personalized
menus in Visio

new for
OfficeXP

Most of what you see in Visio can be customized to better suit the way you like to work. Do the stencils take up too much space on the left side of the screen? You can move them. Does the grid make the page look too busy? You can hide it. And so on. Like other Microsoft Office programs, Visio includes built-in customization in the form of personalized menus, which are the shorter versions of full menus and show only the commands that you frequently use. You can also choose to display the full menus if you prefer by clicking **Customize** on the **Tools** menu.

Window
merging

new for
OfficeXP

In addition, Visio includes many special-purpose windows, which you can reposition on the screen for easy access. For example, the **Shapes** window can be moved to a different part of the screen, which is called **docking** the window. To help customize the view of the drawing page, you can display the **Pan & Zoom** window. This window displays a miniature version of your entire diagram so that you can move to different parts of the drawing page while you work. With the **Size & Position** window, you can enter precise measurements for shape dimensions. You can dock any of these windows where you want, or if you prefer, you can **float** a window, which means to drag it in the middle of your screen or wherever you want it. To dock or float a window, drag it by its title bar. If you choose to display several windows at once, you can save space by **merging** one window inside another. Visio displays tabs at the bottom of each window so that you can switch among them.

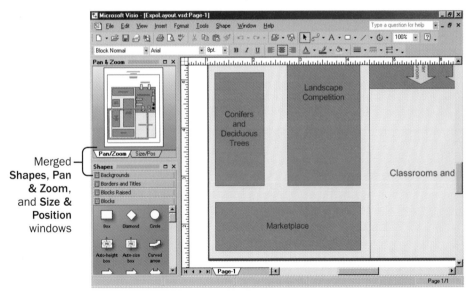

Merged
**Shapes, Pan
& Zoom**,
and **Size &
Position**
windows

Tip

You can also dock and float any toolbar and the entire menu bar.

ExpoLayout

In this exercise, you use different methods to customize the Visio drawing window. You start by opening a sample drawing that shows the proposed layout for the gardening expo, hosted by The Garden Company. Throughout this book, you'll see references to The Garden Company, a fictitious garden design store. You'll create an assortment of drawings and diagrams related to The Garden Company and its weekend expo.

1 Start Visio.

Open

2 On the Standard toolbar, click the **Open** button.

The **Open** dialog box appears.

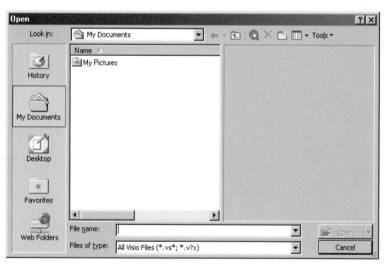

3 Click the **Look in** down arrow, and then click **(C:)**.

4 In the list of files and folder names, double-click the **SBS** folder, and then double-click the **Visio** folder.

The contents of the folder are displayed.

5 Double-click **Creating**, and then double-click **ExpoLayout**.

Visio opens a diagram showing the layout of a gardening expo and the four block diagram stencils.

Your screen should resemble the figure shown on the following page.

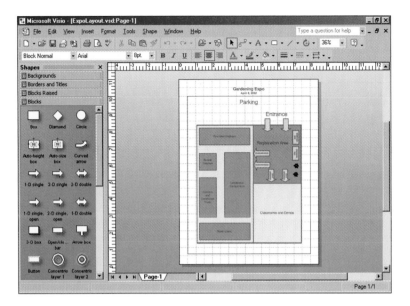

6   On the **View** menu, click **Rulers** to hide the horizontal and vertical rulers.

7   On the **View** menu, click **Grid** to display the drawing page without the grid.

8   On the **Tools** menu, click **Customize**.

The **Customize** dialog box appears and displays the **Options** tab.

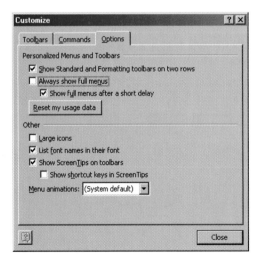

Troubleshooting

The **Customize** dialog box opens with the tab that was last displayed. If the **Options** tab doesn't appear on top automatically, click it to display it.

9   Select the **Always show full menus** check box, and then click **Close**.

Visio restores the complete set of commands to the menus.

10   On the **View** menu, click **Pan & Zoom Window**.

Visio opens the **Pan & Zoom** window and docks it in the upper right corner of the drawing window (or wherever it last appeared).

11   In the **Pan & Zoom** window, drag to draw a rectangle around the green area in the upper right corner.

Visio zooms in to show the enclosed area, which is highlighted in red in the **Pan & Zoom** window. The **Zoom** box on the Standard toolbar displays the new zoom level.

12   In the **Pan & Zoom** window, drag a corner of the red box to enlarge the selection.

Visio changes the level of zoom in the drawing window so that more of the page is visible.

AutoHide

13   On the title bar of the **Pan & Zoom** window, click the **AutoHide** button.

Visio slides the window out of sight until only its title bar is visible.

14   Point to the **Pan & Zoom** title bar.

Visio opens the window. As long as the mouse pointer points to the window, it stays open.

15   Click the **AutoHide** button.

Visio turns off the AutoHide feature so that the window stays open.

16   Drag the **Pan & Zoom** window by its title bar into the **Shapes** window.

Visio merges the **Pan & Zoom** window into the **Shapes** window. Depending on where you released the mouse button, the **Pan & Zoom** window will appear above or below the **Shapes** window.

17 Point to the horizontal border between the **Pan & Zoom** window and the **Shapes** window until a two-headed pointer appears.

18 With the two-headed pointer, drag to make the **Pan & Zoom** window slightly smaller.

Close

19 Click the **Close** button in the **Pan & Zoom** window.

Visio hides the **Pan & Zoom** window and enlarges the **Shapes** window to fill the space.

Open Stencil

20 On the Standard toolbar, click the **Open Stencil** down arrow.

Visio displays a menu of diagram types.

Troubleshooting

If you click the folder icon on the **Open Stencil** button rather than the down arrow, the **Open Stencil** dialog box appears. The same diagram types are listed, but they instead appear as folders that you can open.

21 Point to **Visio Extras**, and then click **Callouts**.

Visio opens the **Callouts** stencil and displays it on top in the **Shapes** window. Callout shapes are designed to annotate any type of drawing. Most callouts include text and a box or line.

22 On the **Callouts** stencil, click the green stencil icon in the title bar.

Visio displays a menu for the stencil.

23 Click **Icons Only**.

Visio displays the master shape icons without the names.

24 Click the stencil icon, and then click **Icons and Names**.

Visio displays both the master shape icons and the shape names.

25 On the **File** menu, click **Close**.

Visio prompts you to save your changes.

26 Click **No**.

Visio closes the sample drawing.

Customizing Colors and Other Options

If you would like to personalize the look of Visio, you can take customization a step further. For example, if you get tired of the green stencil window or the white drawing page, you can change these and other colors used by Visio. To choose different colors, click **Options** on the **Tools** menu, and then click the **View** tab in the **Options** dialog box that appears. The options for these changes are listed under **Color Settings**.

Like other Microsoft Office programs, Visio includes toolbars that you can customize. You can even create a new toolbar and add to it the commands you use most. Click **Customize** on the **Tools** menu to view the options for customizing toolbars.

Keep in mind that the more you customize Visio, the less your screen will match the illustrations shown in this book.

Getting Diagram Help

Ask A
Question box

new for
OfficeXP

Visio offers a variety of ways to get help while you're working. The quickest way—and a new feature in Visio 2002—is to use the Ask A Question box on the Microsoft Visio menu bar. You type a keyword in the box and press the [Enter] key, and then Visio searches through its Help topics to find the ones related to the keyword.

The **Microsoft Visio Help** window looks and works like other Microsoft Office applications. One difference is in how the information is organized. In the Help **Contents**, Visio includes the **Drawing Types** topics, which describe tasks specific to a particular template. Suppose you want to start a diagram with a template you haven't used before, but you aren't sure how to get started. The **Drawing Types** topics give you a jump start by telling you which shapes to add to the page first, which formatting commands will work best for that diagram type, and so on. Other topics in Microsoft Visio Help describe the tasks that are common to most diagram types, such as how to format shapes.

Tip

Help

When you open a dialog box in Visio, you can display a Help topic about each option by clicking the **Help** button in that dialog box (usually located in the lower left corner).

ExpoHelp

In this exercise, you start with the ExpoHelp drawing and search for a Help topic about pages. Then you locate the **Drawing Types** topics for block diagrams, adjust the size of the **Help** window, and **tile** the **Help** window and drawing page window, which means to arrange them side by side.

Open

1 On the Standard toolbar, click the **Open** button to display the **Open** dialog box.

2 In the **Look in** box, navigate to the **SBS\Visio** folder.

The contents of the folder are displayed.

3 Double-click **Creating**, and then double-click **ExpoHelp.**

Visio opens the gardening expo block diagram and its stencils.

4 On the Microsoft Visio menu bar, click in the Ask A Question box, type pages, and then press Enter.

Visio displays a list of topics about pages.

5 Click **About the drawing page**.

The **Microsoft Visio Help** window opens on top of the drawing window, displays the topic you selected, and shows the topic's location in the navigation pane on the **Contents** tab.

Troubleshooting

Show

If you don't see the navigation pane and the **Contents** tab, click the **Show** button on the toolbar in the **Microsoft Visio Help** window.

6   On the **Contents** tab, drag the scroll bar to the top if necessary, and then click the plus (**+**) sign next to **Drawing Types**.

Visio expands the list of Help topics about drawing types.

7   Expand **Block Diagram**.

Visio lists each template in the **Block Diagram** category.

8   Expand **Block diagrams**.

Visio displays the Help topics about creating block diagrams.

9   Click **Create a block diagram**.

Visio displays the steps for creating a block diagram.

Hide

10   Click the **Hide** button.

The navigation pane is hidden, and the **Hide** button becomes the **Show** button.

Auto Tile

11   Click the **Auto Tile** button.

Visio tiles the **Help** and drawing page windows so that both are visible.

Close

12   On the **Microsoft Visio Help** title bar, click the **Close** button.

The **Help** window closes, and the drawing page window is resized.

13   On the **File** menu, click **Close**.

Visio closes the ExpoHelp drawing.

14   On the **File** menu, click **Exit**.

Visio closes.

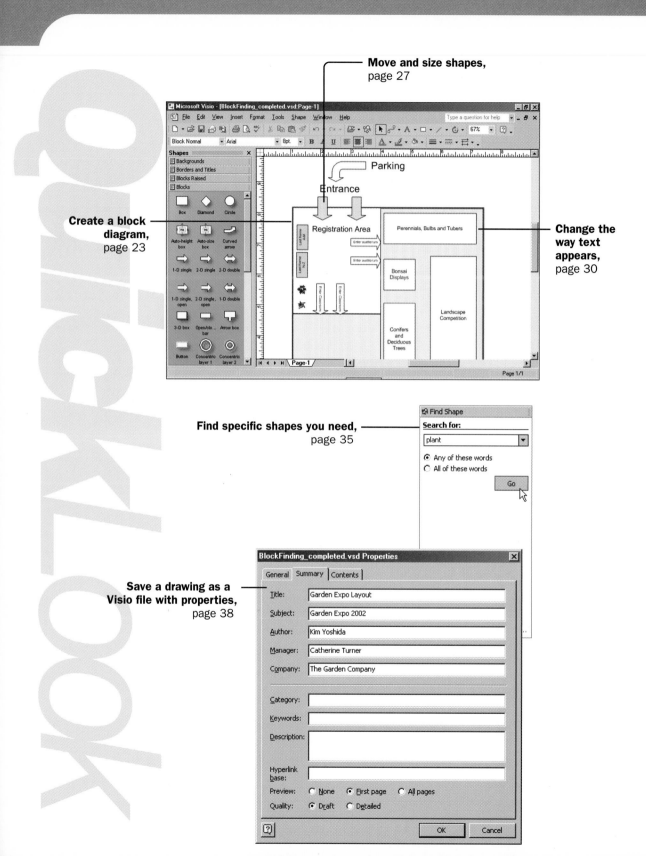

Move and size shapes,
page 27

Create a block diagram,
page 23

Change the way text appears,
page 30

Find specific shapes you need,
page 35

Save a drawing as a Visio file with properties,
page 38

Chapter 2
Adding Shapes to Diagrams

After completing this chapter, you will be able to:

✔ **Create a diagram using block shapes.**

✔ **Add text to shapes and change the way text appears.**

✔ **Move and resize shapes.**

✔ **Find specific shapes you need.**

✔ **Save a drawing as a Visio file.**

✔ **Record information when saving a drawing.**

Microsoft Visio comes with thousands of shapes to help you quickly create drawings. Shapes in Visio represent both conceptual graphics, such as arrows and boxes, and real-world objects, such as office furniture. Shapes can be as simple as a rectangle that represents a step in a process flowchart. Or shapes can be complex, such as a network hub in a network diagram. Because shapes are designed to look like the objects they represent, many include unique behavior or built-in options that help you create a particular type of drawing, whether that's a flowchart, a network diagram, or something else.

After you add shapes to the Visio drawing page, you'll probably have to make changes to your drawing from time to time. Shape "smarts" help you revise drawings easily. For example, after you create an organization chart, you can update it as personnel changes occur. Shapes that represent managers and their employees can be rearranged to fit your organization's structure. You can also customize shapes to suit your personal style by modifying text, color, and other shape **attributes**.

In this chapter, you'll create a diagram that shows the layout for the gardening expo, hosted by The Garden Company, by starting with the **Block Diagram** template. Block diagrams use simple box and arrow shapes to represent a variety of concepts and processes and so are one of the most commonly used diagram types in Visio.

This chapter uses the practice files BlockMoving, BlockEditing, and BlockFinding that you installed from the CD-ROM. For details about installing the practice files, see "Using the Book's CD-ROM" at the beginning of this book.

Understanding Shapes

Shapes are the building blocks of all Visio diagrams. By understanding a few fundamental shape attributes, you'll be able to work more efficiently with any type of shape. Despite their variety, all Visio shapes are either **one-dimensional** (1-D) or **two-dimensional** (2-D). The difference affects both the way shapes look and the way you work with them. For example, a line is a 1-D shape; it has two **endpoints** you can drag to resize the shape in any direction. In addition, a 1-D shape can show order, because endpoints indicate a beginning and an ending, which you see when you select a 1-D shape. A **begin point** is displayed with a plus (+) sign, and an **end point** is shown with an x symbol.

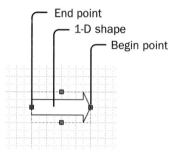

A 2-D shape has **selection handles** rather than endpoints. When you click a 2-D shape, a rectangular **selection box** appears around the shape to show that the shape is selected. You can drag the corner selection handles to resize a 2-D shape proportionally—something you can't do to a 1-D shape—or drag a middle selection handle to stretch or shrink the shape vertically or horizontally.

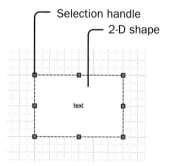

Whether 1-D or 2-D, all shapes have one thing in common: you use **dragging**, the most basic action in Visio, to add or move them. Notice that when you drag a shape to the drawing page, the shape automatically **snaps** to the nearest grid line. Snapping pulls shapes toward the grid for perfect alignment. By default, shapes snap to rulers and grid lines.

As you drag, a shape snaps
to the grid line.

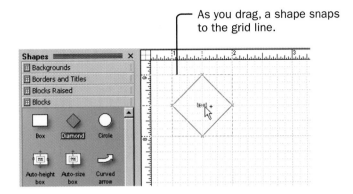

After you know how to drag shapes, you can create any type of drawing. In this short exercise, you practice dragging a few shapes to the drawing page.

1   On the **File** menu, point to **New**, point to **Block Diagram**, and then click **Block Diagram**.

Visio opens a new, blank drawing page and four stencils.

2   On the **View** menu, make sure that both the **Rulers** and **Grid** commands are checked.

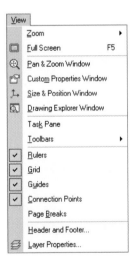

Troubleshooting

If no check mark appears beside either the **Rulers** or **Grid** command on the **View** menu, the grid or the rulers have been hidden. To display them again, click the command.

3   Pause the pointer over the **Box** shape on the **Blocks** stencil.

A ScreenTip appears that indicates how to use the shape.

4   Drag the shape onto the drawing page, and then release the mouse button.

An instance of the shape appears on the drawing page surrounded by eight selection handles to show that the shape is selected. The word *text* appears in the shape.

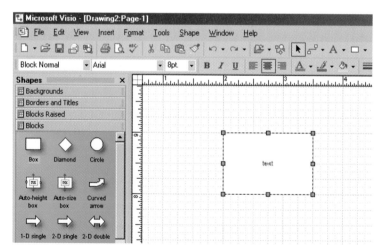

5   Drag the **1-D single** shape from the **Blocks** stencil onto the drawing page.

An instance of the shape appears on the drawing page. The shape is selected, displaying an endpoint on the left and right edges as well as a selection handle on the top and bottom edges.

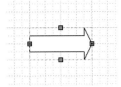

6   Drag additional shapes the from the **Blocks** stencil onto the drawing page.

Important

As you drag shapes, notice how the shapes snap to the grid on the drawing page for precise placement.

7   On the **File** menu, click **Close**.

Visio displays a message asking if you want to save your changes.

8   Click **No** to close the drawing without saving changes.

Starting a Block Diagram

Like most business professionals, you probably spend a portion of your day planning. Block diagrams are useful in the planning process, because they let you represent complex concepts and systems in a simplified manner. Most block diagrams consist of basic 2-D shapes, such as triangles, squares, circles, ellipses, and arrows; and connectors. Yet with just these shapes you can organize ideas and show layers of information in a visual form that's suitable for reports and presentations.

Like most Visio drawings, block diagrams typically contain text as well as shapes. In Visio, almost any shape can include text. You don't necessarily have to select a special tool or spend time arranging text in a drawing, because you can type right in a shape. The area in a shape where text appears is called a **text block**. To add text to a shape, you simply select the shape and then type.

In any Visio drawing, it helps to become familiar with the Pointer tool—the tool for completing most tasks. Use the Pointer tool to drag, select, and move shapes. The pointer changes appearance depending on what you are doing.

Pointer	Task	Description
	Select a shape	Select a shape and type to add text, or select and drag a shape to move it.
	Duplicate a shape	Hold down the ⌈Ctrl⌉ key, and then click and drag a shape to duplicate it.
	Resize a shape	Position the pointer over a selection handle, and then click and drag a shape to resize it.
	Zoom in and out	Hold down the ⌈Ctrl⌉ + ⌈Shift⌉ keys and left-click to zoom in or right-click to zoom out.

BlockStarting

In this exercise, you continue a drawing, BlockStarting, that's been started using the **Block Diagram** template. You drag shapes from the stencil to the drawing page, select shapes to add text, move shapes, and then save the drawing to update a Visio drawing file.

Open

1 On the Standard toolbar, click the **Open** button.

The **Open** dialog box appears.

2 Navigate to the **SBS\Visio\Adding** folder on your hard disk, and double-click the **BlockStarting** file.

The **BlockStarting** file opens at 100% zoom with the **Blocks, Blocks Raised, Borders and Titles**, and **Backgrounds** stencils open.

3 Drag the **2-D single** arrow shape from the **Blocks** stencil onto the drawing page directly below the **Enter auditorium** arrow shape.

An instance of the shape appears on the drawing page and remains selected.

Tip

Notice how the shape snaps to the grid even though the grid is obscured by the white **Registration Area** shape.

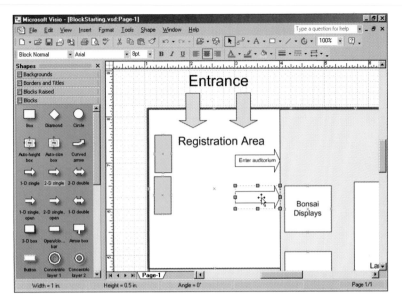

4 With the arrow shape selected, type **Enter auditorium**.

The pointer changes to a blinking I-beam as you type, and the shape's text block is highlighted with a dotted green line.

5 Click outside of the shape.

Visio cancels the selection of the text block and displays the arrow pointer.

6 Click to select the top gold box shape. Type **Last name**, press the `Enter` key, and then type **A–M**.

As you type, Visio displays the text block horizontally so that the text appears upright.

7 Click outside the shape.

Visio cancels the selection of the text block and displays the text vertically in the shape.

Tip

After you type in a shape, press the `Esc` key to display the pointer again.

8 Repeat steps 6 and 7 for the bottom box shape, but type **Last name**, press [Enter], type **N–Z**, and then click outside the shape.

The text is added to the lower arrow shape, and Visio displays the pointer again.

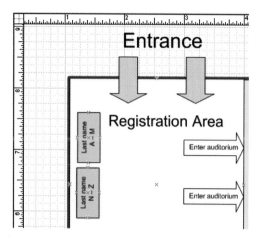

9 Drag the **Box** shape from the **Blocks** stencil until it appears directly above the **Bonsai Displays** box.

10 When the shape snaps to the grid, release the mouse button.

11 With the box shape selected, type **Perennials, Bulbs, and Tubers**.

Visio adds the text to the shape, automatically wrapping the lines to fit.

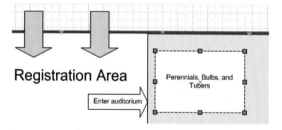

12 Click outside the shape.

Visio cancels the selection.

Save

13 On the Standard toolbar, click the **Save** button.

Visio saves your changes.

14 On the **File** menu, click **Close**.

BlockStarting closes.

Moving and Sizing Shapes

Once you create a drawing, you are likely to spend time revising it. Whether you want to add a box shape to represent a new step in a process, or reconfigure an office layout after you receive a new piece of furniture, you need to know how to move and size shapes. You must first **select** a shape before you move or modify it. There are a number of ways to select a shape, depending on what you want to do. To select one shape, you simply place the pointer over the shape, and then when the pointer changes to a four-headed arrow, you click the shape. You know the shape is selected because the green selection handles appear.

Moving shapes in Visio is a simple matter of dragging shapes into place—as long as you don't inadvertently resize the shape as you move it. By looking at the pointer, you can easily avoid this. When the pointer turns to a four-headed arrow, you know you can drag the shape to where you want it.

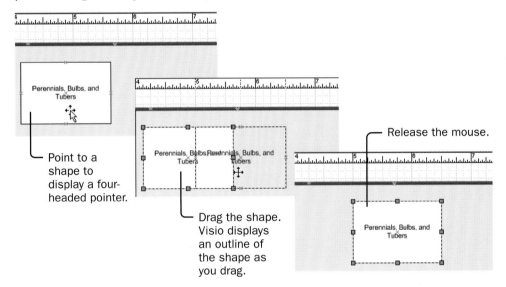

Point to a shape to display a four-headed pointer.

Drag the shape. Visio displays an outline of the shape as you drag.

Release the mouse.

Important

If you resize a shape accidentally when you move it, you can immediately cancel the action by clicking **Undo** on the **Edit** menu.

Moving multiple shapes as a unit is a two-step process. First you select the shapes, and then you drag them to the new position. To select multiple shapes, you click the first shape and then hold down [Shift] as you click to select the other shapes. The first shape you select is the **primary shape**. Its selection handles remain green, while the other shapes, called **secondary shapes**, have blue selection handles.

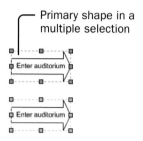

Primary shape in a multiple selection

Tip

Another method for selecting multiple shapes is to use the Pointer tool to draw a rectangle around the shapes you want to select.

The way you resize a shape depends on whether the shape is 1-D or 2-D. You can drag a 1-D shape's endpoints in any direction to stretch the shape. With a 2-D shape, you can change just the height or width, or you can resize the entire shape proportionally, depending on which selection handle you drag.

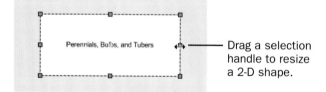

Drag a selection handle to resize a 2-D shape.

BlockMoving

In this exercise, you continue an existing drawing that's based on the **Block Diagram** template. You resize shapes using selection handles. Then you select multiple shapes and move them to another position on the drawing page.

Open

1 On the Standard toolbar, click the **Open** button.

The **Open** dialog box appears.

2 Navigate to the **SBS\Visio\Adding** folder, and double-click the **BlockMoving** file.

BlockMoving opens at 100% zoom with the **Blocks**, **Blocks Raised**, **Borders and Titles**, and **Backgrounds** stencils open.

3   Click the **Perennials, Bulbs, and Tubers** box to select it.

4   Position the pointer over the middle selection handle on the right.

The pointer turns to a two-headed arrow.

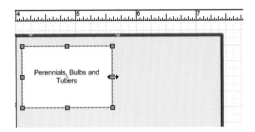

5   Drag the section handle until the right side of the box is aligned with the right side of the **Landscape Competition** box.

6   For a better look, position the pointer in the middle of the **Perennials, Bulbs, and Tubers** box. Hold down `Ctrl`+`Shift` and then click.

Visio zooms in, and the **Zoom** box displays the current level of zoom.

7   If you need to slightly adjust the size of the box, select the box shape, and then drag the right middle handle to the left or right.

8   Hold down `Ctrl`+`Shift`, and then right-click to zoom out.

9   Click the top **Enter auditorium** shape, hold down `Shift`, and then click the bottom **Enter auditorium** shape.

Both shapes are selected. The selection handles of the top shape are green, because it is the primary shape.

10   Point to the top shape until the four-headed pointer appears, and then drag to move both shapes down approximately one inch.

As you drag, tick marks appear on the horizontal ruler to show you the shape's position.

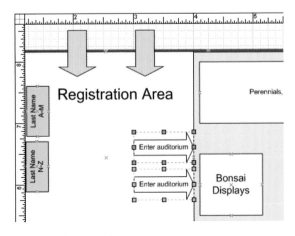

29

Tip

To drag a shape in a perfectly straight line, hold down Shift as you drag.

Save

11 On the Standard toolbar, click the **Save** button.

12 Visio saves the changes.

13 On the **File** menu, click **Close**.

BlockMoving closes.

Editing Shapes

Pointer Tool

To refine your drawing, you can edit shapes in a variety of ways. For example, after you add a box shape to a block diagram, you can edit the shape by adding text to describe the purpose of the shape. By default, most shapes appear without text or with placeholder text when you place them in your drawing. Adding text to any Visio shape is easy—you select the shape and type. By selecting the shape with the Pointer tool, which you activate by clicking the **Pointer Tool** button on the Standard toolbar, you also select any existing text.

Text Tool

When you start typing, the new text replaces the existing text. To select only part of the existing text, use the Text tool, which you activate by clicking the **Text Tool** button on the Standard toolbar. The Text tool opens the shape's text block so that you can add new text without replacing the existing text. When you click with the Text tool, the pointer is replaced by the insertion point, which shows where text appears when you type. The insertion point looks like a blinking vertical I-beam. You can also display the insertion point with the Pointer tool by double-clicking to select the text and then clicking again where you want to place the insertion point.

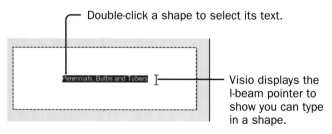

Double-click a shape to select its text.

Visio displays the I-beam pointer to show you can type in a shape.

An efficient way to revise multiple shapes at once is to edit just one shape and then duplicate it. You can duplicate a shape quickly using the keyboard and mouse. Select the shape you want to duplicate, hold down Ctrl, and then drag away from the shape. When you release the mouse button, the duplicate shape appears.

Some shapes let you further fine-tune their look with special handles called **control handles**. When you drag a control handle, the control handle performs an action unique to that shape. For example, the **Line-Curve Connector** shape has a control handle that adjusts the curvature of the arc. To read a ScreenTip that explains what a control handle does, pause the pointer over a control handle.

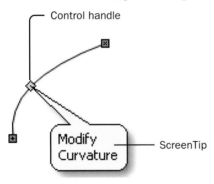

Control handle

Modify Curvature — ScreenTip

BlockEditing

In this exercise, you continue an existing drawing based on the **Block Diagram** template. You drag and rotate an arrow shape. After you type text in the shape, you duplicate it by using the keyboard and mouse shortcut. You also edit existing text by using the Text tool. Finally, you modify a shape by dragging a control handle.

Open

1 On the Standard toolbar, click the **Open** button.

The **Open** dialog box appears.

2 Navigate to the **SBS\Visio\Adding** folder, and double-click the **BlockEditing** file.

BlockEditing opens at 100% zoom with the **Blocks**, **Blocks Raised**, **Borders and Titles**, and **Backgrounds** stencils open.

Pointer Tool

3 On the Standard toolbar, click the **Pointer Tool** button.

4 Drag the **2-D single** arrow shape from the **Blocks** stencil and position it below the **Last Name N–Z** box.

The shape is selected.

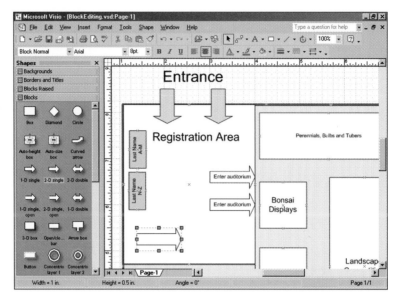

5 Type **Enter Classroom** to position the text in the shape.

6 Press Esc.

The insertion point is replaced by the pointer, and the shape is selected.

7 Right-click the shape, point to **Shape** on the shortcut menu, and then click **Rotate Right**.

The arrow shape is rotated clockwise 90 degrees and remains selected.

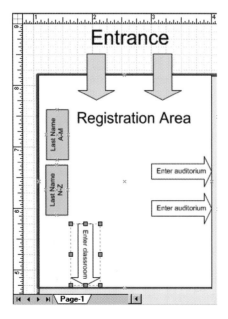

8   Place the pointer over the arrow (or **Enter classroom** shape), hold down Ctrl, and then drag to the right. Release the mouse button.

A duplicate arrow shape appears to the right of the original shape.

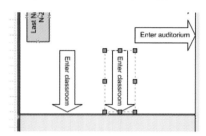

9   Click the drawing page away from the shapes to cancel the selection.

10 Drag the vertical scroll bar down until the **Classrooms and Demos** shape is visible.

Text Tool

A

11 On the Standard toolbar, click the **Text Tool** button.

The pointer changes to display a text box icon.

12 In the **Classroom and Demos** shape, click to the left of the letter *C* in *Classroom*.

The blinking cursor indicates the insertion point.

13 Type **Gardening**, press Space , and then click outside of the box shape.

The new text appears in the box.

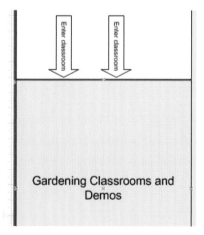

14 Drag the vertical scrollbar up until the **Perennials, Bulbs, and Tubers** box is visible, and then click the **Pointer Tool** button on the Standard toolbar.

15 Click the **Perennials, Bulbs, and Tubers** shape.

Selection handles appear around the shape.

Font Size

8pt. ▾

16 On the Formatting toolbar, click the **Font Size** down arrow to display a list of sizes.

17 Click **12 pt** in the box.

The font size of the selected shape is increased to 12 points.

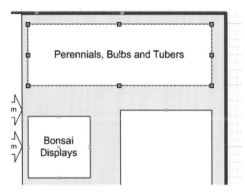

18 Drag the vertical scrollbar up until the **Parking** label is visible.

19 From the **Blocks** stencil, drag the **Curved arrow** shape to the left of the **Parking** label.

20 On the **Shape** menu, point to **Rotate or Flip**, and then click **Flip Horizontal**.

The shape is flipped across its horizontal center.

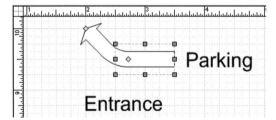

21 Pause the pointer over the top yellow control handle.

A ScreenTip labeled *Reposition Arrowhead* is displayed.

22 Drag the **Reposition Arrowhead** control handle downward until it points toward the **Entrance** label.

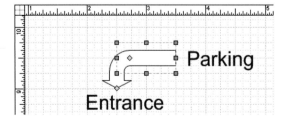

23 Release the mouse button, and then click outside of the shape to cancel the selection.

Save

24 On the Standard toolbar, click the **Save** button.

Visio saves the changes.

25 On the **File** menu, click **Close**.

BlockEditing closes.

Finding and Adding Shapes

Find Shape
command

There might come a time when you need to find a shape that is located on a stencil other than on the one you have open. Say you create a flowchart and want to include a text callout to highlight a step in the process. Because there are thousands of Visio shapes, how do you find the one you need? With the new **Find Shape** command, you can quickly search through the all the stencils in Visio to find that shape you're looking for. Searching for shapes is an easy way to locate shapes without opening additional Visio stencils.

Find Shape

To search for shapes, you click the **Find Shape** button on the Standard toolbar. Visio opens the **Find Shape** window and docks it with the stencils. The **Find Shape** window includes a **Search For** box that you use to type keywords associated with the type of shape you want to locate. For example, to locate furniture shapes, you might type *desk* or *chair*. When you click the **Go** button, Visio searches the stencils installed on your hard disk for the shapes that match the keyword you've typed.

The **Find Shape** window locates
shapes based on keywords you type.

BlockFinding

In this exercise, you continue an existing drawing based on the **Block Diagram** template. You use the **Find Shape** command to locate a shape and then you drag the shape to the drawing page.

Open

1 On the Standard toolbar, click the **Open** button.

The **Open** dialog box appears.

2 Navigate to the **SBS\Visio\Adding** folder, and double-click the **BlockFinding** file.

BlockFinding opens at 50% zoom with the **Blocks**, **Blocks Raised**, **Borders and Titles**, and **Backgrounds** stencils open.

Find Shape

3 On the Standard toolbar, click the **Find Shape** button.

The **Find Shape** window appears.

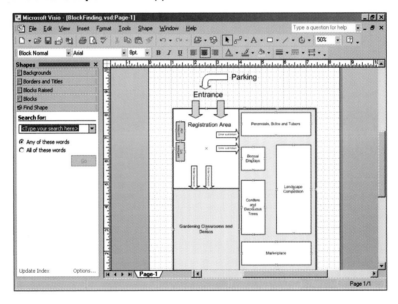

4 In the **Search for** box, type **plant**.

5 Click the **Go** button.

Visio searches for plant shapes and displays the shapes it finds along with the name of the stencil containing the shapes.

6 From the **Office Accessories** stencil in the **Find Shape** window, drag the **Large plant** shape onto the drawing page directly below the **Last Name N–Z** shape.

Visio adds the shape to the drawing page just as if you had dragged it from a stencil window.

Troubleshooting

You might need to scroll down in the **Find Shape** window to display the shapes on the **Office Accessories** stencil.

7 Select the **Plant** shape in the **Find Shape** window, and drag it directly below the **Large Plant** shape on the drawing page.

Find Shape icon

8 On the **Find Shape** title bar, click the icon in the left corner.

A shortcut menu appears.

9 On the shortcut menu, click **Close**.

The **Find Shape** window closes.

Save

10 On the Standard toolbar, click the **Save** button.

Visio saves the changes.

11 On the **File** menu, click **Close**.

BlockFinding closes.

Saving Drawings

Saving in Visio is just like saving in any other Microsoft Office application. You click the **Save** button on the Standard toolbar or click **Save** on the **File** menu. The first time you save your drawing, the **Save As** dialog box appears. After you type a file name and then click **Save**, the **Properties** dialog box appears. A number of options are available in the dialog box that allow you to record information about your drawing, such as file description, author, manager, and company. This information is useful when creating a drawing you plan to distribute to other employees. For example, typing your name in the Author box of the **Properties** dialog box alerts others who open your diagram that you are the person who created the file.

Tip

You can type up to 63 characters for most options in the **Properties** dialog box.

The best way to avoid losing data is to save often. After you initially save your drawing in Visio, click the **Save** button on the Standard toolbar every time you make significant changes.

In this exercise, you start a new drawing and save it. Then you type information in the **Properties** dialog box. You don't need any practice files to complete this exercise.

New

1 On the Standard toolbar, click the **New** down arrow.

2 In the drop-down list that appears, point to **Block Diagram**, and then click **Block Diagram**.

3 Drag a few shapes from the **Blocks** stencil to the drawing page.

Save

4 On the Standard toolbar, click the **Save** button.

The **Save As** dialog box appears.

5 In the **File name** box, type BlockSaving, and then click **Save**.

The **Properties** dialog box appears with the **Summary** tab selected. The drawing file name appears selected in the **Title** box. Based on your computer's settings, other properties might appear as well.

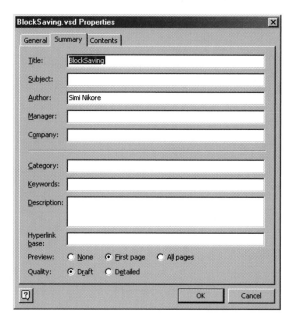

6   In the **Title** box, type Garden Expo Layout over the highlighted text.

The new text replaces the file name.

7   In the **Subject** box, type Garden Expo 2002.

8   In the **Author** box, select the existing text and type Kim Yoshida.

9   In the **Manager** box, type Catherine Turner.

10   In the **Company** box, type The Garden Company.

11   Click **OK** to save the file.

The **Properties** dialog boxes closes.

Tip

To save changes to a file that has been previously saved, press the Ctrl+S keys.

12   To view the information you just typed, click **Properties** on the **File** menu.

The **Properties** dialog box appears and displays the information you typed.

13   On the **File** menu, click **Close**.

BlockSaving closes.

14   On the **File** menu, click **Exit**.

Visio closes.

Make your drawing more appealing with a color scheme, page 52

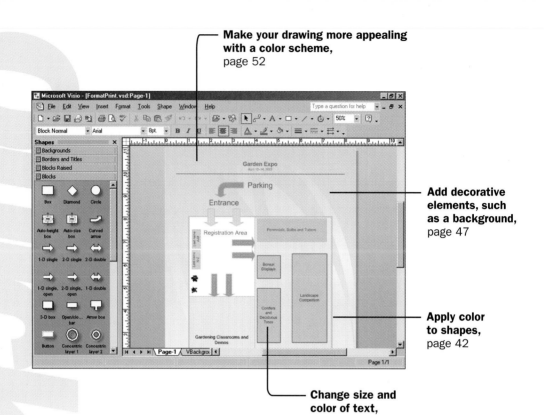

Add decorative elements, such as a background, page 47

Apply color to shapes, page 42

Change size and color of text, page 43

Preview drawings in the Print Preview window, page 56

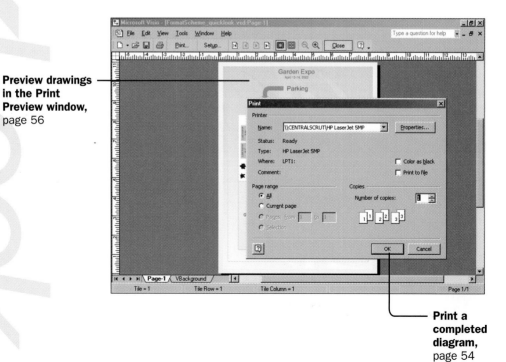

Print a completed diagram, page 54

Chapter 3
Formatting Shapes and Diagrams

After completing this chapter, you will be able to:

✔ Format a shape's line, fill, and text.
✔ Add decorative elements.
✔ Make your drawing more appealing with a color scheme.
✔ Preview and print a completed diagram.

Microsoft Visio shapes come ready to use—you simply drag them to the drawing page. However, there will be times when you want to adjust the way shapes look to make your drawing more effective. For example, say you create a flowchart that you want to include in a presentation for a meeting. To make sure your flowchart draws the attention of your colleagues, you could add colors to the process shapes that coordinate with your slides and increase the font size of the text to make it more readable. Or perhaps you want to customize some shapes to meet your organization's design specifications. With Visio, formatting shapes and drawings is easy.

In this chapter, you'll learn the quickest methods for formatting shapes and adding the finishing touches to a drawing. For example, you can add a professional look to a drawing with decorative elements such as ornamental borders and attractive title shapes. You can even format your drawing with coordinated colors that complement a corporate color scheme. Then you'll be ready to preview and print your work.

 This chapter uses the practice files FormatShapes, FormatDecorate, FormatScheme, and FormatPrint that you installed from this book's CD-ROM. For details about installing the practice files, see "Using the Book's CD-ROM" at the beginning of this book.

Formatting Shapes

Formatting is the way you modify the look of shapes. The right formatting can add emphasis and depth to make your drawing communicate more effectively. For example, you can draw attention to important steps in a process by adding high-contrast colors to particular shapes or add overall polish with something as simple as a shadow behind the shapes so that they stand out to your audience.

Every shape in Visio includes a combination of attributes that you can format, including the thickness and color of the **line** bordering the shape; the color and pattern of a 2-D shape's interior, called its **fill**; and text size, style, and color. Although 1-D shapes do not have fill, they do include an additional line attribute—**line ends**, which are the arrowheads or other ornaments that you can add to either end of a line. By formatting a shape's line, fill, and text, you can subtly or radically change its look to better suit your message.

When you drag any shape from a stencil to the drawing page, the shape is already formatted even if it doesn't necessarily appear to be. For example, the **Box** shape on the **Blocks** stencil has white fill and is bordered by a 1-point solid line. Text that you type in this shape is black and set to 8-point Arial.

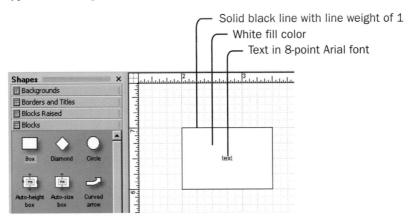

What if you want something livelier than a black and white shape? Visio makes it easy to format shapes with the buttons on the Formatting toolbar, which appears by default at the top of the window, below the Standard toolbar. Most of these buttons have drop-down lists that include options you can select. To view the options for a specific button, click the down arrow to the right of the button. For example, to change a shape's fill color, select the shape, click the down arrow on the **Fill Color** button to see a palette of colors that you can apply, and then click the color you want.

Important

Not all formatting options appear as toolbar buttons. Visio also includes commands on the **Format** menu for formatting a shape's line, fill, and text.

When you format a shape, you can also change the appearance of its text. The built-in formatting of most shape text is designed for readability on a printout. However, when drawings are used in presentations or added to other documents, a different text format might be more suitable. For example, when you create a drawing for a presentation, the text must be must larger to be viewed when projected. You can change the format of text by choosing a different font, font size, or font color. Typically, you select a shape, and then you choose a text format to affect all the text in a shape. You can, however, selectively format words or lines of text in a shape by selecting the text first rather than selecting the shape. When you double-click most shapes, Visio selects all the text in the shape, and the pointer changes to an I-beam that you can use to select a particular word or line of text.

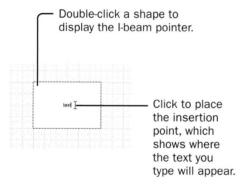

Double-click a shape to display the I-beam pointer.

Click to place the insertion point, which shows where the text you type will appear.

Tip

Pause the pointer over a toolbar button to display a ScreenTip that describes its purpose.

Format Painter

In a drawing with many shapes, you can save time by copying formats from one shape to another. Inconsistent formatting can distract readers from your message. To help you maintain a consistent look, the Format Painter tool copies all the fill, line, and text attributes of one shape and applies them to another. When you click the **Format Painter** button on the Standard toolbar, the format of the selected shape is copied. You then click the shape you want to format. If you double-click the **Format Painter** button, you can format multiple shapes on the page by clicking them in succession.

FormatShapes

In this exercise, you refine a drawing in progress that shows the conference hall layout for a gardening expo hosted by The Garden Company. You start by opening an existing drawing, FormatShapes, that is based on the **Block Diagram** template. You apply a new fill color and line weight to a block shape that represents an area of the showroom floor. You use the Format Painter tool to copy the formatting from one shape to another. Then you change the font size and color of other shapes.

Open

1 Start Visio.

2 On the Standard toolbar, click the **Open** button.

The **Open** dialog box appears.

3 Click the **Look in** down arrow, navigate to the **SBS\Visio\Formatting** folder, and then double-click the **FormatShapes** file.

The FormatShapes drawing opens at 100% and opens the following four stencils: **Blocks**, **Blocks Raised**, **Backgrounds**, and **Borders and Titles**.

4 Click the **Perennials, Bulbs, and Tubers** box to select it.

Fill Color

5 On the Formatting toolbar, click the **Fill Color** down arrow.

The **Fill Color** palette appears.

6 Pause the pointer over a color in the palette to see the ScreenTip that identifies the color.

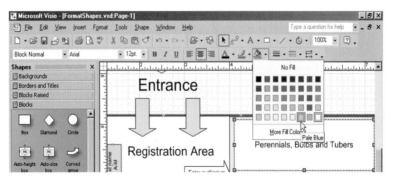

7 Click **Pale Blue** in the palette.

The shape is filled with pale blue, which also appears on the **Fill Color** button.

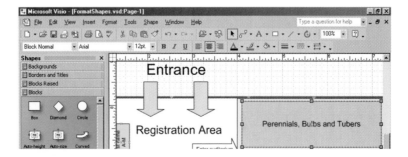

Line Weight

8 On the Formatting toolbar, click the **Line Weight** down arrow to display a list of line weights.

9 Pause the pointer over an item in the list to see the ScreenTip that describes it.

10 Click **Line Weight 5** in the list.

The box now has a thicker border around it. The shape remains selected.

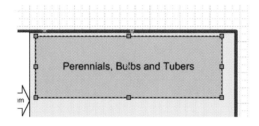

Format Painter

11 On the Standard toolbar, double-click the **Format Painter** button.

The pointer displays a paintbrush icon to indicate that the Format Painter tool is selected.

12 One at a time, click the following four boxes: **Bonsai Displays**, **Landscape Competition**, **Conifers and Deciduous Trees**, and **Marketplace**.

Visio copies the formatting to the shapes, changing their fill color to pale blue and their line weight to 5. On the Standard toolbar, the blue border around the **Format Painter** button indicates that the tool is still in effect.

13 On the Standard toolbar, click the **Format Painter** button.

The Format Painter tool is replaced with the Pointer tool.

14 Position the pointer above and to the left of the **Last name A-M** box.

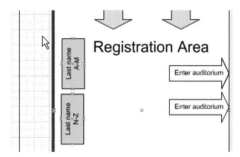

15 Starting slightly outside the left border, drag around the shapes labeled **Last name A-M** and **Last name N-Z**.

As you drag, Visio displays the selection box. When you release the mouse, the two shapes are selected.

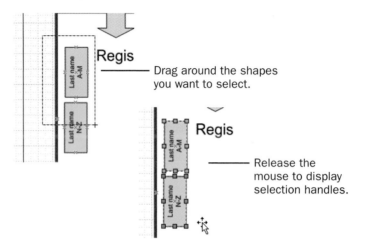

Drag around the shapes you want to select.

Release the mouse to display selection handles.

Font Size

8pt.

16 On the Formatting toolbar, click the **Font Size** down arrow, and then click **10 pt.** in the list.

Visio increases the text size for both selected shapes.

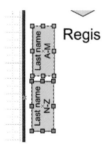

Tip

You can type a number in the **Font Size** box on the Formatting toolbar to change text size rather than clicking an option in the list.

17 Click the top **Enter auditorium** arrow shape.

18 Holding down Shift, click the remaining three arrow shapes with text.

The first shape you select (the primary shape) has green selection handles; the other shapes' handles are displayed in blue.

Text Color

19 On the Formatting toolbar, click the **Text Color** down arrow to display the color palette.

20 Click **Gold** in the palette.

Visio changes the text in the four selected arrows to gold.

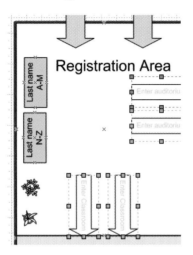

21 Click outside the drawing to deselect the shapes.

Save

22 On the Standard toolbar, click the **Save** button.

Visio saves the changes.

23 On the **File** menu, click **Close**.

FormatShapes closes.

Adding Decorative Elements

In addition to formatting shapes, you can in effect format an entire drawing by adding decorative elements, such as borders, title blocks, and backgrounds. A border is a design that appears around some or all of the edges of the drawing page. A title block adds a formatted title to your drawing and can include other information, such as the date. A background is an overall pattern that appears behind a drawing, much like wallpaper on the Microsoft Windows desktop. Borders, title blocks, and backgrounds are all special types of shapes whose purpose is to add a professional look to your drawing. You'll find these shapes on the **Backgrounds** and **Borders and Titles** stencils that open with many of the business-oriented templates in Visio, including the **Block Diagram** template. You can add a border, title, or background at any time, but typically these shapes are added as a finishing touch just before you print or distribute your drawing.

Visio comes with dozens of border, title block, and background designs. You add one to a drawing much as you would add any shape—by dragging. When you drag a border to the page, it is automatically sized to fit the page. Most borders include text in the form of a title and page number. Visio supplies the page number automatically, but you can type to replace the generic *Title* text. For a less elaborate title, use one of the title block shapes, which also include the word *Title* as a placeholder for your drawing's title. Some borders and title blocks display the date as well, which, like page numbers, are added automatically.

Like borders, background shapes are sized to fit a page. However, after you add a background shape to a drawing, you'll see a new page in your drawing labeled *Vbackground* on the page tab at the bottom of the drawing page window. Visio adds the background shape to this new background page so that the background doesn't get in the way as you move and format shapes. The background shows through and is printed with the drawing page.

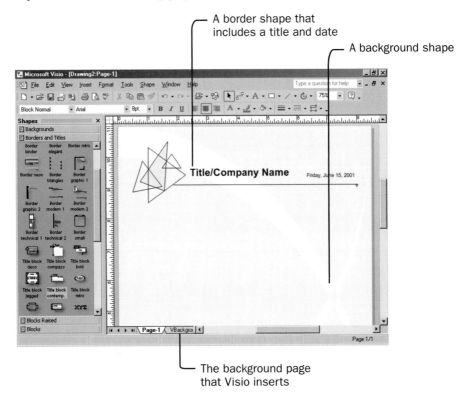

A border shape that includes a title and date

A background shape

The background page that Visio inserts

<table>
<tr><td>Format-
Decorate</td><td>In this exercise, you fine-tune the appearance of the gardening expo layout. You start by opening the FormatDecorate drawing, which is based on the **Block Diagram** template. You then experiment with border, title block, and background shapes to find just the right look for the drawing.</td></tr>
</table>

Open

1 On the Standard toolbar, click the **Open** button.

The **Open** dialog box appears.

2 Navigate to the **SBS\Visio\Formatting** folder, and double-click the **Format-Decorate** file.

The FormatDecorate drawing opens at 100% zoom and opens the following four stencils: **Blocks**, **Blocks Raised**, **Backgrounds**, and **Borders and Titles**.

3 From the **Borders and Titles** stencil, drag the **Border Classic** shape to the drawing page.

You can drop the border anywhere on the drawing page, and it automatically snaps into place. Visio adds a shape with the word *Title* and the date at the top of the page and a page number at the bottom.

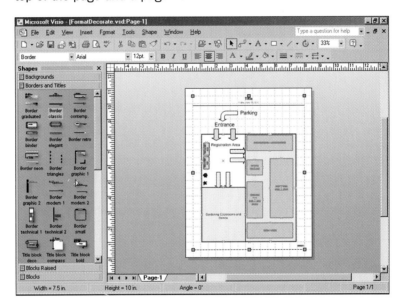

Zoom

33% ▾

4 On the Standard toolbar, click the **Zoom** down arrow, and then click **100%** in the list.

Visio zooms in to the center of the selected shape.

5 Scroll up until the word *Title* is visible, and then press the `F2` key.

Visio selects the shape's text. When you hold the mouse pointer over the shape, the pointer changes to an I-beam.

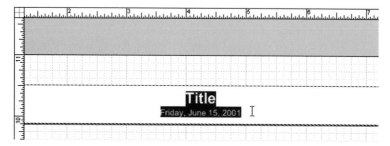

6 Drag across the word *Title* in the text block to select just that word, and then type **Garden Expo**.

Visio replaces the word *Title* with the text you typed.

Troubleshooting

Text Tool

If you select a title block shape and type, you might inadvertently replace the automatic date text as well as the title. If this happens, immediately press the `Ctrl`+`Z` keys (or click **Undo** on the **Edit** menu). Make sure to select just the word *Title*, and then type. Sometimes this is easier to do if you select the text using the Text tool, which you access by clicking the **Text Tool** button on the Standard toolbar.

7 Click the date to select it.

8 Type **April 12–14, 2002**.

Visio replaces the date with the text you type.

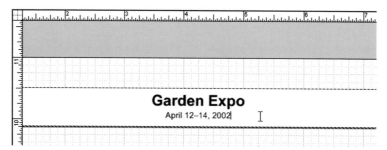

9 From the **Backgrounds** stencil, drag the **Background Rain** shape to the drawing page.

The **Make Background** dialog box appears.

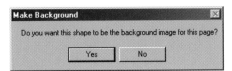

10 Click **Yes**.

Visio inserts a new page called **Vbackground** and adds the **Background Rain** shape, which appears behind the drawing page.

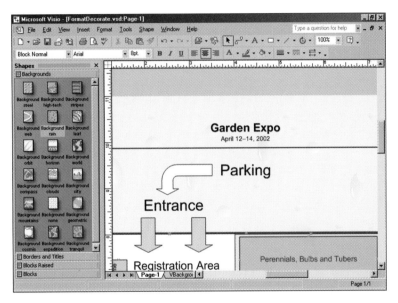

11 To undo the results, press <kbd>Ctrl</kbd>+<kbd>Z</kbd>.

Visio removes the background image from the drawing.

12 From the **Backgrounds** stencil, drag the **Background Leaf** shape to the drawing page.

The **Make Background** dialog box appears.

13 Click **Yes**.

Visio reinserts a page labeled **Vbackground** and adds the new background shape, which appears behind the drawing.

Save

14 On the Standard toolbar, click the **Save** button to save the changes.

15 On the **File** menu, click **Close**.

FormatDecorate closes.

Using Shapes with Dates

Many of the title block and border shapes display a date when you add them to the drawing page. This text is actually a field, a type of placeholder text that Visio replaces with the current date or page number based on your computer's date and time settings. Page numbers are also a type of field. A date field can display the date in several different formats, which are predetermined by the master shape you select. However, you can edit date fields to display the date in a different format—a useful technique to know if you like a particular shape but prefer a different style of date. For more information about fields, type **text field** in the Ask A Question box on the menu bar, and then press [Enter]. In the list of topics, click **About Text Fields**.

Adding a Color Scheme

The quickest way to add polish to a diagram is to use a **color scheme**, a set of coordinated colors that Visio applies wholesale to your shapes and text. If you're pressed for time, you can click the **Color Schemes** command on the **Tools** menu, apply a new color scheme, and change the look of your entire drawing. A color scheme applies colors to the text, line, fill, and shadows of all a drawing's shapes, including background and border shapes. You choose a color scheme by a name that suggests the result; for example, choose **Forest** to apply earth tones or **Steel** to apply shades of gray. If you don't like the result, you can simply choose a different color scheme from the **Color Schemes** dialog box.

If you have already formatted shapes in your drawing with color, you can apply a color scheme without changing existing colors. The **Color Schemes** dialog box includes an option that preserves existing formatting. If you don't select this option, though, the new colors of the color scheme replace your formats—a fast way to provide a consistent look to your drawing.

Troubleshooting

Color schemes are designed to work with business-oriented diagrams, such as flowcharts. If you start a diagram with a template that does not support color schemes, the **Color Schemes** command does not appear on the **Tools** menu.

FormatScheme

In this exercise, you add pizzazz to a drawing that represents the layout of the gardening expo hosted by The Garden Company. You start by opening an existing drawing, FormatScheme, based on the **Block Diagram** template. Then you apply several color schemes until you find one that you want.

Open

1   On the Standard toolbar, click the **Open** button.

The **Open** dialog box appears.

2   Navigate to the **SBS\Visio\Formatting** folder, and double-click the **FormatScheme** file.

FormatScheme opens at 100% zoom with the following four stencils: **Blocks**, **Blocks Raised**, **Backgrounds**, and **Borders and Titles**.

3   On the **Tools** menu, click **Color Schemes** to open the **Color Schemes** dialog box.

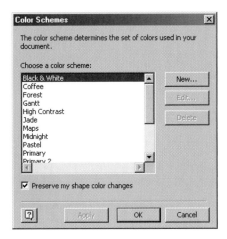

Tip

If you are editing a drawing that supports the use of color schemes, you can right-click the drawing page to display a shortcut menu that includes the **Color Scheme** command.

4   In the **Choose a color scheme** list, click **Forest**.

5   Make sure the **Preserve my shape color changes** check box is selected, and then click **Apply**.

Visio applies the color scheme, and the dialog box remains open.

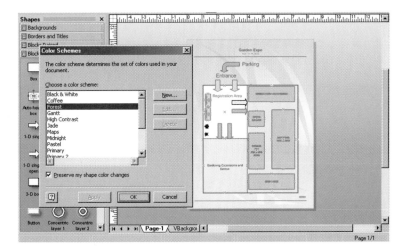

Important

Notice that when you apply a color scheme, Visio changes the color of the background as well as the fill and text color of some—but not all—shapes. When the **Preserve my shape color changes** check box is selected, Visio does not apply the color scheme to shapes have been formatted manually.

6 In the **Choose a color scheme** list, click **Jade**, and then click **Apply**.

Visio applies the new color scheme.

7 To accept the color scheme, click **OK**.

The **Color Scheme** dialog box closes.

8 Select the jade-colored arrow labeled **Enter auditorium**.

Selection handles appear around the shape.

Format Painter

9 On the Standard toolbar, click the **Format Painter** button, and then click the white arrow labeled **Enter auditorium**.

Visio applies the color scheme formats to the shape, overwriting its previous formatting.

Save

10 On the Standard toolbar, click the **Save** button.

Visio saves the changes.

11 On the **File** menu, click **Close**.

FormatSchemes closes.

Tip

To remove a color scheme and revert to the default black and white shapes, apply the **Black & White** color scheme.

Printing a Diagram

Print Page

Most people share their Visio drawings and diagrams by printing them. Like other Microsoft Office applications, Visio includes a **Print Preview** command that shows you exactly how your drawing will look when it is printed, as well as a **Print Page** button on the Standard toolbar that you can click to print one page of your drawing. For more printing options, such as to print multiple copies of a drawing, you can use the **Print** command on the **File** menu.

Where Visio differs from other Office applications is in the way the size of the drawing page affects printed output. For example, in Microsoft Word, you choose the page size when you print. In Visio, you can choose the size of your drawing page independently of the size of the paper in your printer. As a result, if your drawing page is larger, smaller, or oriented differently than your printer's paper, you must make adjustments when you print. Fortunately, Visio takes care of this for you in drawings based on a template. The template sets up your drawing page to be printed correctly on the letter-sized paper most often found in office printers.

You can change the size of the drawing page and choose the size of your printer's paper in one place: the **Page Setup** dialog box, which you open by clicking **Page Setup** on the **File** menu. The **Page Setup** dialog box includes a welter of options on several tabs, but the following two are the most important ones to know about when you print:

■ **Print Setup** tab, where you can select the size and orientation of your printer's paper.

■ **Page Size** tab, where you can change the size and orientation of the drawing page on the screen.

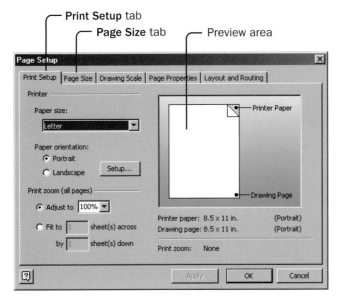

The **Page Setup** dialog box includes a miniature preview that helps you see the effect of various settings. Another way to preview a drawing before you print is to display **page breaks**, gray lines that show you where Visio will break up a large drawing to fit on your printer's paper. If your drawing page matches the size of your printer's paper, no page breaks appear. For the most detailed preview that shows you exactly how and where your shapes will be printed, use the **Print Preview** command. If you have a black and white printer, Visio even previews your drawing in shades of gray just as it will look when printed.

Fixing Page Orientation Problems

The most common problem that people encounter when printing Visio drawings occurs when the drawing page is oriented differently than the printer's paper. For example, if the drawing page is wider than it is tall (landscape orientation), but the printer paper uses the typical portrait orientation (taller than wide), Visio displays a message box that says one or more drawing pages are oriented differently than the printer paper. To correct this problem, click the **Print Setup** command on the **File** menu, and then do one of the following:

■ Change the drawing page to match the printer's paper: click the **Page Size** tab, and then click the **Same as printer paper size** option.

■ Change the printer's paper to match your drawing: click the **Print Setup** tab, and then click the option under **Paper orientation** that matches the preview of the drawing page shown.

FormatPrint

In this exercise, you practice previewing and printing a diagram that shows The Garden Company's gardening expo. You start by opening the FormatPrint file, a drawing based on the **Block Diagram** template. You view page breaks first, and then you preview the drawing in the **Print Preview** window. Finally, you compare the printer paper size with the drawing size in the **Page Setup** dialog box and then print the drawing.

Important

To complete this exercise, a printer must be installed and connected to your computer.

Open

1 On the Standard toolbar, click the **Open** button.

The **Open** dialog box appears.

2 Navigate to the **SBS\Visio\Formatting** folder, and double-click the **Format-Print** file.

FormatPrint opens at 100% zoom and opens the following four stencils: **Blocks**, **Blocks Raised**, **Backgrounds**, and **Borders and Titles**.

3 On the **View** menu, click **Page Breaks**.

No page breaks are displayed, because the drawing will fit on the printed page as is without breaking the pages.

4 On the **File** menu, click **Print Preview**.

The **Print Preview** window opens and displays the Print Preview toolbar.

Important

If you have a color printer, your screen will not match the following illustration, which previews the drawing when a black and white printer is selected.

Print Preview toolbar

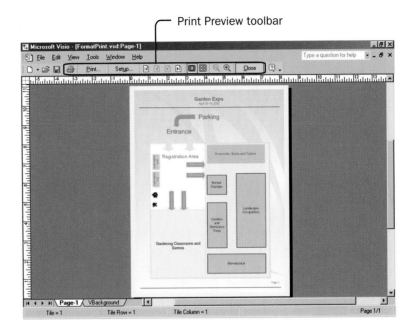

5   On the Print Preview toolbar, click **Setup**.

The **Page Setup** dialog box appears and displays the **Print Setup** tab.

6   Make sure the **Paper size** option is set to **Letter** and the **Paper orientation** option is set to **Portrait.**

Tip

Use the preview area in the **Page Setup** dialog box to verify that the printer paper and drawing page match in size and orientation. The current size and orientation settings are listed below the preview picture as well.

7 Click the **Page Size** tab.

Settings for the drawing page appear.

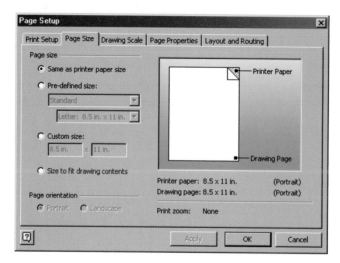

8 Make sure that **Same as printer paper size** is selected, and then click **OK**.

The **Page Setup** dialog box closes.

9 On the Print Preview toolbar, click **Print**.

The **Print** dialog box opens. Notice that **Page range** is set to **All** and that **Number of copies** is set to **1**.

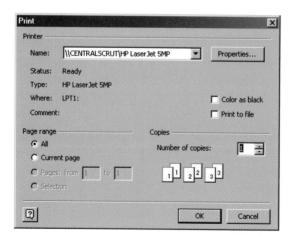

Troubleshooting

Make sure you click the **Print** button. If you click the **Print Page** button instead, Visio does not display the **Print** dialog box but rather prints the current page.

10 Click **OK** to print.

Visio prints your drawing.

Troubleshooting

To troubleshoot any problems you may encounter when printing, refer to Microsoft Visio's online Help. In the Ask A Question box, type troubleshoot and then press ⏎ Enter . In the list of results, click **Troubleshoot printing** to open that topic in Microsoft Visio Help.

11 On the Print Preview toolbar, click **Close**.

The **Print Preview** window closes, and the drawing page is displayed.

Save

12 On the Standard toolbar, click the **Save** button.

Visio saves your changes.

13 On the **File** menu, click **Exit**.

Visio closes.

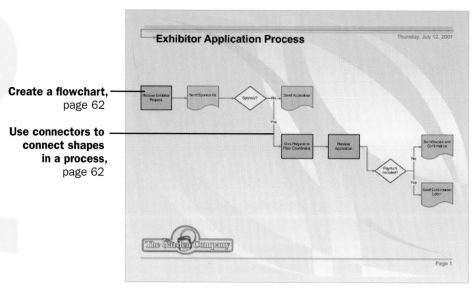

Create a flowchart, page 62

Use connectors to connect shapes in a process, page 62

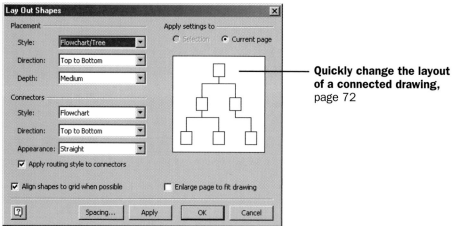

Quickly change the layout of a connected drawing, page 72

Revise groups and locked shapes, page 77

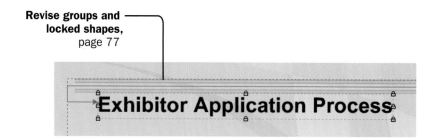

Chapter 4
Connecting Shapes

After completing this chapter, you will be able to:

✔ **Create a diagram using flowchart shapes.**

✔ **Create and modify connectors between shapes.**

✔ **Change the layout of a connected drawing.**

✔ **Adjust the spacing between shapes by distributing them evenly.**

✔ **Edit Visio shapes that are groups.**

Many types of diagrams in Microsoft Visio depict related ideas, relationships, or a sequence by showing shapes that are connected by lines. These diagrams are referred to collectively as **connected drawings** and include flowcharts, organization charts, and network diagrams. For example, a flowchart shows the steps in a process as a series of shapes connected by lines. Visio makes it easy to create connected drawings with smart shapes called **connectors**, which are 1-D lines that attach automatically to 2-D shapes, such as the process shapes in a flowchart. If you rearrange connected shapes, the connectors stay connected—Visio reroutes the connector lines for you, so you don't waste time redrawing lines.

Visio comes with several templates that include shapes for creating connected drawings. This chapter shows you how to create a flowchart, but the techniques you use to connect flowchart shapes apply to other types of connected drawings as well. As you arrange connected shapes, you can take advantage of several layout tools that help you align and position shapes evenly. Visio can even change the orientation of a connected drawing for you; for example, you can change a flowchart that reads from top to bottom to a left-to-right layout.

This chapter uses the practice files ConnectModify, ConnectLayout, and Connect-Group that you installed from this book's CD-ROM. For details about installing the practice files, see "Using the Book's CD-ROM" at the beginning of this book.

Connecting Shapes in a Flowchart

Flowcharts are ideal for visually representing business processes. For example, if you need to show how a customer order flows through various departments within your organization, you can create a flowchart to show this, adding shapes that depict receipt of the order, logging the order in a database, and so on. Although Visio includes several different flowchart templates, the most common type of flowchart shows uses simple shapes to indicate a process step (the **Process** shape), a decision (the **Decision** shape), a step that results in documentation (the **Document** shape), and a step that requires data (the **Data** shape). Connectors between the shapes show the relationship between the steps. Connectors can also include text to clarify the process being depicted. When you move a shape that is connected to another shape, the shapes stay attached and the connector moves around other shapes if necessary.

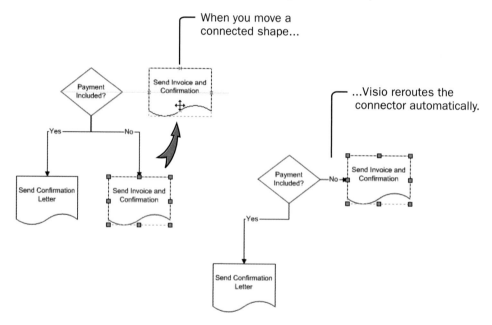

When you move a connected shape...

...Visio reroutes the connector automatically.

Connector Tool

Visio includes a number of methods for connecting shapes. For flowchart shapes, the simplest method is to use the Connector tool, which you access by clicking the **Connector Tool** button on the Standard toolbar. There are two ways to use the Connector tool:

- You can add shapes to the drawing page first, and then use the Connector tool to draw connectors between shapes.

- You can use the Connector tool to drag shapes from a stencil onto the drawing page so that each shape you drag is connected to the selected shape on the page. That is, Visio adds the connectors for you.

Important

To connect shapes as you add them, make sure to select the Connector tool *before* you drag shapes to the drawing page. To connect shapes *after* you add them, make sure to drag with the Connector tool in the direction that the process follows—that is, from step one to step two and so on.

The attribute that makes a connector stay attached to shapes is called **glue**. When you select a connector that is glued to a shape, the connector's endpoints are displayed in red. The red endpoints, as the following illustration shows, are your clue that the connector will stay attached when you move shapes.

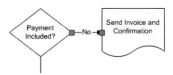

In this exercise, you start a new drawing using the **Basic Flowchart** template. You drag several shapes to the drawing page and connect them using the Connector tool. Then you add text to the connectors to indicate a *yes* or *no* decision.

1 Start Visio.

2 On the **File** menu, point to **New**, point to **Flowchart**, and then click **Basic Flowchart**.

The **Basic Flowchart** template opens and displays the **Basic Flowchart Shapes** stencil, the **Borders and Titles** stencil, and the **Backgrounds** stencil.

Connector Tool

3 On the Standard toolbar, click the **Connector Tool** button.

The pointer displays a connector icon.

4 Drag the **Process** shape from the **Basic Flowchart Shapes** stencil and position it near the top of the drawing page.

5 Drag the **Decision** shape from the **Basic Flowchart Shapes** stencil and position it below the **Process** shape.

As you drag, dotted lines called the **dynamic grid** appear, showing you how to align the new shape with respect to the shape already on the page. After you drop the shape in place, a connector appears between the shapes.

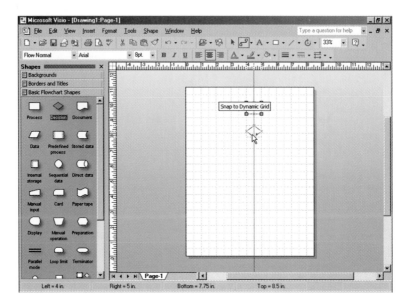

6   Drag the **Document** shape from the **Basic Flowchart Shapes** stencil and position it to the right of the diamond-shaped **Decision** shape. Use the dynamic grid to align the top of the **Document** and **Decision** shapes.

A connector appears between the **Decision** and **Document** shapes.

7   Click the **Decision** shape to select it.

Green selection handles appear around the shape.

8   Drag another **Process** shape from the **Basic Flowchart Shapes** stencil and position it below the **Decision** shape.

All four shapes are connected.

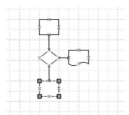

Pointer Tool

9   Click the **Pointer Tool** button on the Standard toolbar.

Troubleshooting

If you try to move or modify shapes with the Connector tool, you might sometimes mistakenly create another connector instead of moving the shape. If this happens, click **Undo** on the **Edit** menu, and then click the **Pointer Tool** button and move the shape.

10 Click the top **Process** shape to select it.

Zoom

33% ▼

11 On the Standard toolbar, click the **Zoom** down arrow, and then click **100%**.

Visio zooms in on the selected shape.

12 Type **Contact workshop presenters**.

The text is added to the process shape.

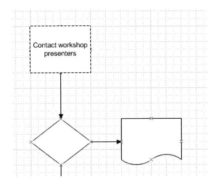

13 Select the **Decision** shape, and then type **Presenter available?**

14 Select the **Document** shape, and then type **Send presenter kit and contract**.

15 Select the bottom **Process** shape, and then type **Contact exhibitors**.

16 Select the connector between the **Decision** shape and the **Document** shape.

The connector is selected and displays red handles where the endpoints are glued to the shapes.

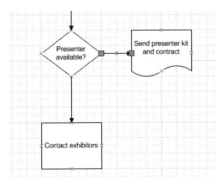

65

17 Type **Yes**.

As you type, the connector's text box is displayed.

18 Select the connector between the **Decision** shape and the bottom **Process** shape, and then type **No**.

The text is added to the connector.

19 Click the drawing page away from the shapes.

The selection is canceled. The completed flowchart should look similar to the following illustration.

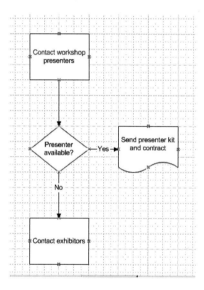

Save

20 On the Standard toolbar, click the **Save** button.

The **Save As** dialog box appears.

21 In the **File name** box, type **ConnectFlowchart**, and then click the **Save** button.

Visio saves your flowchart as a drawing file and displays the **Properties** dialog box.

22 Click **OK**.

The **Properties** dialog box closes.

23 On the **File** menu, click **Close**.

ConnectFlowchart closes.

Modifying Shapes in Connected Drawings

Visio makes it easy to connect shapes, but what do you do if you need to insert a new shape into an existing flowchart or other connected drawing? Creating a flowchart can help you see a process more clearly, and as a result, you probably will spend more time revising the diagram than you did to create it. Perhaps you need to add a missing step or to revise a series of steps to make a process more efficient. Moving, adding, reconnecting, and realigning shapes are common tasks associated with flowcharts and other types of connected drawings.

Visio helps you by keeping connected shapes connected even when you move them, but sometimes you need to disconnect shapes to insert new ones into a flowchart. When you add shapes to an existing connected drawing, you can use the Connector tool to redraw the connectors. However, the way you draw with the Connector tool can have two very different results, because you can connect either shapes or specific points on shapes. Connecting entire shapes provides the most flexibility, because when you move shapes, Visio can route the connector between the two closest points. This is called a **shape-to-shape** connection, and it's the best type to use for flowcharts. If you connect specific points on shapes, Visio makes sure that the connector remains attached to those points regardless of where you move the shapes. This is called a **point-to-point** connection, and it's useful when you don't want connectors to jump around on a shape. When you select a connector, the size of the endpoints tell you the type of connection that's used, as the following illustration shows.

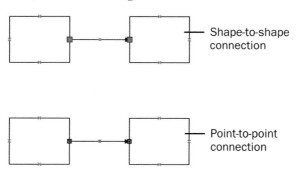

Shape-to-shape connection

Point-to-point connection

When you move a shape that has a shape-to-shape connection, Visio reroutes the connector around other shapes on the page. In addition, if you place a new shape between two connected shapes, the connector is rerouted to avoid passing through the middle shape.

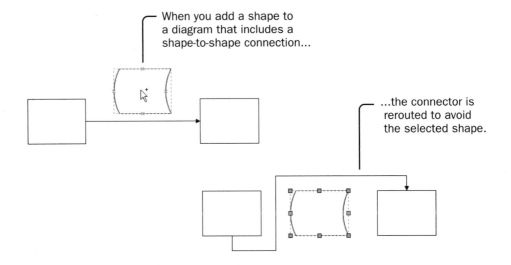

When you add a shape to a diagram that includes a shape-to-shape connection...

...the connector is rerouted to avoid the selected shape.

After you move a shape, you might need to adjust its position slightly. In Visio, you can move a shape in small increments using the arrow keys on your keyboard, which "nudge" a shape into position.

Tip

To nudge a shape by even smaller increments, hold down [Shift] as you press an arrow key.

ConnectModify

In this exercise, you open an existing drawing, ConnectModify, that is based on the **Basic Flowchart** template. You move a flowchart shape to a new position to see how the connector moves along with the shape. Then you drag a new shape to the drawing and use the Connector tool to connect it to the flowchart.

Open

1 On the Standard toolbar, click the **Open** button.

The **Open** dialog box appears.

2 Navigate to the **SBS\Visio\Connecting** folder, and double-click the **Connect-Modify** file.

The ConnectModify drawing opens at 100% zoom and displays the **Basic Flowchart Shapes** stencil, the **Borders and Titles** stencil, and the **Backgrounds** stencil.

3 Drag the **Receive Exhibitor Request** shape approximately one inch up.

The connector stretches to stay attached to the shape.

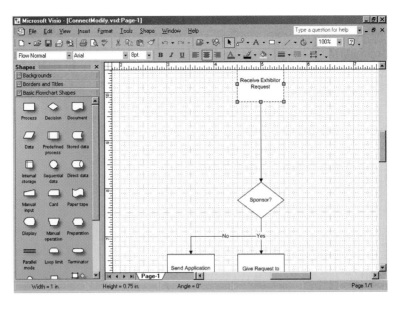

4 Click the connector between the **Receive Exhibitor Request** shape and the **Sponsor?** shape.

The connector is selected.

5 Press ⌷Del⌷.

The connector is deleted.

6 Drag the **Document** shape from the **Basic Flowchart Shapes** stencil to the drawing page, using the dynamic grid to help you position it between the **Receive Exhibitor Request** and the **Sponsor?** shapes.

The document shape is selected.

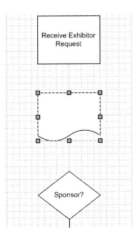

7 Type **Send Sponsor Kit**.

The text is added to the document shape, and the insertion point remains in the shape's text block.

Connector Tool

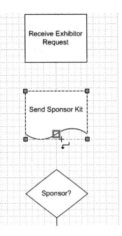

8 Click the **Connector Tool** button on the Standard toolbar.

Selection handles appear around the document shape.

9 Point to the bottom of the **Send Sponsor Kit** shape.

A red square highlights a point on the shape to indicate that a point-to-point connection will be created if you drag.

10 Point to the middle of the **Send Sponsor Kit** shape.

A red outline appears around the shape to indicate that a shape-to-shape connection will be created if you drag.

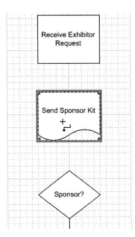

Troubleshooting

If a red border appears around just one connection point rather than the entire shape, move the pointer closer to the center of the shape to create a shape-to-shape connection.

11 Drag to the middle of the **Sponsor?** shape until you see a red outline around the shape, and then release the mouse button.

Visio creates a shape-to-shape connection between the shapes.

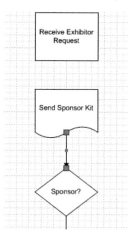

Troubleshooting

If the endpoints on the new connector display + or x symbols, you've created a point-to-point connection. Click **Undo** on the **Edit** menu, and then repeat steps 10 and 11 to create a shape-to-shape connection with solid red endpoints as the illustration above shows.

12 Point to the middle of the **Receive Exhibitor Request** shape until you see a red outline around the shape.

13 Drag to the middle of the **Send Sponsor Kit** shape until you see a red outline around the shape, and then release the mouse.

Visio creates a shape-to-shape connection between the shapes.

Save

14 On the Standard toolbar, click the **Save** button.

Visio saves the changes.

15 On the **File** menu, click **Close**.

The drawing closes.

Changing the Layout of Connected Drawings

Although flowcharts frequently appear as documents that you read from top to bottom, you can connect shapes from left to right, right to left, or even in a circular fashion depending on what you want to show. For example, a top-to-bottom flowchart that you intend to add to a presentation slide might look better oriented from left to right. You can change the direction of a connected drawing such as a flowchart in one step with the **Lay Out Shapes** command on the **Shape** menu. As long as you've created shape-to-shape connections throughout a diagram, Visio can change the entire layout and reroute connectors as the following illustration shows.

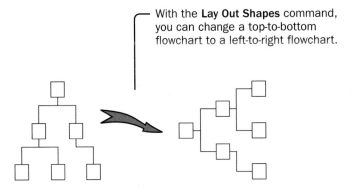

With the **Lay Out Shapes** command, you can change a top-to-bottom flowchart to a left-to-right flowchart.

In addition, if you need to update a large flowchart to include a new process, you can use the **Lay Out Shapes** command to realign the drawing. For example, say you add a new shape to an existing flowchart in the approximate location you want. After you connect the new shape to the appropriate shapes in the flowchart, you can use the **Lay Out Shapes** command to adjust the layout and realign all the shapes.

Troubleshooting

When you change the layout of a drawing, you might find that it no longer fits on the page. In this case, you can change the page size or orientation by clicking **Page Setup** on the **File** menu. When the dialog box opens, click the **Page Setup** tab, and select a different page size or orientation.

Another way to fine-tune the layout of a connected drawing is to use the **Distribute Shapes** command on the **Shape** menu to adjust the spacing between shapes evenly. You can distribute three or more selected shapes at a time. When you distribute shapes vertically, the spacing is defined by the top and bottom shapes in the selection. When you distribute shapes horizontally, the spacing is defined by the left most and right most shapes in the selection.

Tip

When you distribute shapes, the order in which you select the shapes is not important.

ConnectLayout

In this exercise, you open the ConnectLayout drawing, a flowchart based on the **Basic Flowchart** template. You use the **Lay Out Shapes** command to change the top-to-bottom layout to a left-to-right layout. Then you distribute several shapes so that they are evenly spaced.

Open

1 On the Standard toolbar, click the **Open** button

The **Open** dialog box appears.

2 Navigate to the **SBS\Visio\Connecting** folder, and double-click the **ConnectLayout** file.

The ConnectLayout drawing file opens and displays the **Basic Flowchart Shapes** stencil, the **Borders and Titles** stencil, and the **Backgrounds** stencil.

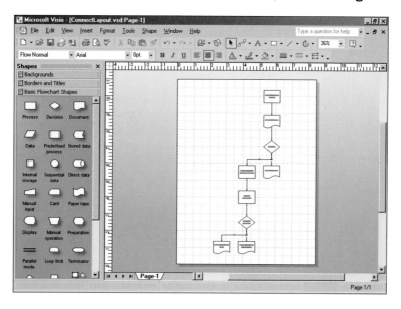

3 On the **Shape** menu, click **Lay Out Shapes**.

The **Lay Out Shapes** dialog box appears.

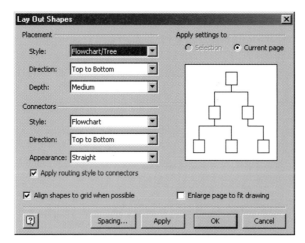

4 In the **Placement** area, click the **Direction** down arrow, and then click **Left to Right.**

A preview of the layout appears in the area to the right.

5 Click **OK**.

Visio changes the flowchart layout, but some shapes extend beyond the drawing page onto the pasteboard.

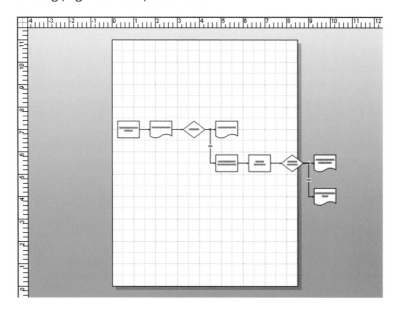

6 On the **File** menu, click **Page Setup**.

The **Page Setup** dialog box appears and displays the **Print Setup** tab, which indicates that the paper orientation is **Portrait** (taller than wide).

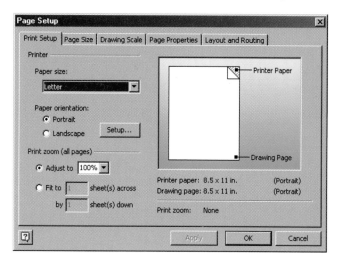

7 Click **Landscape**, and then click **OK**.

The drawing page is now wider than it is tall; however, the flowchart is slightly off center.

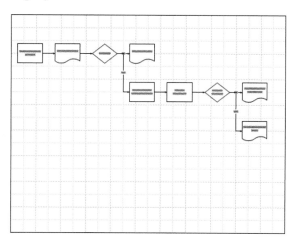

8 On the **Shape** menu, click **Center Drawing**.

The flowchart is centered on the drawing page.

Zoom

33% ▾

9 On the Standard toolbar, click the **Zoom** down arrow, and then click **100%**.

Visio zooms in to the center of the drawing page.

10 Drag the horizontal scrollbar until you can see the right edge of the drawing page.

The **Payment Included** shape, the **Select Confirmation Letter** shape, and the **Send Invoice and Confirmation** shape become visible.

11 Hold down ⟨ Shift ⟩, and then click the **Payment Included** shape, the **Select Confirmation Letter** shape, and the **Send Invoice and Confirmation** shape.

The shapes are selected.

12 On the **Shape** menu, click **Distribute Shapes**.

The **Distribute Shapes** dialog box appears.

13 In the **Up/Down** area, click the leftmost button, and then click **OK**.

The shapes are distributed evenly at their centers.

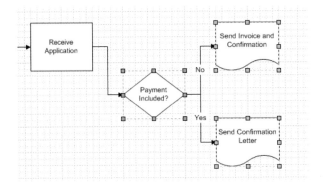

Save

14 On the Standard toolbar, click the **Save** button.

Visio saves the changes.

15 On the **File** menu, click **Close**.

ConnectLayout closes.

Using Groups and Locked Shapes

Many shapes you use in Visio, including borders and titles, are **groups**, which are a collection of shapes that function as a unit. For instance, the **Title Block Deco** shape on the **Borders and Titles** stencil is a group composed of three shapes: a decorative box, a shape that says *Title*, and a shape that displays the date. With a group, each shape can be formatted differently and yet the group moves and is sized as a single unit. In the **Title Block Deco** shape, for example, the *Title* shape is formatted with 18-point type, whereas the date shape uses 6-point type. When you click a group, the entire group is selected. If you then click a shape in the group, you **subselect** that shape, which allows you to format just that shape.

Groups and other Visio shapes are often **locked**, which means they're protected against specific changes. When you select a locked shape, the selection handles appear as **padlocks**. Shapes in a group are often locked to prevent you from deleting or inadvertently moving them when you move the group.

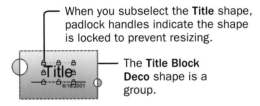

When you subselect the **Title** shape, padlock handles indicate the shape is locked to prevent resizing.

The **Title Block Deco** shape is a group.

ConnectGroup

In this exercise, you open the ConnectGroup drawing, a flowchart based on the **Basic Flowchart** template. You drag a grouped shape to the drawing page. To format the group, you subselect existing text and type a title, and then you subselect a line and change its color and thickness.

Open

1 On the Standard toolbar, click the **Open** button.

The **Open** dialog box appears.

2 Navigate to the **SBS\Visio\Connecting** folder, and double-click the **Connect-Group** file.

ConnectGroup file opens at 50% zoom and displays the **Basic Flowchart Shapes** stencil, the **Borders and Titles** stencil, and the **Backgrounds** stencil.

3 From the **Borders and Titles** stencil, drag the **Border Neon** shape to the drawing page.

You can position the border anywhere on the drawing page—it automatically snaps into place. The border is selected.

4 On the **Format** menu, click **Special**.

The **Special** dialog box appears and identifies the selected shape.

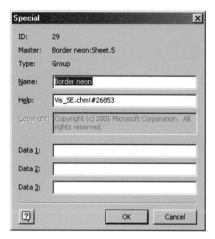

5   Notice that for **Type**, **Group** is displayed, which indicates that the selected border shape is a group.

6   Click **OK** to close the **Special** dialog box.

The border shape remains selected.

7   Click the word **Title** to subselect it.

Padlock handles appear around the shape, indicating that it is locked. In this case, the locks prevent you from moving the subselected shape.

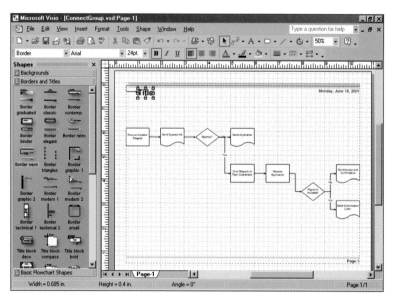

8   Type **Exhibitor Application Process**.

Visio replaces the word *Title* with the new text. The insertion point remains in the text block.

9 Click a blank area of the drawing page to deselect the shape.

10 Click the border, and then click the arrow pointing to the title to subselect the line.

Padlock handles appear around the shape, indicating that it is locked.

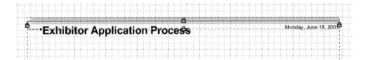

Line Color

11 On the Formatting toolbar, click the **Line Color** down arrow, and then click **Green**.

The subselected line turns green.

Line Weight

12 On the Formatting toolbar, click the **Line Weight** down arrow, and then click line weight **13**.

The subselected line increases in thickness.

13 Click a blank area of the drawing page to deselect the shape.

The formatted group should now look similar to the following.

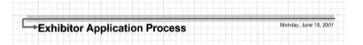

Save

14 On the Standard toolbar, click the **Save** button.

Visio saves the changes.

15 On the **File** menu, click **Exit**.

Visio closes.

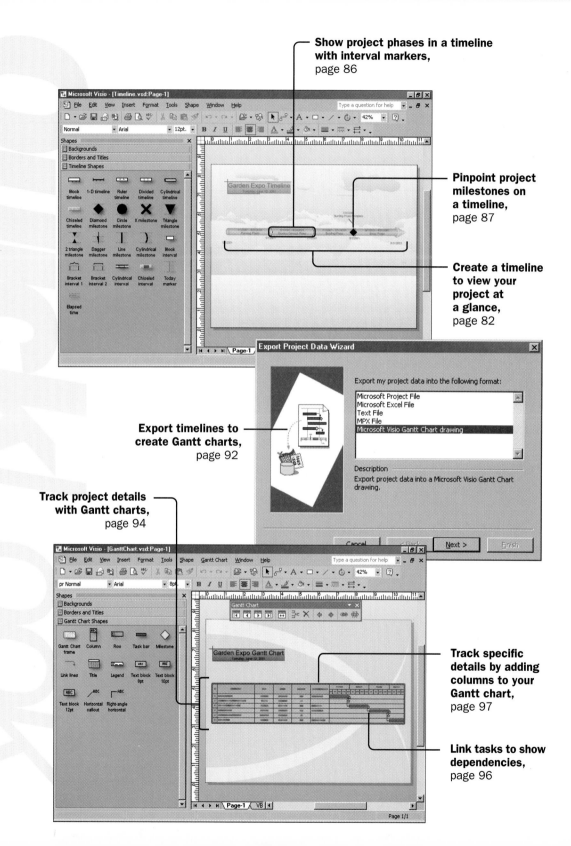

Show project phases in a timeline with interval markers, page 86

Pinpoint project milestones on a timeline, page 87

Create a timeline to view your project at a glance, page 82

Export timelines to create Gantt charts, page 92

Track project details with Gantt charts, page 94

Track specific details by adding columns to your Gantt chart, page 97

Link tasks to show dependencies, page 96

Chapter 5
Creating Project Schedules

After completing this chapter, you will be able to:

✔ Create timelines to view your project at a glance.

✔ Export timelines to create Gantt charts.

✔ Track project details with Gantt charts.

Effective project schedules are vital to a successful project. Project schedules help you track project dates, milestones, phases, and tasks, and they let you assess the progress of your project. Although each organization has a unique method of creating project schedules, there is one element that successful methods share: visualizing the progress of the project from the big picture down to the details.

In Microsoft Visio, you can use **timelines** to visualize your overall project and present this information to executives and others who need to grasp it quickly. On the other hand, for project managers or team members who need more detail, **Gantt charts** provide project specifics in a visual form that's easy to comprehend. Timelines and Gantt charts can help you keep your project on track, and they ultimately contribute to the success of your project.

In this chapter, you'll learn how to use Visio timelines and Gantt charts to visualize and track The Garden Expo project. You'll learn how to create a timeline to view the project at a glance, export the timeline data to create a Gantt chart, and track project details with the Gantt chart.

This chapter uses the practice files Timeline, NewGantt, and GanttChart. For details about installing the practice files, see "Using the Book's CD-ROM" at the beginning of this book.

Creating Timelines to View Your Projects at a Glance

When you're planning a project, timelines help you visualize the big picture and identify the project's scope. They come in handy when you want to present high-level project information to those who need to view this information at a glance. You can begin creating your timelines during brainstorming sessions and then modify them as your project plans develop.

A **timeline** is a visual that represents a specific period of time and the events that occur during that time. Timelines are particularly good at showing an overview of a project—project status, a history of events, and what's to come. Timelines usually include milestones and interval markers. **Milestones** represent significant events or dates in a schedule, such as the date the building phase of The Garden Expo project is to be completed. They can pinpoint dates when you want to evaluate the progress of your project and make necessary decisions or adjustments. **Interval markers** specify a length of time. Use them to represent the beginning and end of a process or phase. For example, you could use an interval marker to represent the building phase in The Garden Expo project.

Interval markers can specify the beginning and end of a process or phase.

Milestones pinpoint important dates or events so that you can evaluate the progress of your project.

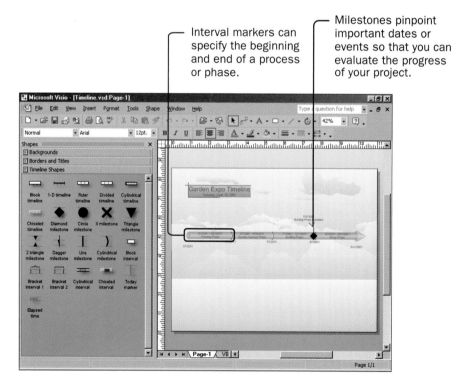

You create timelines using the **Timeline** template and the **Timeline Shapes** stencil by dragging shapes that represent milestones and interval markers from the stencil to a timeline. After you add shapes to your timeline, you can reposition them by dragging them. Then Visio updates the date on the shape according to its position on the timeline.

Tip

If you already have project data in a Microsoft Project, Microsoft Excel, or text file format, you can import it into Visio using the **Import Project Data Wizard**. On the **Tools** menu, point to **Macros**, point to **Project Schedule**, and then click **Import Project Data Wizard**. Follow the steps in the wizard to import the project data and create a Visio timeline or Gantt chart.

In this exercise, you create a timeline, add interval markers, add a milestone, and add a title and background.

1   Start Visio.

2   On the **File** menu, point to **New**, point to **Project Schedule**, and then click **Timeline**.

Visio opens the **Timeline** template, which opens a blank drawing page and the **Timeline Shapes** stencil, the **Borders and Titles** stencil, and the **Backgrounds** stencil.

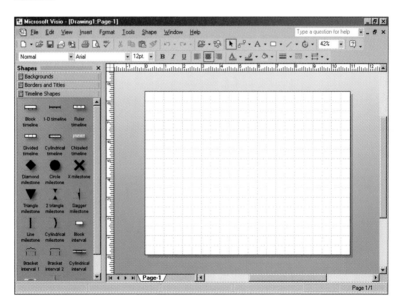

3   From the **Timeline Shapes** stencil, drag the **Cylindrical timeline** shape to the drawing page.

The **Configure Timeline** dialog box appears.

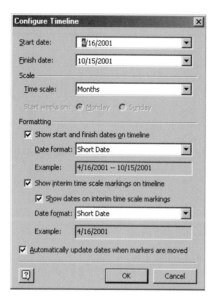

4   In the **Start date** box, click the down arrow to display a monthly calendar. In the calendar, click the left or right arrow to display the month of May, and then select the start date for the timeline by clicking **1**.

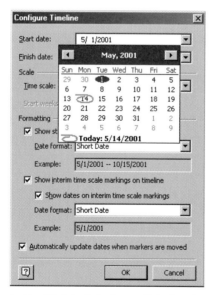

5   In the **Finish date** box, click the down arrow to display a monthly calendar. In the calendar, click the left or right arrow to display the month of August, and then select the finish date for the timeline by clicking **31**.

6 Click **OK**.

The dialog box closes, and Visio positions the timeline on the drawing page.

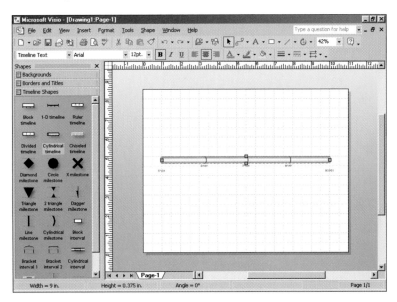

7 To add a decorative arrowhead on the right end of the timeline, right-click the timeline, and then click **Show Right Arrowhead**.

Visio adds an arrowhead to the right end of the timeline.

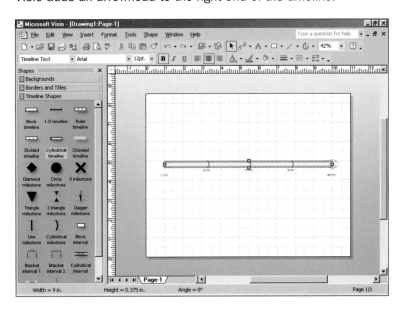

8 Drag a **Cylindrical interval** shape anywhere on the timeline.

The **Configure Interval** dialog box appears.

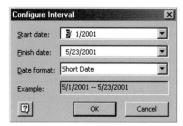

9 In the **Start date** box, click the down arrow to display a monthly calendar. In the calendar, click the left or right arrow to display the month of May, and then select the start date for the interval by clicking **1**.

10 In the **Finish date** box, click the down arrow to display a monthly calendar. In the calendar, click the left or right arrow to display the month of May, and then select the finish date for the timeline by clicking **31**.

11 Click **OK**.

The dialog box closes, and Visio positions the interval shape in the correct position on the timeline.

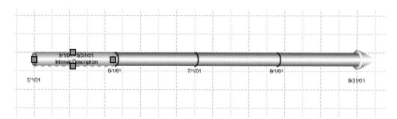

12 With the **Cylindrical interval** shape selected, press [F2] to edit the text.

Visio selects the text and zooms in on it so you can see it better.

13 Select the text *Interval Description*, and then type a new label, **Planning Phase**.

14 Press ⎋.

Visio zooms back out again so that you can see the entire timeline.

15 Drag three more **Cylindrical interval** shapes to the timeline and configure them as shown in the table below.

Start date	Finish date	Label
June 1	June 30	Develop Concept Phase
July 1	July 31	Building Phase
August 1	August 31	Setup Phase

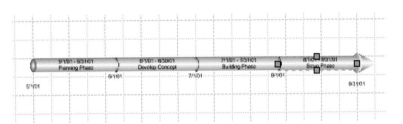

16 Drag a **Diamond milestone** shape anywhere on the timeline.

The **Configure Milestone** dialog box appears.

17 In the **Milestone date** box, click the down arrow to display a monthly calendar. In the calendar, click the left or right arrow to display the month of July, and then select the milestone date by clicking **31**.

18 Click **OK**.

The dialog box closes, and Visio correctly positions the milestone shape on the timeline.

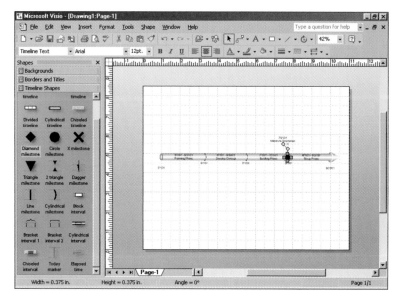

19 With the milestone selected, press F2.

Visio selects the text and zooms in on it so that you can see it better.

20 Select the text *Milestone Description*, and then type a new label, **Building Phase Complete**.

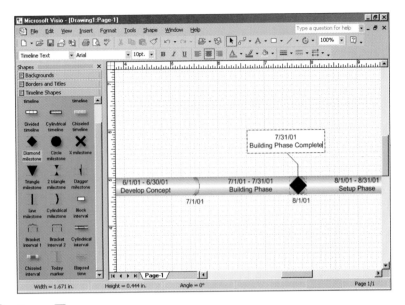

21 Press ⟦Esc⟧.

Visio zooms back out again so that you can see the entire timeline.

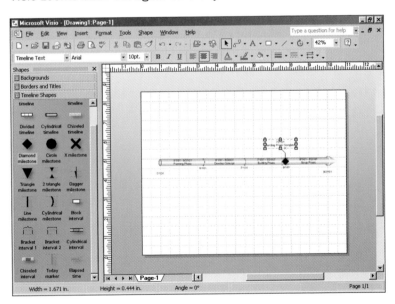

22 To add a background to your drawing, click the **Backgrounds** stencil to make it active, and then drag the **Background mountains** shape to the drawing page.

The **Make Background** dialog box appears.

23 Click **Yes**.

Visio creates a mountain background for your drawing.

24 To add a title to your drawing, click the **Borders and Titles** stencil to make it active, and then drag the **Title block contemp.** shape to the upper left corner of the drawing page.

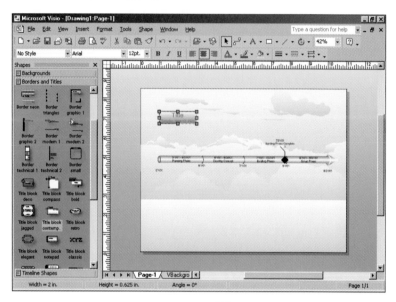

25 With the title shape selected, press ⟨F2⟩.

26 Select the word *Title*, and then type a new title, **Garden Expo Timeline**.

The **Title block contemp**. shape expands to fit your title.

27 Press ⟨Esc⟩.

28 Click the title shape, and then drag it to align it with the left edge of the timeline.

29 To add a color scheme to your timeline, right-click the drawing page, and then click **Color Schemes**.

The **Color Schemes** dialog box appears.

30 In the **Choose a color scheme** list, click **Forest**, and then click **OK**.

The dialog box closes, and Visio changes the color scheme of your drawing.

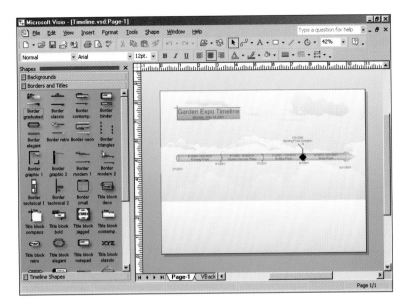

31 On the **File** menu, click **Save As**.

The **Save As** dialog box appears.

32 In the **File name** box, type **Timeline**, and then click **Save**.

The **Properties** dialog box appears.

33 Click **OK**.

Visio saves the drawing.

34 On the **File** menu, click **Close**.

The drawing closes.

Tip

After you create a timeline, you can modify it or any of the shapes you added to it by right-clicking the timeline or a shape. Then, on the shortcut menu, click the appropriate command. For example, to reconfigure a milestone, right-click it, and then click **Configure Milestone**. To change the milestone type to a diamond, circle, X, or triangle, right-click the milestone, and then click **Set Milestone Type**. For more information on creating timelines, type **Timeline** in the Ask A Question box in the upper right corner of the Visio window.

Exporting Timelines to Create Gantt Charts

Export Project
Data Wizard

new for
OfficeXP

When you use Visio drawings to schedule your projects, you usually start by visualizing the big picture with timelines, and then you create Gantt charts to view project details. Instead of creating a Gantt chart for a project from scratch, you can export your timeline data and, with this data, create a Gantt chart using the **Export Project Data Wizard**. Then you can flesh out the details of your project with the Gantt chart.

Timeline

In this exercise, you open an existing Garden Expo timeline, and then you use the **Export Project Data Wizard** to export the timeline data and create a Gantt chart from that data.

Tip

As you revise your Gantt charts, you'll no doubt make changes to the overall schedule as well. Just as you can export timeline data to create Gantt charts, you can also export Gantt chart data to create new timelines using the **Export Project Data Wizard**.

Open

1 On the Standard toolbar, click the **Open** button.

The **Open** dialog box appears.

2 Navigate to the **SBS\Visio\Projects** folder, and then double-click the **Timeline** file.

The Timeline drawing opens. The **Timeline Shapes** stencil, **Borders and Titles** stencil, and **Backgrounds** stencil are displayed.

3 On the **Tools** menu, point to **Macros**, point to **Project Schedule**, and then click **Export Project Data Wizard**.

The **Export Project Data Wizard** dialog box appears.

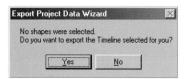

4 Click **Yes**.

The **Export Project Data Wizard** starts.

5 On the first **Export Project Data Wizard** page, click **Microsoft Visio Gantt Chart drawing**, and then click **Next**.

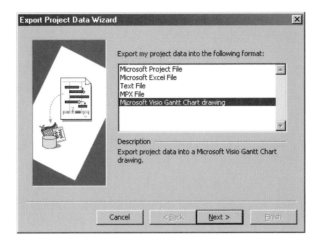

6 On the second **Export Project Data Wizard** page, click **Next** to accept the default selection.

7 On the third **Export Project Data Wizard** page, click **Next** to accept the default selection.

8 On the fourth and last **Export Project Data Wizard** page, click **Finish**.

Microsoft Visio exports the timeline data, opens the **Gantt Chart** template and the **Gantt Chart Shapes** stencil, the **Borders and Titles** stencil, and the **Backgrounds** stencil, and then lays out the Gantt chart on a new drawing page.

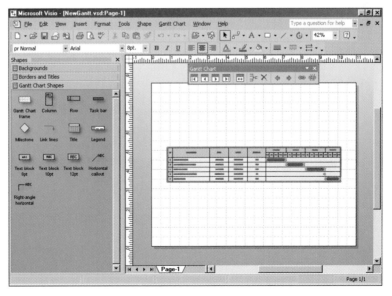

9 On the **File** menu, click **Save As**.

The **Save As** dialog box appears.

10 In the **File name** box, type **NewGantt**, and then click the **Save** button.

The **Properties** dialog box appears.

11 Click **OK**.

Visio saves the drawing.

12 On the **File** menu, click **Close**.

The drawing closes.

Tracking Project Details with Gantt Charts

While Visio timelines help you view your project at a glance, Gantt charts help you manage its details. With Gantt charts, you can track the details of each project task, create task dependencies, see how changes to one task affect another, and quickly identify task owners and status. A **Gantt chart** includes a list of project tasks and details about the tasks, **Gantt bars** that represent the duration of each task, and a timescale. With Gantt charts, you can visualize and track the project specifics that project managers and project members need to complete their tasks and keep the project on schedule.

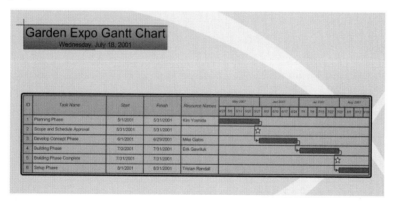

You can create Gantt charts from existing timeline data using the **Export Project Data Wizard** or from scratch using the **Gantt Chart** template. To create a Gantt chart from scratch, on the **File** menu, point to **New**, point to **Project Schedule**, and then click **Gantt Chart**. The **Gantt Chart Options** dialog box appears. Use it to configure and format your Gantt chart.

After you create a Gantt chart from existing data or from scratch, you add rows and columns to the chart. Each row represents a task, and each Gantt bar in a row represents the duration of the task. Each column represents project data you want to track, such as start date, end date, percentage complete, resource name, and task notes.

You can also show that one task can't start until another ends by creating a task dependency. To create a task dependency, you select the Gantt bar for the task that starts first, and then the bar for the task that can't start until the other ends. Then you link the bars. Visio draws arrows between the linked tasks.

New Gantt

In this exercise, you open an existing Gantt chart. You track task details for the Garden Expo project by creating task dependencies, inserting columns, and creating new tasks. For visual appeal, you also add a title and background to your drawing.

1 On the Standard toolbar, click the **Open** button.

The **Open** dialog box appears.

2 Navigate to the **SBS\Visio\Projects** folder, and then double-click the **NewGantt** file.

The NewGantt drawing opens. The **Gantt Chart Shapes** stencil, the **Borders and Titles** stencil, and the **Backgrounds** stencil are displayed. This drawing was created with the **Gantt Chart** template, so you'll also see the **Gantt Chart** menu on the menu bar and the Gantt Chart toolbar.

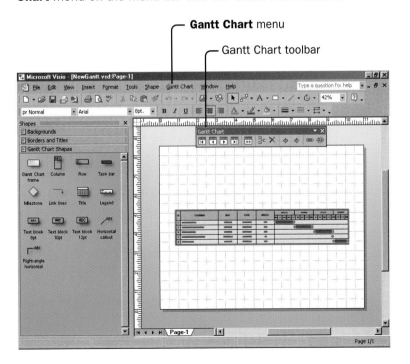

Gantt Chart menu

Gantt Chart toolbar

3   On the **View** menu, click **Connection Points** to turn them off so that they don't obscure your view of the Gantt chart.

4   Select the first blue Gantt bar in the Gantt chart.

5   Hold down [Shift] while you select the three other Gantt bars, from top to bottom.

Important

The order in which you select and link the tasks is important. Select the Gantt bar for the task that starts first, and then the bar for the task that can't start until the other ends, and so on.

6   To create task dependencies, on the **Gantt Chart** menu, click **Link Tasks**.
Visio links the selected tasks.

7   Press [Esc] to deselect everything.

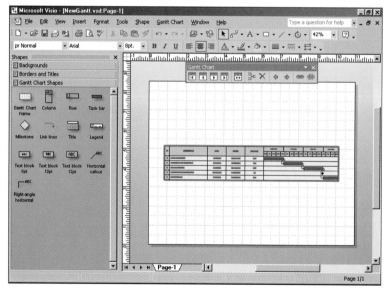

8   Hold down [Shift] + [Ctrl] as you click the Gantt chart to zoom in for a better view.

9 To track more task details, right-click the **Duration** column, and then click **Insert Column**.

The **Insert Column** dialog box appears.

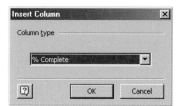

10 To add column with which you can track each task owner, click the down arrow, click **Resource Names** in the list, and then click **OK**.

Visio inserts a column after the **Duration** column.

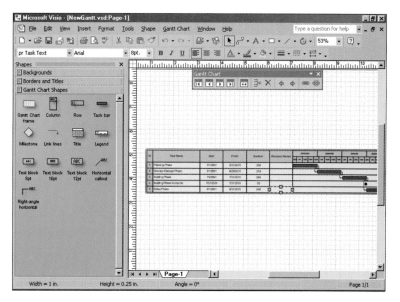

11 On the **Shape** menu, click **Center Drawing**.

Visio centers the Gantt chart on the drawing page.

12 Select the first cell in the **Resource Names** column, and then type
Kim Yoshida.

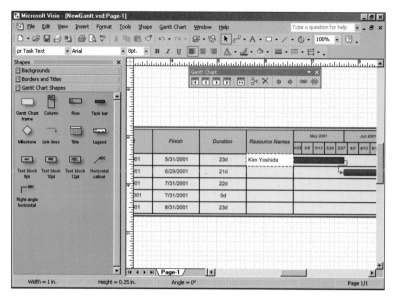

13 Select the second cell in the **Resource Names** column, and then type
Mike Galos.

14 Select the third cell in the **Resource Names** column, and then type
Erik Gavriluk.

15 Skip the fourth cell, select the last cell in the **Resource Names** column, and
then type Tristan Randall.

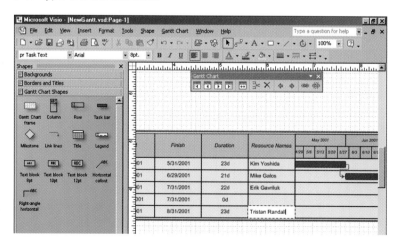

16 In the Visio window, scroll to the left until you can see the **Task Name** column.

17 To add one more milestone to the Gantt chart, right-click the second row that represents the **Develop Concept Phase** task, and then click **New Task**.

Visio inserts a new row for a new task above the **Develop Concept Phase** task row.

Tip

You can add more tasks to the end of your Gantt chart by selecting the Gantt chart frame and dragging it down. You can delete tasks at the end of the chart by dragging the Gantt chart frame back up.

18 With the **Task Name** cell for the new milestone selected, type **Scope and Schedule Approval**.

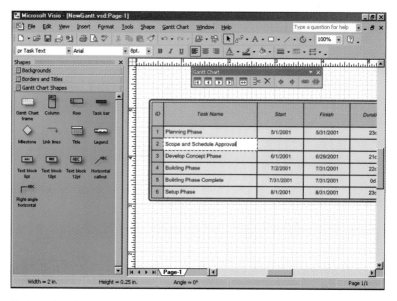

19 Select the **Start** cell for the new milestone.

Visio inserts default task information for you.

20 Type **5/31**, and then click outside the Gantt chart.

Visio changes the finish date to match the start date.

21 In the Visio window, scroll to the right until you can see the **Duration** column.

22 To make this task a milestone, select the **Duration** cell for the new milestone, type **0** because milestones don't have a duration, and then click outside the Gantt chart.

Visio changes the Gantt bar to a diamond.

23 To zoom out and fit the drawing page in the Visio window, hold down ⌃ while you press ⊞.

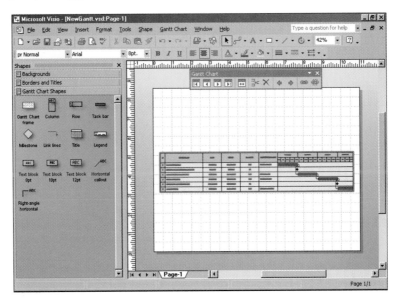

24 To change the milestone type to a star for all the milestones in the Gantt chart, on the **Gantt Chart** menu, click **Options**.

The **Gantt Chart Options** dialog box appears.

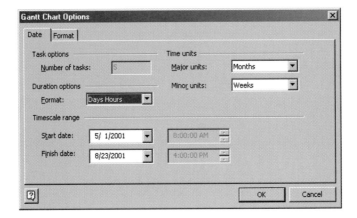

25 Click the **Format** tab, and then under **Milestones**, for **Shape**, click **Star**.

26 Click **OK**.

Visio changes the milestone shapes in the Gantt chart to stars.

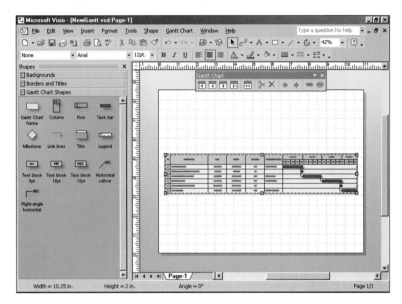

27 To add a background to your drawing, click the **Backgrounds** stencil to make it active, and then drag the **Background web** shape to the drawing page.

The **Make Background** dialog box appears.

28 Click **Yes**.

Visio creates a background for your drawing.

29 To add a title to your drawing, click the **Borders and Titles** stencil to make it active, and then drag the **Title block contemp.** shape to the upper left corner of the drawing page.

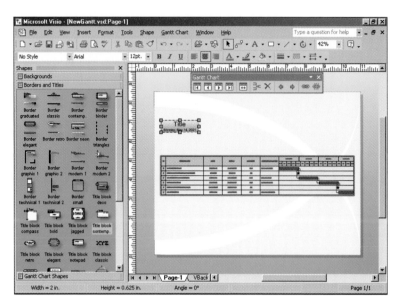

30 With the title shape selected, press [F2].

31 Select the word *Title*, and then type a new title, **Garden Expo Gantt Chart**.

The **Title block contemp.** shape expands to fit your title.

32 Press [Esc].

33 Click the title shape, and then drag it to align it with the left edge of the Gantt chart.

34 To add a color scheme to your timeline, right-click the drawing page, and then click **Color Schemes**.

The **Color Schemes** dialog box appears.

35 In the **Choose a color scheme** list, click **Coffee**, and then click **OK**.

The dialog box closes, and Visio changes the color scheme of your drawing.

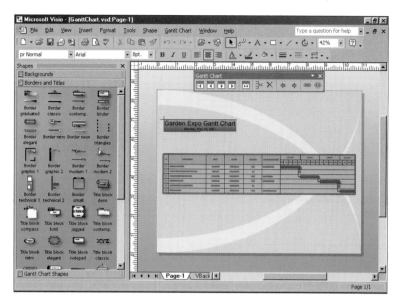

36 On the **File** menu, click **Save As**.

The **Save As** dialog box appears.

37 In the **File name** box, type **GanttChart**, and then click **Save**.

The **Properties** dialog box appears.

38 Click **OK**.

Visio saves the drawing.

39 On the **File** menu, click **Close**.

The drawing closes.

Tip

For more information on creating Gantt charts, type **Gantt chart** in the Ask A Question box in the upper right corner of the Visio window.

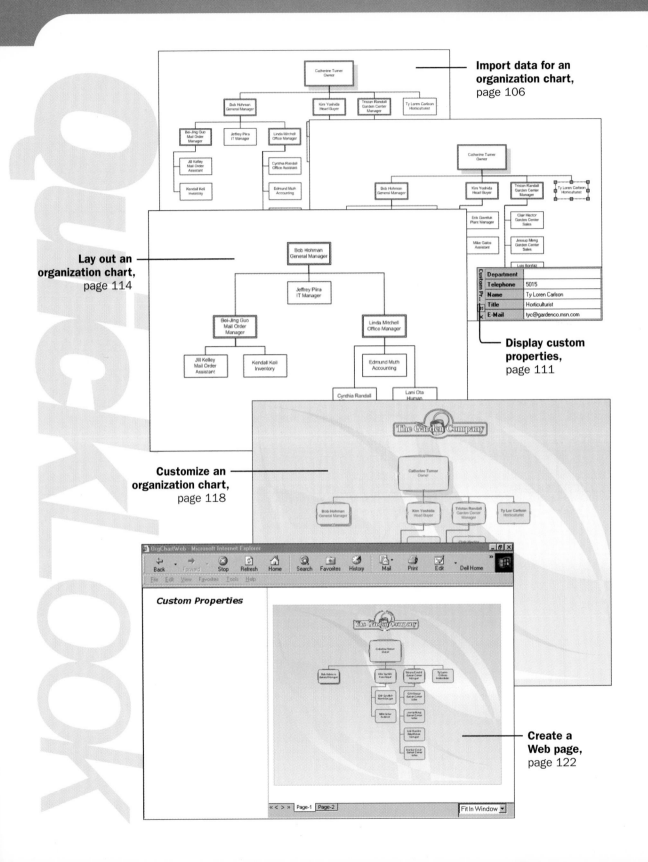

Import data for an
organization chart,
page 106

Lay out an
organization chart,
page 114

Display custom
properties,
page 111

Customize an
organization chart,
page 118

Create a
Web page,
page 122

Chapter 6
Creating an Organization Chart

After completing this chapter, you will be able to:

✔ Import data from a file to create an organization chart.

✔ Store and display employee information with an organization chart.

✔ Connect and lay out organization chart shapes.

✔ Customize an organization chart.

✔ Save an organization chart as a Web page.

Organization charts are used in almost every kind of business to visually document employee groups and their reporting relationships. The **Organization Chart** templates in Microsoft Visio let you quickly and easily create simple or complex organization charts. With the basic template, you can create an organization chart by dragging specialized position shapes, which represent people within the organization, onto the drawing page. By taking advantage of the intelligent behavior of the position shapes you choose, you can quickly show employee relationships within the organization. For example, if you drop a multiple position shape on a manager shape, Visio will lay out and connect as many positions (up to 50) as you specify to that manager. The **Organization Chart Wizard** template provides a step-by-step approach to building an organization chart from existing information stored in data files or information you provide to the wizard.

The position shapes in a Visio organization chart store information about the people and relationships within the organization. You can change the display to show any combination of stored data without having to re-create the entire chart.

In this chapter, you import existing human resources data from a Microsoft Excel spreadsheet to create an organization chart for The Garden Company. You view the additional data stored with each shape, edit the data, and then modify the layout. After adding color and a background to enhance the appearance of your chart, you save it as a Web page.

This chapter uses the practice files TGC Employees, OrgChart, OrgChartLayout, OrgChartCustom, and OrgChartWeb that you installed from this book's CD-ROM. For details about installing the practice files, see "Using the Book's CD-ROM" at the beginning of this book.

Importing Data for an Organization Chart

Today, many businesses maintain human resources information in electronic format. By using the **Organization Chart Wizard**, you can create an organization chart by importing employee information already stored in corporate data sources such as databases and data files. Then, if the organizational structure changes, you simply update the chart, rather than re-create it. This saves time and effort, especially for large organizations, and reduces the potential for error. You can import from the following data sources: a Microsoft Excel spreadsheet (.xls), a text file (.txt), Microsoft Exchange Server directories, Active Directory data, a Microsoft Access database (.mdb), or any ODBC (Open Database Connectivity)-compliant database application.

For the **Organization Chart Wizard** to work, the source data must be in the proper format and include, at minimum, data identifying unique employee names and the managers to whom they report. In an Excel spreadsheet, columns of information represent data fields that can be imported to your organization chart. For example, a human resources spreadsheet might include columns listing name, manager, department, title, e-mail address, phone, and office number.

With the **Organization Chart Wizard**, you first specify the data source from which you will import the data, and then you determine which columns contain the information that the wizard will use to structure the organization chart. In a typical chart, Visio uses an employee name field and a "reports to" field (the manager name) to specify how the reporting structure will be generated. That means that every employee name in the data source must also be associated with the name of the manager to whom the employee reports (except for the person at the very top of the organization). For example, if employee Luis Bonifaz reports to manager Bob Hohman, the data source must include both pieces of information so that Visio can structure the organization chart accurately.

Next, you select the data fields you want to appear on the organization chart (such as name and title) and identify additional fields you want to import as **custom properties**. A custom property is information that might not be displayed on the chart but that provides additional information about each position. For example, your organization chart might display employee name and title. Additional custom property data stored with each position shape might include phone number, e-mail address, and office number.

TGC Employees

In this exercise, you import data from an existing Excel spreadsheet to generate an organization chart for The Garden Company. In addition to importing the **Name** and **Reports to** fields, you also import data identifying the title, telephone number, and e-mail address for each employee. You do not need Excel to complete this exercise.

Tip

For help creating organization charts, type **organization chart** in the Ask A Question box on the right side of the menu bar.

1 Start Visio.

Visio starts. The **Choose Drawing Type** task pane and the **New Drawing** task pane appear.

2 Under **Category** in the **Choose Drawing Type** task pane, click **Organization Chart**.

The **Organization Chart** and the **Organization Chart Wizard** templates are listed in the **Template** area.

Tip

On the **File** menu, click **New**, and then click **Choose New Drawing** for another way to open the **Organization Chart Wizard**.

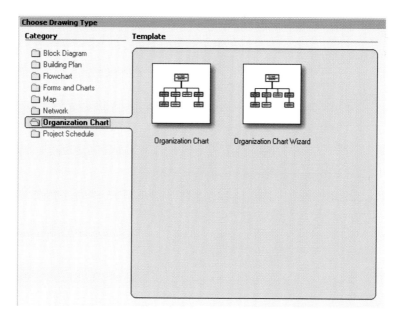

3 Under **Template**, click **Organization Chart Wizard**.

The template opens, displaying the drawing page, three stencils, and the first page of the **Organization Chart Wizard**.

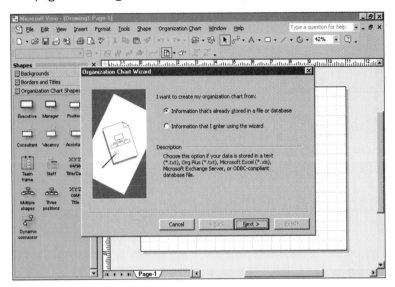

4 Make sure the **Information that's already stored in a file or database** option is selected, and then click **Next**.

The next wizard page appears, asking you to identify the type of data source you will be importing from.

5 Make sure the **A text, Org Plus (*.txt), or Microsoft Excel file** option is selected, and then click **Next**.

The next wizard page appears, asking you to locate the file you will use.

6 Click **Browse**, and then navigate to the **SBS\Visio\OrgChart** folder, and double-click **TGC Employees.xls**.

The wizard page reappears with the file and its path displayed.

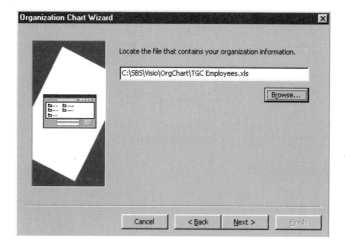

7 Click **Next**.

The next wizard page appears, asking you to choose the columns in the spreadsheet that contain the information the wizard will use to define the organization.

8 In the **Name** box, make sure **Name** is displayed; in the **Reports to** box, make sure **Manager** is displayed. Click **Next**.

The next wizard page appears, asking you to choose the fields you want to display on your organization chart.

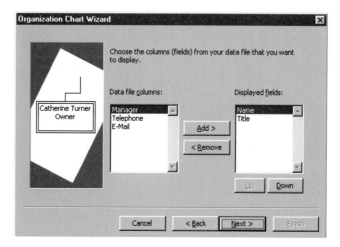

9 Make sure the **Displayed fields** list displays **Name** and **Title**. Click **Next**.

The next wizard page appears, asking you to choose additional columns (or fields) to import into your organization chart as custom properties.

10 In the **Data file columns** box, click **Telephone**, and then click **Add** to move it to the **Custom Property fields** box.

Telephone is listed in the **Custom Property fields** box.

11 Repeat step 10 to add **E-Mail**. Click **Next**.

The next wizard page appears, asking whether you want Visio to break your organization across pages.

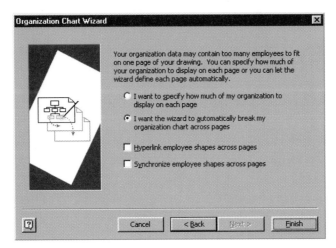

12 Make sure the **I want the wizard to automatically break my organization chart across pages** option is selected, and click **Finish**.

The wizard imports the data according to the specifications you entered, and the organization chart appears on the drawing page.

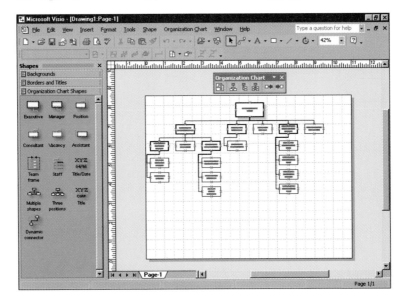

Zoom

33% ▼

13 On the Standard toolbar, click the **Zoom** down arrow, and click **75%**.

The drawing page displays the drawing at 75 percent of its actual size.

14 On the **File** menu, click **Close**, but don't save your changes.

Your drawing file closes.

Displaying Custom Properties

In Visio, you can store specific data about a shape as custom properties. For example, network equipment shapes are assigned custom properties for manufacturer, product number, part number, product description, asset number, serial number, location, and more. Each of these custom properties can contain data associated with the specific equipment shape in your diagram. In the case of a Visio organization chart, custom properties provide more descriptive information about the person in the job. Name, title, department, and telephone custom property fields are already assigned to position shapes. However, you can add an unlimited number of other custom property fields to store as much information as you need.

Although your organization chart might display only the names and titles for each position shape, you can view additional custom property fields by opening the **Custom Properties** window and then selecting a particular shape. If you want to display a different combination of custom properties, you can change the display without re-creating the entire chart.

OrgChart

In this exercise, you open an organization chart. You view the custom properties of two shapes and edit a telephone number in one of them. Then you change the display to add e-mail information to each shape.

Open

1 On the Standard toolbar, click the **Open** button.

The **Open** dialog box appears.

2 Navigate to the **SBS\Visio\OrgChart** folder, and double-click **OrgChart**.

OrgChart opens, displaying the names and titles of employees of The Garden Company.

3 On the **View** menu, click **Custom Properties Window**.

The **Custom Properties** window appears with no data displayed.

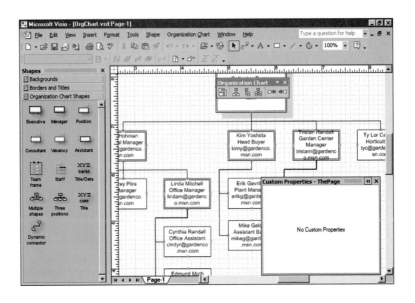

Tip

You can also open the **Custom Properties** window by clicking the **Custom Properties Window** button on the View toolbar. To display the View toolbar, right-click anywhere on the toolbar and click **View**.

Zoom

33% ▼

4 On the Standard toolbar, click the **Zoom** down arrow, and click **75%**.

The drawing page displays the drawing at 75 percent of its actual size.

5 Click the **Catherine Turner** position shape.

The **Custom Properties** window displays the telephone, name, title, and e-mail information for Catherine Turner.

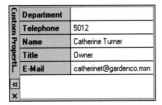

Department	
Telephone	5012
Name	Catherine Turner
Title	Owner
E-Mail	catherinet@gardenco.msn

6 Click the **Ty Loren Carlson** position shape.

7 In the **Custom Properties** window, click the **Telephone** box, type **5025**, and press `Enter`.

The **Telephone** box displays the changed number.

8 On the **Organization Chart** menu, click **Options**.

The **Options** dialog box appears.

9 In the **Options** dialog box, click **Set Display Fields**.

The **Set Display Fields** dialog box appears.

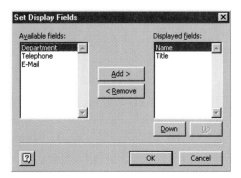

10 In the **Available Fields** list, click **E-Mail**, and then click **Add** to move it to the **Displayed Fields** list. Click **OK** twice.

The **Set Display Fields** dialog box closes. A message box appears, asking if you want the shape height adjusted to accommodate the additional information.

11 Click **Yes**.

The **Options** dialog box closes, and the shapes on your organization enlarge to display the name, title, and e-mail address for each position.

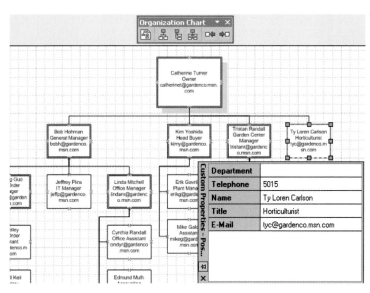

Close

12 For an unobstructed view of your organization chart, click the **Close** button on the **Custom Properties** window.

Tip

To hide the **Custom Properties** window, click the pushpin, and then move the pointer away.

13 On the **File** menu, click **Close**, but don't save your changes.

The OrgChart drawing closes.

Laying Out an Organization Chart

If your organization chart changes or if you plan to use it for more than one purpose, you might want to rearrange the way the position shapes are placed on the drawing page. Visio provides a number of tools to help you rearrange your organization chart, allowing you to modify the way it looks without changing the reporting structure. For example, the Organization Chart toolbar contains buttons for arranging all the shapes or groups of shapes in horizontal, vertical, or side-by-side layouts. You can also use this toolbar to quickly change the order of the position shapes reporting to a particular manager.

Charts for large or complex organizations can be arranged on several pages. You can quickly build a multi-page organization chart by creating **synchronized copies** of each department displayed on the original page and placing them on other pages in your drawing. Each synchronized copy duplicates the positions and reporting relationships for an employee group, and any changes to the text or custom properties of any synchronized shape then apply to all synchronized copies of the shape on other pages. This is a real time-saver and prevents inaccuracies from creeping into your drawing.

Synchronized copies are often used to create the detailed staffing pages for each department of a large organization. The original page can then be simplified to display only the top executive and his or her key managers, with the details for each department hidden.

Using hyperlinks, you can link a shape or entire page to another shape, a page within your drawing, an intranet or Internet URL, or a file. In addition to helping you navigate quickly within your drawing—for example, between the overview and the departmental pages in your organization chart—hyperlinks add more depth to shapes or pages. For example, you could link a company's customer service department page to the departmental Web site on the corporate intranet, providing access to more information about the group.

OrgChartLayout

In this exercise, you choose a layout for your organization chart. You create a synchronized copy of one department on another page and then insert a hyperlink linking the manager shape on the original page to its copy on the other page.

Open

1 On the Standard toolbar, click the **Open** button.

The **Open** dialog box appears.

2 Navigate to the **SBS\Visio\OrgChart** folder, and double-click **OrgChartLayout**.

OrgChartLayout opens, displaying the employees of The Garden Company.

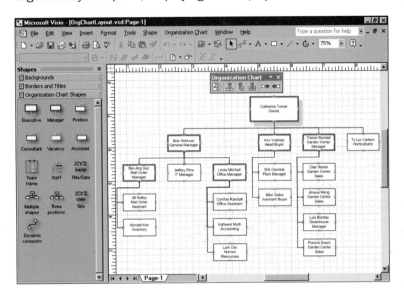

Vertical Layout

3 Select the **Bob Hohman General Manager** shape. On the Organization Chart toolbar, click **Vertical Layout**, and then click **Align Left**.

The subordinates in Bob Hohman's department are realigned. Some shapes drop below the bottom of the drawing page.

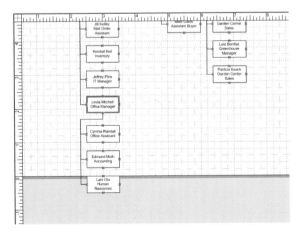

115

Tip

Another way to change the layout of your entire organization chart, or portions of your chart, is to select the position shape at the highest level of the staffing group you want to change, and then on the **Organization Chart** menu, click **Arrange Subordinates**. Click the layout style you want, and then click **OK**.

4 With the Bob Hohman shape selected, click **Create Synchronized Copy** on the **Organization Chart** menu.

The **Create Synchronized Copy** dialog box appears, asking whether you want your copy placed on a new page.

5 Make sure the **New page** option is selected. Select the **Hide subordinates on original page** check box, and click **OK**.

The dialog box closes, and Visio inserts a second page displaying Bob Hohman's department. The drawing is zoomed out so that you can see the entire drawing page. The Bob Hohman shape is selected.

Horizontal
Layout

6 On the Organization Chart toolbar, click **Horizontal Layout**, and then **Center**.

The subordinates in Bob Hohman's department are realigned.

7 On the **Edit** menu, click **Select All**, and when the pointer changes, drag the shapes to the center of the page.

Zoom

33% ▾

8 On the Standard toolbar, click the **Zoom** down arrow, and click **75%**.

The drawing page displays Bob Hohman's department at 75% of its actual size.

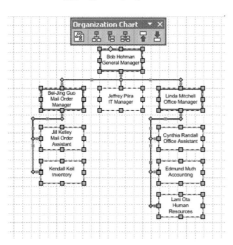

9 Click a blank area on the page to cancel the entire selection, and then select the **Bob Hohman** shape.

10 On the **View** menu, click **Custom Properties Window**.

The **Custom Properties** window opens, displaying the information for Bob Hohman.

11 Click the **Telephone** box, type **5041**, and press ⌷Enter⌷ to change the telephone number.

12 Click the **Page-1** tab, and select the **Bob Hohman** shape to view the custom properties for the shape.

The custom property information for Bob Hohman displays the new phone number, and his subordinates are now hidden from view.

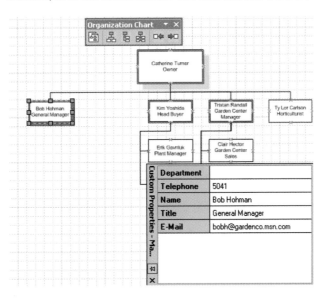

Important

Changes to the text and custom properties of a shape apply to all synchronized copies of the shape. However, changes such as adding, deleting, or moving a shape apply only to the page on which you are working.

13 With the Bob Hohman shape selected, click **Hyperlinks** on the **Insert** menu.

The **Hyperlinks** dialog box appears.

14 Click **Browse** next to the blank **Sub-address** box.

The **Hyperlink** dialog box appears.

15 Click the **Page** down arrow, and click **Page-2**. Click **OK**.

The **Hyperlink** dialog box closes, and the **Hyperlinks** dialog box shows Page-2 in the **Sub-address** box.

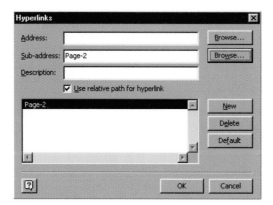

16 Click **OK**.

The **Hyperlinks** dialog box closes.

17 Pause the pointer over the **Bob Hohman** shape.

The pointer changes to indicate that a hyperlink is associated with the shape. A ScreenTip identifies the name of the link as *Page-2*.

18 Right-click the **Bob Hohman** shape, and on the shortcut menu that appears, click **Page-2**.

Visio navigates to Page-2 of your organization chart, displaying Bob Hohman's department with all subordinates showing.

19 On the **File** menu, click **Close**, but don't save your changes.

The OrgChartLayout drawing closes.

Customizing an Organization Chart

With Visio, you can add color and a background, change the design, or insert a company logo or other graphic to enhance the appearance of your organization chart. Visio provides 17 predesigned color schemes, which eliminate the need to choose colors for each individual element in your organization chart. Combined with one of 18 backgrounds, you can quickly find the color scheme that works best for your purpose. Plus, the organization chart templates provide five **themes**, which are formatting options that change the overall design of the shapes and text in your drawings.

OrgChartCustom

In this exercise, you change the look of your organization chart by choosing a different design theme and adding color and a background. Then you insert The Garden Company logo as a finishing touch.

Open

1 On the Standard toolbar, click the **Open** button.

The **Open** dialog box appears.

2 Navigate to the **SBS\Visio\OrgChart** folder, and double-click **OrgChartCustom**.

OrgChartCustom opens, displaying the employees of The Garden Company.

3 Click the **Backgrounds** stencil, and drag the **Background leaf** shape to the drawing page.

The **Make Background** dialog box appears, asking if you want the shape to be the background for the page.

4 Click **Yes**.

The **Leaf** background shape appears on Page-1. A **Vbackground** tab appears at the bottom of the page.

Tip

When you add a background shape to a page, Visio also adds a page to your drawing called **Vbackground**. The **Vbackground** page can contain all the visual items you might want to include in your background, including Visio shapes, text, and graphics such as clip art, pictures, and logos. You can assign this background to any page in your drawing.

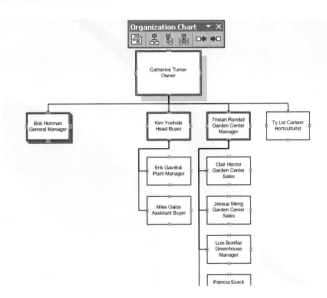

5 Click the **Page-2** tab at the bottom of your drawing, and then click **Page Setup** on the **File** menu.

The **Page Setup** dialog box appears.

6   To apply the background to Page-2 also, click the **Page Properties** tab, click the **Background** down arrow, and click **Vbackground**. Click **OK**.

The background is applied to Page-2.

7   On the **Tools** menu, click **Color Schemes**. In the **Color Schemes** dialog box, click **Forest** in the **Choose a color scheme** list, and then click **OK**.

The shapes, text, and background colors change to the new color scheme.

8   On the **Organization Chart** menu, click **Options**.

The **Options** dialog box appears.

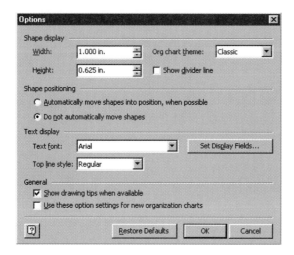

9   In the **Shape display** area, click the **Org chart theme** down arrow, and then click **Retro**.

10 In the **Text display** area, click the **Top line style** down arrow and then click **Bold**. Click **OK**.

The organization chart appears, displaying the new Retro design. Each person's name is shown in bold type.

11 Click the **Vbackground** tab on the drawing page. On the **Insert** menu, point to **Picture**, and click **From File**.

The **Insert Picture** dialog box appears.

12 Navigate to the **SBS\Visio\OrgChart** folder, and then double-click **TGC Logo.gif**.

The Garden Company logo appears in the center of your drawing.

13 Drag a corner selection handle to make the logo smaller, and then move it to the upper center of your drawing. Press the [Esc] key to clear your selection.

Your background page should look similar to the figure on the following page.

Tip

Graphics added to the background page appear in the same place on every page assigned with that background.

14 Click the **Page-1** tab on the drawing page. Click the **Close** button on the Organization Chart toolbar for an unobstructed view of your completed organization chart.

Your organization chart should look similar to this.

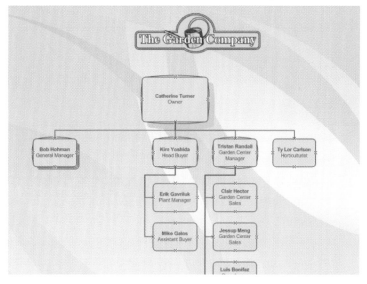

15 On the **File** menu, click **Close**, but don't save your changes.

The OrgChartCustom drawing closes.

Saving a Drawing as a Web Page

By saving your Visio drawings in HTML (Hypertext Markup Language) format, you can share information via the Internet or a corporate intranet. Many organizations use this method to make information available to employees across the company. Visio drawings published to the Web are accessible to any employee with a browser and the proper permission to access to the intranet—even if they don't have Visio.

Web-based organization charts can help employees understand the relationships between staffing groups and can visually explain organizational changes. Each shape also stores custom property information about its position so that the charts can be a source for up-to-date employee information, such as office location, telephone number, or e-mail address.

When you save a Visio drawing as a Web page, Visio creates the HTML source code for the shapes and data. Navigation elements included in your drawing, such as hyperlinks and page tabs, are retained in the new Web page.

Visio saves your drawing so that it is compatible with recently released Web browsers such as Microsoft Internet Explorer 5 and later as well as older browsers. Some features in Visio 2002, such as page tabs, do not work with Netscape or earlier versions of Microsoft Internet Explorer.

The results of saving your drawing as a Web page are an .htm format file and a folder containing the graphic elements that support your drawing online.

OrgChartWeb

In this exercise, you save an organization chart as a Web page. Then you view the results and navigate to other pages of the chart using a hyperlink and the page tabs.

Important

You will need a Web browser, such as Microsoft Internet Explorer, to complete this exercise.

Open

1 On the Standard toolbar, click the **Open** button.

The **Open** dialog box appears.

2 Navigate to the **SBS\Visio\OrgChart** folder, and double-click **OrgChartWeb**.

The OrgChartWeb drawing opens, displaying the employees of The Garden Company.

3 On the **File** menu, click **Save as Web Page**.

The **Save As** dialog box appears with OrgChartWeb displayed in the **File name** box.

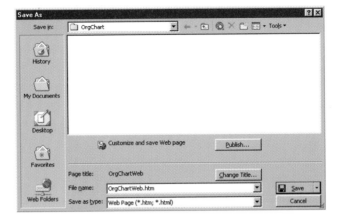

Tip

The file name will be displayed in the title bar of the browser when you view your drawing as a Web page. To change the title displayed on the Web page, click the **Change Title** button in the **Save As** dialog box.

4   In the **Save As** dialog box, click **Publish**.

The **Save As Web Page** dialog box appears.

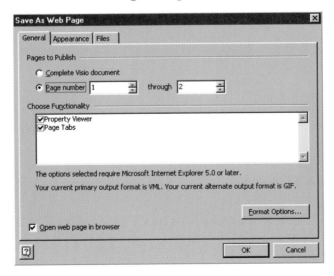

5   In the **Pages to Publish** area, make sure the **Page number 1 through 2** option is selected.

6   In the **Choose Functionality** area, make sure the **Property Viewer** and **Page Tabs** check boxes are selected.

The **Property Viewer** option adds a frame that displays the diagram's custom properties. The **Page Tabs** option adds tabs to the Web page for displaying all the pages in a multiple-page drawing.

7   Make sure the **Open web page in browser** check box is selected, and then click **OK**.

A progress bar appears as Visio saves your drawing in HTML format. The drawing opens in your browser, showing the blank **Custom Properties** pane at the left and the organization chart at the right.

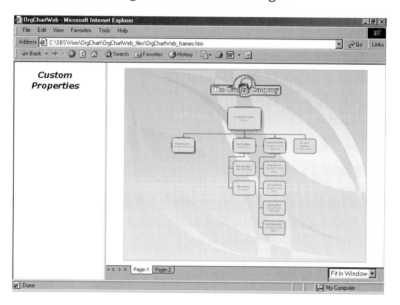

Troubleshooting

Unless your Web browser is Microsoft Internet Explorer 5 or later, you might not see the **Custom Properties** Pane.

8   Click the **Fit In Window** down arrow in the lower right corner, and then click **200%**.

The organization chart increases in size.

Custom
Properties
pane

9   Pause the pointer over the **Catherine Turner** shape, and view the **Custom Properties** pane.

new for
OfficeXP

Catherine Turner's employee information is displayed. You might have to resize the **Custom Properties** pane to see the complete display.

Custom Properties

Field	Value
Name	Catherine Turner
Title	Owner
E-Mail	catherinet@gardenco.msn.com
Department	
Telephone	5012.0000

10 Pause the pointer over the **Bob Hohman** shape.

The pointer changes to a hand to indicate a hyperlink.

11 Click the **Bob Hohman** shape.

Visio navigates to Page-2, which contains Bob Hohman's department detail.

12 Click the **Page-1** tab at the bottom of the drawing to return to the company overview page.

13 On the **File** menu in your browser, click **Close**.

Your Web page closes, and your original Visio drawing appears.

On the **File** menu in Visio, click **Close**, but don't save your changes.

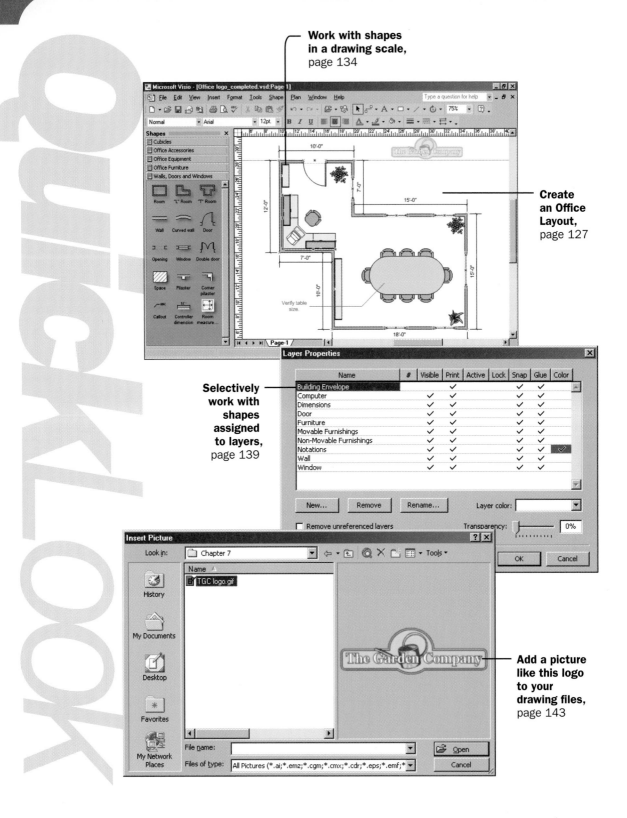

**Work with shapes
in a drawing scale,**
page 134

**Create
an Office
Layout,**
page 127

**Selectively
work with
shapes
assigned
to layers,**
page 139

**Add a picture
like this logo
to your
drawing files,**
page 143

Chapter 7
Laying Out Office Space

After completing this chapter, you will be able to:

✔   **Create a scaled office layout.**

✔   **Use door, window, and furniture shapes in a scaled drawing.**

✔   **Organize shapes with layers.**

✔   **Import pictures into an existing drawing.**

Think of something big—a house, an office building, or your backyard. In Microsoft Visio, you can diagram a large object on a small page by using a **drawing scale**, which represents the relationship between an object's size in the real world and its size on the page. Like a map that depicts a 10-mile stretch of highway with a 1-inch line, a scaled drawing represents objects at a ratio or a fraction of their size. A drawing scale isn't for large objects only—you can also draw very small objects, such as a watch mechanism or printed circuit, at a larger scale as well. When you start a Visio drawing with a scaled template, the drawing scale is set up for you, and the shapes conform to that scale automatically. All you have to do is drag and drop them.

In this chapter, you create a diagram of a furnished office for the head gardener of The Garden Company, who gives frequent lectures in the adjoining conference space. You work with the **Office Layout** template to create a replica of the building shell—its walls, doors, and windows—and then add furniture shapes. This chapter introduces a new concept, layers, which provide a method of organizing shapes. As a finishing touch, you import a graphic file that contains The Garden Company logo.

 This chapter uses the practice files OfficeWalls, OfficeFurnished, and OfficeLogo that you installed from the CD-ROM. For details about installing the practice files, see "Using the Book's CD-ROM" at the beginning of this book.

Creating an Office Layout

The **Office Layout** template makes it easy to create an accurate floor plan with architectural details, such as pilasters (rectangular wall projections like columns) and door swing (the space needed to open or close a door). If your goal is simply to experiment with different furniture arrangements in a room, you might not need the level of detail that Visio provides. However, because Visio is designed to provide architectural and engineering precision, your scaled diagrams are as accurate as your measurements.

All Visio templates have a pre-set drawing scale, but for most business diagrams, such as flowcharts or organization charts, that scale is 1:1—that is, no scale. In the **Office Layout** template, the drawing scale is ½ inch to 1 foot, which means that a shape that appears ½ inch high on the drawing page represents an object that is 1 foot tall. Visio sets up the drawing page using the template's scale and **units of measure**, which are typically inches (although Visio includes metric templates as well). If you prefer to measure shapes in yards or meters or some other measurement unit, you can by using the **Page Setup** command on the **File** menu, which is also how you set the drawing scale. In addition, the **Office Layout** template also adds a new menu: the **Plan** menu, which includes commands specifically for working in this type of drawing.

When you start a drawing with a scaled template, the drawing page reflects the measurement units of that scale much as a map reflects the scale shown in its legend. The units of measure for the drawing scale appear on the rulers and the grid and are displayed automatically in the dimension line shapes that you can add to walls. Part of what you have to do when working in an office layout or any scaled drawing is grow accustomed to measuring distance in real-world units. For example, if your drawing scale is ½ inch to 1 foot on letter-sized paper (11 by 8½ inches), the rulers show that the page is 22 feet long and 17 feet high. That's because the rulers display the real-world measurements so that you position and size shapes in terms of the physical space or object you're designing. When you print the page, however, Visio ensures that it fits on regular letter-sized paper.

Rulers reflect the drawing scale.
Dimension lines display measurements automatically.
The **Plan** menu appears.
Guides help you align and move shapes.

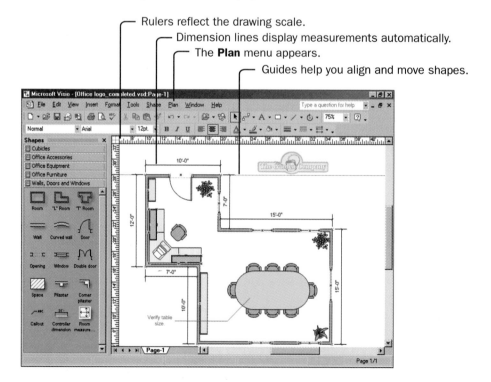

After you set up the drawing scale you want, you start by adding shapes that represent the structure of your building. One way to do this is to drag wall shapes onto the page and rotate them into position. Where two walls meet, Visio joins their corners automatically for a smooth look. All the other structural shapes, such as doors and windows, are designed to snap to the wall shapes in a building layout. However, when you're planning a new space, you can instead use the **Space** shape, which represents a 10-foot-by-10-foot area. You can lay out a patchwork of space shapes, and then combine them into a single area by using the **Union** command, which merges shapes to create a new shape. Then you can convert the space into walls. Although this technique sounds like it takes several steps, most people find it easier to lay out rooms and create walls in this fashion rather than drag out individual wall shapes.

When you need to measure areas precisely, Visio offers several helpful shortcuts. Some shapes display their size—for example, the **Space** shape displays *100 sq. ft*. The status bar below the drawing page reflects the real-world units of measure, so you can see at a glance how large shapes really are and exactly where a wall goes. Guide lines can help you align shapes to an exact point as well. Shapes connect to guides to ensure perfect alignment, and you can even drag a guide to move all the shapes connected to it—a very efficient technique. Visio's built-in connection behavior also helps you attach dimension lines to the walls they measure. As you move or resize walls, the dimension lines stay connected and update measurements as they change.

In this exercise, you start a new office layout with the **Office Layout** template and use the **Page Setup** command to customize the drawing scale. You rough out the area you want to show with **Space** shapes, which you then combine into a single shape and convert to walls—a faster way of creating the outline of a building than simply dragging wall shapes onto the page.

1 Start Visio.

2 On the **File** menu, point to **New**, point to **Building Plan**, and then click **Office Layout**.

Visio starts a blank drawing with the **Office Layout** template, which opens the following five stencils: **Walls, Doors and Windows**, **Office Furniture**, **Office Equipment**, **Office Accessories**, and **Cubicles**. The **Plan** menu is added to the menu bar.

3 On the **File** menu, click **Page Setup** to open the **Page Setup** dialog box.

4 Click the **Drawing Scale** tab.

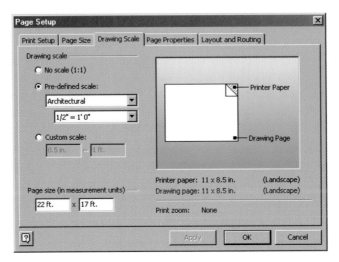

5 Under the **Pre-defined scale** option, click the down arrow on the box that displays **½" = 1'0"**, scroll up, and then click **¼" = 1'0"**.

Visio changes the drawing scale and recalculates the dimensions displayed in the **Page size (in measurement units)** boxes.

6 Click **OK**.

The rulers display the new drawing scale and show that the drawing page represents an area 44 feet wide and 34 feet tall.

7 From the **Walls, Doors and Windows** stencil, drag a **Space** shape onto the page so that its top and left edges are about 10 feet from the page edges as measured by the rulers.

Tip

As you drag a shape, Visio displays dotted lines on the rulers and measurements in the status bar, which show you the shape's exact position on the page.

8 Drag a second **Space** shape onto the page so that its upper left corner overlaps the bottom right corner of the first **Space** shape.

The **Space** shape remains selected. Your screen should look similar to the figure on the following page.

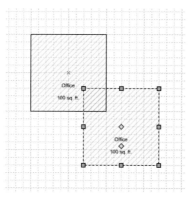

9   On the selected **Space** shape, drag the right middle selection handle to make the shape 20 feet wide, as shown by the **Width** field in the status bar at the bottom of the drawing page window.

Visio updates the measurement displayed on the shape to 200 sq. ft.

10   On the same shape, drag the bottom middle selection handle to make the shape 15 feet high.

Visio updates the measurement displayed on the shape to 300 sq. ft.

11   Hold down ⎡shift⎤ as you click the other **Space** shape so that both shapes are selected.

12   On the **Shape** menu, click **Operations**, and then click **Union**.

Visio combines the two shapes into one shape. The shapes should look similar to the following.

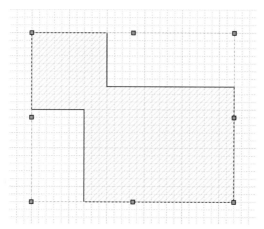

13 On the **Plan** menu, click **Convert To Walls** to display the **Convert To Walls** dialog box.

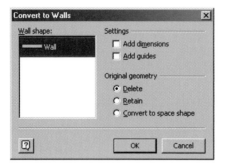

Tip

Another way to create walls is to use the Line or Rectangle tool to draw rough approximations of your walls, and then use the **Convert To Walls** command to convert them into wall shapes.

14 Select the **Add dimensions** check box, and then click **OK**.

Visio displays a status bar as it converts the perimeter of the shape to wall shapes and adds dimension line shapes to each wall.

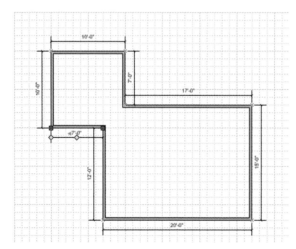

15 Right-click the top 10-foot wall, and click **Add a Guide** on the shortcut menu that appears.

Visio adds a guide to the wall shape's top edge and connects the adjoining walls to the guide so that you can move them together. The guide is selected. Your screen should look similar to the figure on the following page; however, your dimensions might not match exactly.

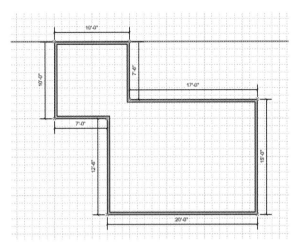

16 Point to the guide until a two-headed arrow appears, and then drag the guide up about 3 feet to the 27-foot mark.

Visio moves the guide and all three walls that are connected to it to the new position and updates the dimension lines. The shapes should look similar to the following.

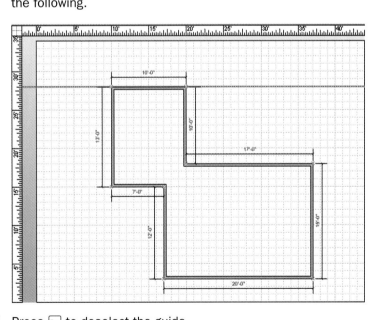

17 Press [Esc] to deselect the guide.

18 On the Standard toolbar, click the **Save** button.

The **Save As** dialog box appears.

19 On the **Places** bar, click **My Documents**.

20 In the **File name** box, type New Office.

21 Click **Save**.

The **Properties** dialog box appears.

22 Click **OK**.

Visio saves the drawing.

23 On the **File** menu, click **Close**.

The drawing closes.

Tip

Although office layouts are a common type of scaled drawing, you can define a scale for any drawing type in Visio. For example, you can create maps, parts drawings, and physical network diagrams to scale by using the **Page Setup** command on the **File** menu to define a drawing scale.

Adding Doors, Windows, and Furniture

You don't have to start with a template to create a scaled drawing, but an advantage of doing so is that the template opens stencils of shapes designed to work in the drawing scale. The **Office Layout** template includes many specialized shapes and tools for working in a drawing scale. Wall shapes join together to form smooth corners. Door and window shapes drop into place on top of walls, rotating if necessary to match the wall's orientation.

One way in which **Office Layout** shapes are unusual is that they're designed to match standard architectural sizes. Because of this, some shapes are locked to prevent you from resizing them with the mouse. To change their size, you must edit the shape's built-in property that controls its dimensions. For example, a **Door** shape has a **Door Width** property that you can set to 24, 28, 30, 36, 48, 60, or 72 inches—standard door widths. Visio resizes the shape based on your selection. You can change a shape's properties from its shortcut menu, which might contain other specialized commands for editing the shape. For example, you can't rotate or flip a door to change its orientation. Instead, you can use the **Reverse In/Out Opening** command or **Reverse Left/Right Opening** command, and Visio does it for you.

Tip

Right-click an office layout shape to see whether its shortcut menu contains special commands for editing the shape.

OfficeWalls

In this exercise, you add doors, windows, and furniture to an office of The Garden Company. You start by opening a sample drawing, OfficeWalls. You work with shape properties and shortcut menu commands to edit door and window shapes. Finally, you add furniture to the rooms.

Open

1 On the Standard toolbar, click the **Open** button to display the **Open** dialog box.

2 Navigate to the **SBS\Visio\OfficeLayout** folder on your hard disk, and then double-click **OfficeWalls**.

Visio opens a diagram showing the outline of two adjoining rooms in a scaled office layout and displays the five office layout stencils.

3 From the **Walls, Doors and Windows** stencil, drag the **Door** shape to the middle of the top 10-foot wall.

When you release the mouse, Visio connects the door to the wall, displaying red selection handles to show that the shapes are connected, and padlock handles to show that the door is locked to prevent resizing.

Zoom

33%

4 On the Standard toolbar, click the **Zoom** down arrow, and then click **100%**.

Visio magnifies the view. The door and wall should look something like this.

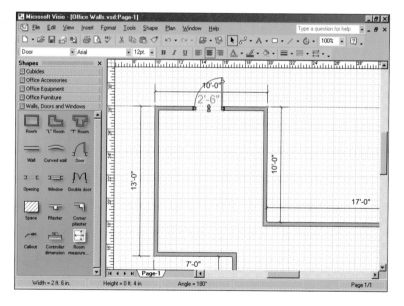

5   Right-click the door to display its shortcut menu, and then click **Properties**.

The **Custom Properties** dialog box appears and lists properties for the door.

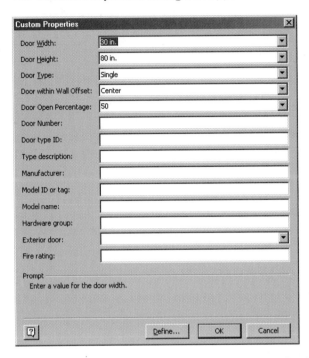

6   In the **Door Width** box, click the down arrow to display a list of dimensions, and then click **36 in**.

7   Click **OK**.

Visio widens the door and updates its dimensions to 3'-0".

8   Right-click the door to display its shortcut menu, and then click **Reverse In/Out Opening**.

Visio flips the door opening so that it swings into the office.

9   From the **Walls, Doors and Windows** stencil, drag the **Window** shape to the vertical wall to the right of the door.

Visio flips the window to match the wall's orientation and then connects the window to the wall shape, displaying red selection handles and padlock handles.

10   Drag the window's lower selection handle until the shape is approximately 3 feet wide.

11 From the **Walls, Doors and Windows** stencil, drag another **Window** shape onto the 17-foot wall.

Visio connects the window to the wall.

12 Hold down [Shift] and [Ctrl] while you drag with the right mouse button to pan the drawing to the left.

The right half of the office space becomes visible.

13 Drag a selection handle on the window you just added to make the shape about 3 feet wide.

Visio updates the window's dimensions.

14 Hold down [Ctrl] while you drag the window along the wall to the right to duplicate the shape.

Visio connects the copied window to the wall. Your drawing page should look similar to the following.

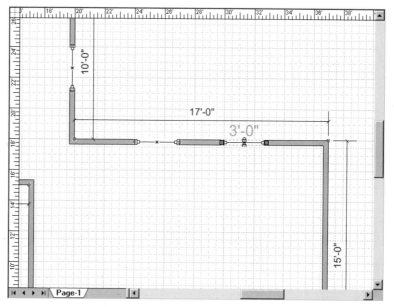

15 Pan the drawing to the right to display the office with the door.

Cubicles
stencil
new for
OfficeXP

16 Click the **Cubicles** stencil to display it on top.

17 From the **Cubicles** stencil, drag the **L workstation** shape into the corner of the office opposite the door.

The shapes should look similar to the figure on the following page.

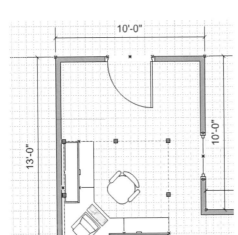

18 Hold down [Shift] and [Ctrl] while you right-click to zoom out.

Visio zooms out to show more of the page.

19 Click the **Office Furniture** stencil to bring it to the top.

20 From the **Office Furniture** stencil, drag the **Multi-chair racetrack** shape into the large empty room.

Visio adds the shape, oriented vertically, to the room. The shape is selected.

21 On the **Shape** menu, point to **Rotate or Flip**, and then click **Rotate Left**.

The **Multi-chair racetrack** shape rotates 90 degrees to the left.

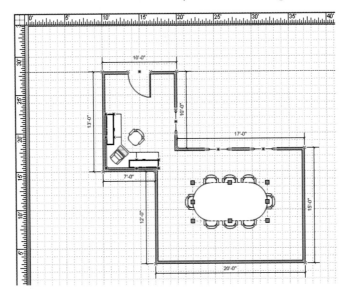

Tip

To quickly rotate a shape 90 degrees to the left, press ⌨Ctrl + ⌨L.

Save

22 On the Standard toolbar, click the **Save** button.

Visio saves your changes.

23 On the **File** menu, click **Close**.

The drawing closes.

Organizing Shapes with Layers

For some drawing types, shapes are pre-assigned to **layers**, categories that help you organize related shapes. Visio can selectively show, hide, lock, print, snap, glue, and color shapes based on their layer assignment, which gives you a great deal of flexibility when editing shapes. For example, it's common to lock the structural shapes like walls, doors, and windows after they're in place so that you don't inadvertently move them while adding furniture to an office layout. Or you can temporarily hide all the annotation shapes, such as dimension lines, to make it easier to see and move furniture shapes.

Layers are often used when different people revise or review a single drawing. For example, in an office layout, the building shell can be locked and then handed off to an electrician, who adds wiring on one layer, and then to a plumber, who adds pipes on another layer. That way, each person can add to the drawing without disturbing another's work. A shape can be assigned to a single layer, to several layers, or to no layer at all. If you use the drawing tools to create a shape, that shape is not assigned to a layer. You can, however, assign a shape to an existing layer or create a new layer. Fortunately, the **Office Layout** shapes are already assigned to layers that are built into the template and added to your drawing.

Tip

If you display the Format Shape toolbar, the **Layer** list shows you which layers a selected shape is assigned to.

Visio includes two commands for working with layers. The **Layer** command on the **Format** menu shows you a shape's layer assignments and allows you to create and remove layers. The **Layer Properties** command on the **View** menu lets you control the appearance and behavior of the shapes assigned to layers.

OfficeFurnished

In this exercise, you add determine which layers shapes are assigned to, and then you change layer properties to affect the way you can interact with shapes in the drawing. You start by opening a sample drawing, OfficeFurnished.

Open

1 On the Standard toolbar, click the **Open** button to display the **Open** dialog box.

2 Navigate to the **SBS\Visio\OfficeLayout** folder on your hard disk, and then double-click **OfficeFurnished**.

Visio opens an office layout diagram and displays the five office layout stencils.

3 Select the conference table, and then on the **Format** menu, click **Layer**.

The **Layer** dialog box appears and highlights the layers to which the shape is assigned. In this case, the conference table (the **Multi-chair racetrack** shape) is assigned to two layers: **Furniture** and **Movable Furnishings**.

4 Click **Cancel** to close the **Layer** dialog box.

5 Select a wall shape, and then on the **Format** menu, click **Layer**.

The **Layer** dialog box appears and highlights the **Building Envelope** layer and the **Wall** layer, indicating that wall shapes are assigned to these layers.

6 Click **Cancel** to close the **Layer** dialog box.

7 From the **Walls, Doors and Windows** stencil, drag the **Callout** shape onto the page to the left of the conference room.

Visio adds a callout that points to the left. The shape is selected.

8 On the **Shape** menu, point to **Rotate or Flip**, and then click **Flip Horizontal**.

The callout now points to the right. The shape remains selected.

9 Type **Verify table size**.

Visio zooms in as you type and adds the text to the callout.

10 Press Esc.

Visio zooms back out. The shape remains selected.

11 Drag the right endpoint of the **Callout** shape to the conference table.

As you drag over the table, Visio highlights the shape with a red border. When you release the mouse, the endpoint turns red, indicating that the callout is connected to the table. The shapes should look similar to those in this figure.

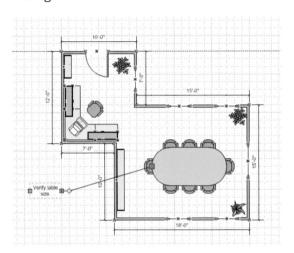

12 On the **View** menu, click **Layer Properties**.

The **Layer Properties** dialog box appears.

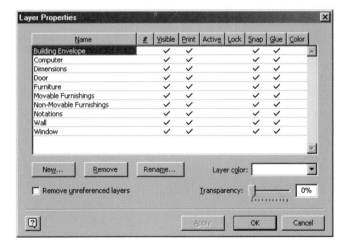

13 In the **Building Envelope** row, click in the **Lock** column.

Visio displays a check mark for **Lock**, indicating that all shapes on the **Building Envelope** layer will be locked to prevent selection.

14 Click in the **Lock** column for the **Door** row, **Wall** row, and **Window** row.

Visio locks the shapes assigned to these layers and displays a check mark for **Lock** in the **Door** row, **Wall** row, and **Window** row.

15 In the **Notations** row, click in the **Visible** column.

Visio clears the check mark in the **Visible** column, indicating that all shapes on the **Notations** layer will be hidden.

16 Click **OK**.

Visio updates the office layout with the new layer properties. The **Callout** shape is no longer visible.

17 In the office layout diagram, click the door shape.

Nothing happens—the shape is locked, so you can't select it. The walls and windows are similarly locked.

18 On the **View** menu, click **Layer Properties** to display the **Layer Properties** dialog box again.

19 In the **Notations** row, click in the **Visible** column to place a check mark there.

20 In the **Notations** row, click in the **Color** column.

Visio places a check mark in the row.

21 In the **Layer Color** box, click the down arrow, scroll up, and then click color **9** (green).

In the **Notations** row, the **Color** check mark is highlighted in green.

22 Click **OK**.

Visio displays the **Callout** shape and text in green.

Save

23 On the Standard toolbar, click the **Save** button.

Visio saves the changes to your drawing.

24 On the **File** menu, click **Close**.

Visio closes the drawing.

Troubleshooting

Many of the shapes in the **Office Layout** template are actually groups, such as the plant shapes on the **Office Accessories** stencil and the multi-chair conference table shapes on the **Office Furniture** stencil. To add color to the individual shapes in the group, you must subselect the shapes: Click to select the group, click a shape in the group to subselect it, and then choose a formatting option. For example, you can subselect a chair in the **Multi-chair racetrack** shape, and then click the **Fill Color** button on the **Formatting** toolbar to apply a color to that chair.

Importing Logos and Other Pictures

Although Visio includes hundreds of shapes as well as several drawing tools, sometimes you simply need an image that was created in a different program. You can import a **picture**—that is, a graphic file—into Visio whether or not you have the application that created the original image. For example, you can import a corporate logo to add it to an existing diagram. Visio can import most of the standard graphic file formats, including popular Web formats such as GIF (Graphic Interchange Format), JPEG (Joint Photographic Expert Group), and PNG (Portable Network Graphics). So there's almost certainly a format that Visio and the graphics application have in common.

There are two ways to import pictures:

Picture
command

new for
OfficeXP

- When you use Visio as a picture editing tool, you can use the **Open** command on the **File** menu to open the file, which creates a drawing page with a picture on it.

- When you want to add a picture to an existing drawing file, you can use the **Picture** command on the **Insert** menu.

Transparent
colors

new for
OfficeXP

Most of the time, you insert pictures into existing drawings. The **Picture** dialog box can even help you locate the correct file, because it can display a preview (sometimes called a thumbnail) of the picture. After you insert a picture, you can edit it somewhat—you can size, position, and **crop** the picture, which means to cut out portions you don't want to see. You can also format picture properties to change a picture's brightness, sharpness, and other qualities that affect appearance. Visio includes a new **Picture** command on the **Format** menu that even previews your changes before you apply them. Another new option that adds visual interest to imported pictures and shapes is transparent colors. By making your picture slightly or very transparent, shapes underneath show through.

You can import files of the following formats in Visio.

File Format	File Extension
Adobe Illustrator File Format	.ai
Compressed Enhanced Metafile	.emz
Computer Graphics Metafile	.cgm
Corel Clipart Format	.cmx
CorelDRAW! Drawing File Format	.cdr
Encapsulated PostScript	.eps
Enhanced Metafile	.emf
Graphics Interchange Format	.gif
IGES Drawing File Format	.igs
JPEG File Interchange Format	.jpg
Macintosh Picture File Format	.pct
Micrografx Designer Version 3.1 File Format	.drw
Micrografx Designer Version 6 File Format	.dsf
Portable Network Graphics	.png
PostScript File	.ps
Tag Image File Format	.tif
Windows Bitmap	.eps and .dib
Windows Metafile	.wmf
ZSoft PC Paintbrush Bitmap	.pcx

Tip

You can insert other types of files as well using different commands. With the **Open** command on the **File** menu, you can open ABC FlowCharter (.af3, .af2) and other files. With the **CAD Drawing** command on the **Insert** menu, you can add Autodesk AutoCAD (.dwg and .dxf) drawings and Bentley Microstation (.dgn) files.

OfficeLogo
TGC Logo

In this exercise, you insert a GIF file of The Garden Company logo into an existing office layout diagram. You start by opening a sample drawing, OfficeLogo. After inserting the logo, you format the picture properties just for fun to make the logo transparent.

Open

1 On the Standard toolbar, click the **Open** button to display the **Open** dialog box.

2 Navigate to **SBS\Visio\OfficeLayout** on your hard disk, and then double-click **OfficeLogo**.

Visio opens an office layout diagram and displays the five office layout stencils.

3 On the **Insert** menu, point to **Picture**, and then click **From File**.

The **Insert Picture** dialog box appears.

4 Navigate to **SBS\Visio\OfficeLayout** on your hard disk, and then click **TGC Logo.gif**.

A preview of the picture appears to the right.

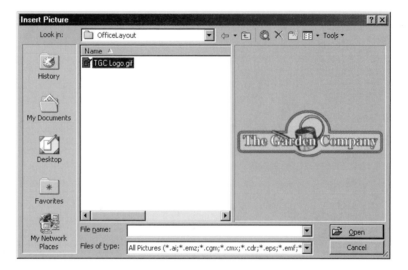

Troubleshooting

Views

If you don't see a preview, in the **Insert Picture** dialog box, click the **Views** down arrow on the **Views** button, and then click **Preview**.

5 Click **Open**.

Visio inserts the logo for The Garden Company in the middle of the page. The logo is selected.

6 Drag the logo graphic to the upper right corner of the drawing page.

Your screen should look similar to the figure on the following page.

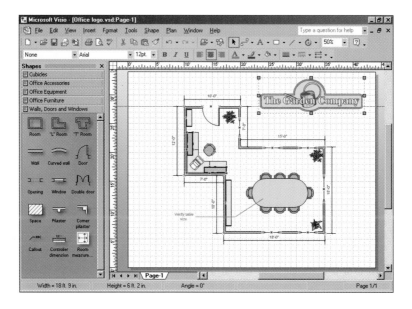

Zoom

7 On the Standard toolbar, click the **Zoom** down arrow, and then click **100%** to zoom in to see the logo.

8 Drag a corner selection handle toward the logo's center to reduce the logo to approximately half its original size.

The logo graphic remains selected.

9 On the **Format** menu, click **Picture**.

The **Picture** dialog box appears and displays a preview of the logo graphic.

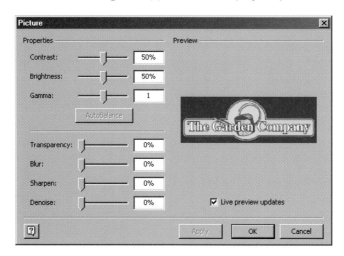

10 Drag the **Transparency** slider to the right until the box indicates 50%.

The preview displays the logo graphic at 50% transparency.

Troubleshooting

The checkerboard pattern in the transparency preview is Visio's way of showing you how transparent the color will be.

11 Click **OK**.

Visio makes the logo graphic transparent so that the grid shows through.

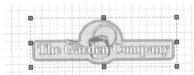

Save

12 On the Standard toolbar, click the **Save** button.

Visio saves the changes to your drawing.

13 On the **File** menu, click **Exit**.

Visio closes.

Tip

Like pictures, shapes can be transparent, too. Select a shape, and then click **Fill** on the **Format** menu. In the **Fill** dialog box, drag the **Transparency** slider to adjust the transparency of the shape's fill color.

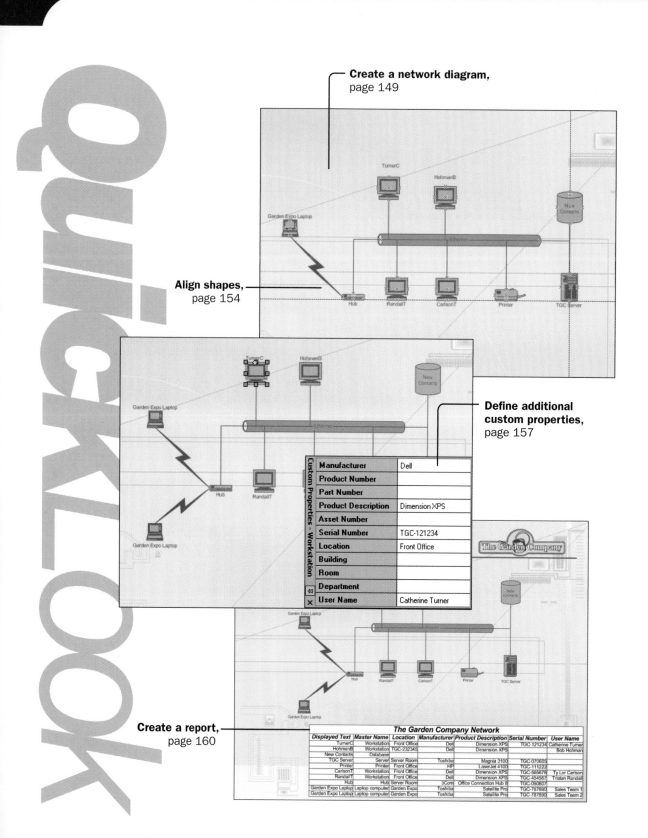

Create a network diagram,
page 149

Align shapes,
page 154

**Define additional
custom properties,**
page 157

Create a report,
page 160

		Dell
Manufacturer		Dell
Product Number		
Part Number		
Product Description		Dimension XPS
Asset Number		
Serial Number		TGC-121234
Location		Front Office
Building		
Room		
Department		
User Name		Catherine Turner

The Garden Company Network

Displayed Text	Master Name	Location	Manufacturer	Product Description	Serial Number	User Name
TurnerC	Workstation	Front Office	Dell	Dimension XPS	TGC-121234	Catherine Turner
HohmanB	Workstation	TGC-232345	Dell	Dimension XPS	TGC-111222	Bob Hohman
New Contacts	Database					
TGC Server	Server	Server Room	Toshiba	Magnia 3100	TGC-070605	
Printer	Printer	Front Office	HP	LaserJet 4100	TGC-111222	
CarlsonT	Workstation	Front Office	Dell	Dimension XPS	TGC-565678	Ty Lor Carlson
RandallT	Workstation	Front Office	Dell	Dimension XPS	TGC-454567	Tristan Randall
Hub	Hub	Server Room	3Com	Office Connection Hub 8	TGC-090807	
Garden Expo Laptop	Laptop computer	Garden Expo	Toshiba	Satellite Pro	TGC-787890	Sales Team 1
Garden Expo Laptop	Laptop computer	Garden Expo	Toshiba	Satellite Pro	TGC-787890	Sales Team 2

Chapter 8
Creating a Network Diagram

After completing this chapter, you will be able to:

✔ Create a network diagram.

✔ Connect and align shapes.

✔ Store information with a shape and create new custom properties.

✔ Create a report based on data from a drawing.

You can use network diagrams to plan, document, and troubleshoot network structures. Microsoft Visio provides the **Basic Network** template and more than 100 computer and network equipment shapes for creating accurate graphic representations of network equipment and connections. In addition to documenting network structures, Visio network diagrams can be used to store data about the equipment in your network, such as serial number, location, manufacturer, and description. This information can be exported to a database or used for reporting purposes.

In this chapter, you assume the role of a consultant hired by The Garden Company to connect workstations at the local gardening expo to the company's network. With these remote connections in place, the sales team can record information in the company's new contacts database about visitors at the company's booth. To present your plan, you create a diagram of the proposed network. Later, you add important information to the shapes in the diagram so that you can create a hardware report.

This chapter uses the practice files Network, NetwkCP, and NetwkRpt that you installed from this book's CD-ROM. For details about installing the practice files, see "Using the Book's CD-ROM" at the beginning of this book.

Creating a Network Diagram

Using Visio to plan a new or improved network allows you to quickly visualize a network structure. After you see how equipment is connected to the network, you can determine the most effective configuration, and then adjust your diagram as necessary. You simply drag shapes to the drawing page, move them around, add more shapes, or delete others until you achieve the result you want. Then you can share the final drawing in presentations and reports.

The first step in creating a network diagram is to determine what hardware to include and what type of **network ring** or **backbone**—the part of the network that handles the major data traffic—you will use. After you decide what you want to diagram, you drag the network ring or backbone to the drawing page followed by each hardware shape. Then you use the dynamic control handles in the ring or backbone to connect the hardware shapes to the network shape.

In this exercise, you diagram The Garden Company's local area network (LAN). You start with an Ethernet backbone, connect workstations and other components directly to the network, and then add a laptop computer as a remote connection from the garden expo booth.

Tip

If you need help creating network diagrams, type **network diagram** in the Ask A Question box located on the menu bar.

1   Start Visio.

The **Choose Drawing Type** task pane and the **New Drawing** task pane appear.

2   In the **Choose Drawing Type** task pane, under **Category**, click **Network**.

The **Basic Network** template appears in the **Template** area.

Tip

On the **File** menu, point to **New**, and then click **Choose Drawing Type** for another way to open the **Basic Network** template.

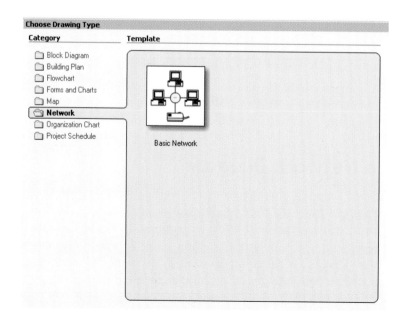

3   Under **Template**, click the **Basic Network** template.

The template opens, displaying the drawing page and five stencils.

Tip

If the **Custom Properties** window is open, click the **Close** button on the window for an unobstructed view of the drawing page.

4   On the **Basic Network Shapes** stencil, drag an **Ethernet** shape to the center of the drawing page, and then drag two **Workstation** shapes above the **Ethernet** shape and drag two **Workstation** shapes below.

The LAN now consists of four **Workstation** shapes and an **Ethernet** shape. Your drawing should look similar to this.

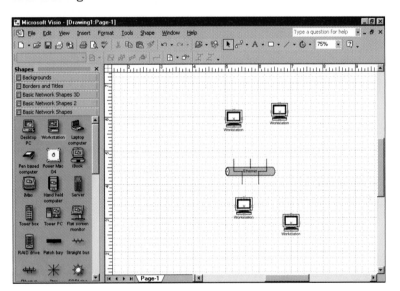

Zoom

33% ▼

5   On the Standard toolbar, click the **Zoom** down arrow, and click **75%** in the list. If necessary, use the scroll bars on the drawing page to see all five shapes.

The drawing page is displayed at 75 percent of its actual size.

6   Click the **Ethernet** shape, and then drag the upper left control handle (indicated by a yellow diamond) and connect it to the bottom of the upper left **Workstation** shape.

When a red square appears at the connection point, the **Workstation shape** is properly connected to the **Ethernet** shape.

Tip

To drag a control handle, pause the pointer over the yellow diamond until it changes to a four-headed arrow. Then drag the handle to the connection point of another shape.

7 Drag control handles from the **Ethernet** shape to connect the remaining **Workstation** shapes.

All four workstations are connected to the network. Four more control handles remain unconnected. Your drawing should look similar to the following.

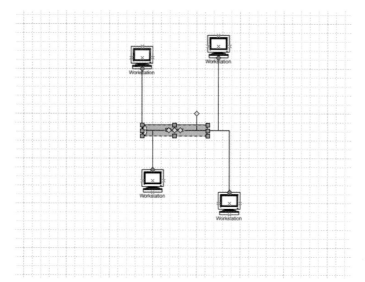

8 From the **Basic Network Shapes** stencil, drag the **Server** shape and a **Database** shape to the right of the **Ethernet** shape, and then drag a **Laptop computer** shape and a **Hub** shape to the left of the local area network shapes.

9 Click the **Ethernet** shape, and then use the control handles to connect the **Server** shape, the **Database** shape, and the **Hub** shape to the **Ethernet** shape.

The **Server** shape, the **Database** shape, and the **Hub** shape are now connected to the local area network.

Tip

You can add more than eight equipment shapes to network topology shapes, such as the **Ethernet** shape, the **Token Ring** shape, or the **Star** shape. First, attach equipment shapes to the eight available control handles. Then drag a second topology shape on top of the first shape. Use the control handles from the second shape to connect up to eight more devices.

10 To indicate the transmission of data from the laptop computer to the network, drag a **Comm-link** shape to the drawing page, and then connect one endpoint to the **Laptop computer** shape and the other to the **Hub** shape.

The diagram now shows a **Laptop computer** shape connected remotely to the local area network via the **Hub** shape. It should look similar to the following.

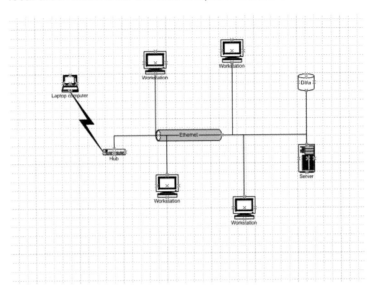

Zoom

33% ▼

11 To help you reposition the **Workstation** label above the **Workstation** shape, click the **Zoom** down arrow, and then click **100%**. Click one of the two **Workstation** shapes located above the **Ethernet** shape, and then move the yellow control handle so that the **Workstation** label is repositioned above the shape.

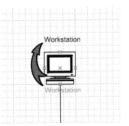

12 Repeat step 11 for the other **Workstation** shape located above the **Ethernet** shape.

Your diagram should look similar to the following.

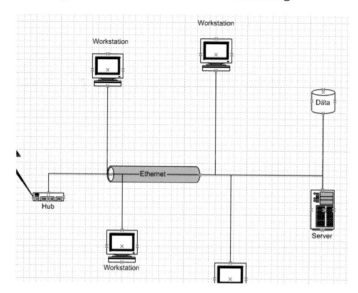

13 On the **File** menu, click **Close**, but don't save your changes.

Your diagram closes.

Aligning Shapes

After you have added all the elements to your drawing, you can easily enhance its appearance. Visio provides special tools for quickly aligning shapes around the network ring or backbone without the effort of moving each shape into position. As with other Visio drawing templates, you can also add a title, background, graphics, and color.

Network

In this exercise, you align hardware shapes around an **Ethernet** shape, and then add a color scheme and a background to your network diagram.

Open

1 On the Standard toolbar, click the **Open** button.

The **Open** dialog box appears.

2 Navigate to the **SBS\Visio\Networks** folder, and double-click **Network**.

The Network drawing opens, displaying a drawing of the structure of a local area network and the equipment connected to it.

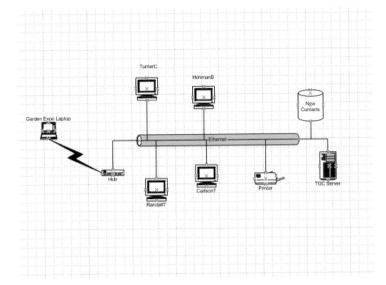

3 Click the **RandallT** shape, hold down [shift], and then click the following four shapes: **CarlsonT**, **Hub**, **Printer**, and **TGC Server**.

The five shapes are selected. The **RandallT** shape has green selection handles because it's the primary shape (that is, it's the first shape selected).

4 On the **Shape** menu, click **Align Shapes** for the dialog box to appear.

Bottom alignment

5 Under **Up/Down alignment**, click the bottom alignment button, and then select the **Create guide and glue shapes to it** check box. Click **OK**.

The five selected shapes align with a horizontal guide that Visio adds at the bottom of the primary shape.

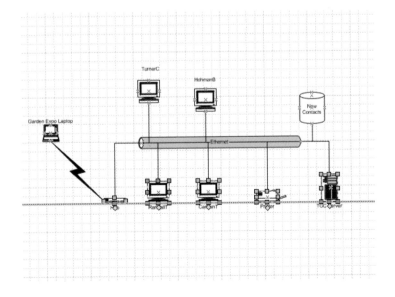

6 Press the ⎋ key to cancel the shape selections.

7 Click the **TGC Server** shape, hold down ⇧, and then click the **New Contacts** database shape.

The two shapes are selected.

8 On the **Shape** menu, click **Align Shapes**.

The **Align Shapes** dialog box appears.

Center
alignment

9 Under **Left/Right alignment**, click the center alignment button (the second button from the left), and then select the **Create guide and glue shapes to it** check box. Click **OK**.

The selected shapes align to the vertical guide that Visio adds at the center of the primary shape.

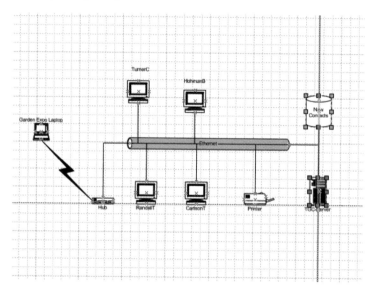

10 Click the **Backgrounds** stencil, and then drag the **Background high-tech** shape to the drawing page.

11 In the **Make Background** dialog box, click **Yes** to make this shape the background image for this page.

The background shape appears behind the network shapes. In addition, a new tab named **VBackground** appears at the bottom of the drawing window.

12 On the **Tools** menu, click **Color Schemes**.

The **Color Schemes** dialog box appears.

13 Click **Forest**, and then click **OK**.

Visio applies the **Forest** color scheme to the shapes in your network diagram. Your drawing should look similar to this.

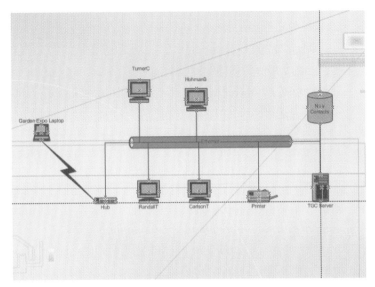

14 On the **File** menu, click **Close**, but don't save your changes.

The Network drawing closes.

Defining New Custom Properties

Custom properties are pre-assigned to many Visio drawing shapes, allowing you to store additional data with the shape. The set of custom properties assigned to a shape is based on how that shape is used and what it represents. For example, a **Position** shape in an organization chart includes custom properties that store the employee's name, telephone number, and department with the shape. Network and hardware shapes contain custom properties reflecting the equipment they represent, such as manufacturer, product number, part number, product description, and serial number. This information can be exported to an electronic file or database or used for reporting purposes.

You might want to store in your drawing additional information that has not been pre-assigned as a custom property. You can do this by defining new custom properties for a specific shape or for all the instances of that shape in your drawing. You can also edit the master shape on a stencil so that the custom property is available in all subsequent drawings.

NetkCP

In this exercise, you view the custom properties assigned to workstations connected to The Garden Company's local area network. For tracking purposes, you create a new custom property to identify which employee uses each computer.

Open

1 On the Standard toolbar, click the **Open** button.

The **Open** dialog box appears.

2 Navigate to the **SBS\Visio\Networks** folder, and double-click **NetwkCP**.

The NetwkCP drawing opens, displaying a drawing of The Garden Company's network layout.

3 On the **View** menu, click **Custom Properties Window**.

The **Custom Properties** window appears. No custom property data is displayed because no shape has been selected.

4 Click the **TurnerC** shape.

5 Resize the **Custom Properties** window so you can see the complete list of custom properties assigned to this shape.

The following boxes contain information: **Manufacturer**, **Product Description**, **Serial Number**, and **Location**.

Manufacturer	Dell
Product Number	
Part Number	
Product Description	Dimension XPS
Asset Number	
Serial Number	TGC-121234
Location	Front Office
Building	
Room	
Department	

6 On the **File** menu, point to **Stencils**, and then click **Document Stencil**.

Document Stencil appears in the stencil pane, displaying each master shape that your drawing includes.

7 In **Document Stencil**, right-click the **Workstation** shape, and then click **Edit Master**.

The master **Workstation** shape appears in the master drawing window. No custom property data is displayed in the **Custom Properties** window.

8 Click the master **Workstation** shape.

The pre-assigned custom property boxes appear in the **Custom Properties** window.

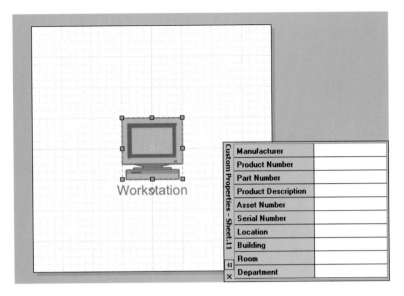

9   Right-click the **Custom Properties** window, and then click **Define Properties**.

10   The **Define Custom Properties** dialog box appears.

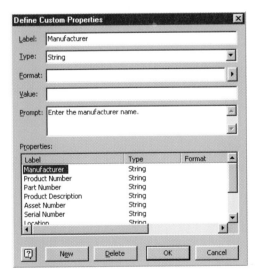

11   Click **New**.

The **Define Custom Properties** dialog box displays **Property11** in the **Label** box.

12   Type User Name in the **Label** box, and then click anywhere in the **Prompt** box. To create a ScreenTip that explains what data to enter in the **User Name** box, type Enter the name of the employee user. Click **OK**.

The **Define Custom Properties** dialog box closes.

13 Scroll to the end of the list in the **Custom Properties** window.

The **User Name** box has been added.

Close Window

14 Click **Close Window** at the right side of the menu bar.

A message appears, asking if you want to update the **Workstation** master shape and all drawing-page instances with the new custom property.

15 Click **Yes** to finish closing the master drawing window.

16 Right-click the **Document Stencil** title bar, and then click **Close**.

Document Stencil closes.

17 Click the **HohmanB** shape, and then scroll to the bottom of the list in the **Custom Properties** window.

The **User Name** box has been added to the **HohmanB** shape. Now you can document the individuals that use each computer in the organization.

Tip

You can quickly create a custom property for use with a single instance of a shape. Rather than editing the master shape in the **Document Stencil**, select the shape on your drawing page. Right-click the **Custom Property** window, and then click **Define Properties**. In the **Define Custom Properties** dialog box, click **New,** and then enter the information for the new property.

18 On the **File** menu, click **Close**, but don't save your changes.

NetwkCP closes.

Creating a Report

You can use custom properties data stored in your diagram for reporting purposes or to export to an electronic file or database. Visio provides several standard report types, such as an Organization Chart report, which includes name, title, and telephone number of employees grouped by department. You can generate a report as a Microsoft Excel spreadsheet, XML file, Web page, or an embedded Microsoft Excel object. You can also create a report in your drawing as a **Visio table shape**, a specialized shape that displays the report data on the drawing page.

Report
command

new for
OfficeXP

Each type of report is defined by a **report definition**, a set of criteria that specifies which shapes and custom properties are included in your report, as well as the format to use. A standard report has a pre-assigned report definition. You can create customized reports or modify existing ones using the **Report Definition Wizard**. The wizard helps you specify the new criteria for your report. Depending on the type of custom properties included in your report, you can also specify calculations, such as a straight count, grand total, average, or median. You can also sort your report by rows and columns.

To generate a report, you select from a list of existing report definitions or create a new one. You can save a new report definition with your drawing or as a separate file (.vrd) in the Samples\Visio Extras folder (installed with Visio 2002). Saving a report definition as a .vrd file allows you to use it again for other drawings.

NetwkRpt

In this exercise, you generate an inventory report of The Garden Company network equipment. You create a new report definition specifying which shapes and custom properties to include, and then you create the report as a **Table** shape to include in your drawing.

Open

1 On the Standard toolbar, click the **Open** button.

The **Open** dialog box appears.

2 Navigate to the **SBS\Visio\Networks** folder, and double-click **NetwkRpt**.

The NetwkRpt drawing opens, displaying a drawing of The Garden Company's network.

3 Click one of the **Garden Expo Laptop** shapes, and then hold down Shift and click the following shapes to include in the report: **TurnerC, HohmanB, New Contacts, TGC Server, Printer, CarlsonT, RandallT, Hub**, and the remaining **Garden Expo Laptop**.

4 On the **Tools** menu, click **Report**.

The **Report** dialog box appears.

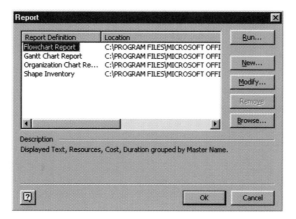

5 Click **New**

The first page of the **Report Definition Wizard** appears.

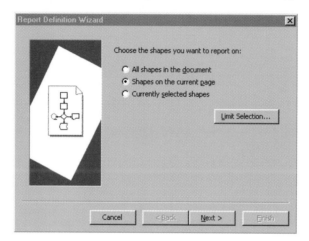

6 Select **Currently selected shapes,** and then click **Next**.

The next page of the wizard appears, asking you to select the properties you want to include as columns in your report.

7 Select the following check boxes representing custom properties for the shapes: **<Displayed Text>**, **<Master Name>**, **Location**, **Manufacturer**, **Product Description**, **Serial Number**, and **User Name**. Click **Next**.

The next page of the wizard appears.

8 In the **Report Title** box, type The Garden Company Network, and then click **Next**.

The next page of the wizard appears.

9 In the **Name** box, type Network Equipment. In the **Description** box, type Includes all network equipment sorted by Master Name.

10 Click the **Save in this drawing** option, and then click **Finish**.

The **Report** dialog box reappears, listing the **Network Equipment** report in the **Report Definition** column.

11 Make sure the **Network Equipment** report is highlighted, and then click **Run**.

The **Run Report** dialog box appears.

Tip

To run an existing report, on the **Tools** menu, click **Report**. Click the **Report Definition** you want, and then click **Run**. In the **Run Report** dialog box, select the format for your report, and click **OK**.

12 In the **Select report format** box, make sure **Visio Table Shape** is selected, and then click **OK**.

Visio generates the report, and the **Report** dialog box appears when the process is complete.

13 To close the **Report** dialog box, click **OK**.

Your Visio drawing, reduced to 42% of actual size, appears with the **Table shape** located at the lower right.

Zoom

33% ▾

14 Press ⟨Esc⟩ to deselect the **Table** shape. On the Standard toolbar, click the **Zoom** down arrow, and then click **50%**.

Your drawing should look similar to this.

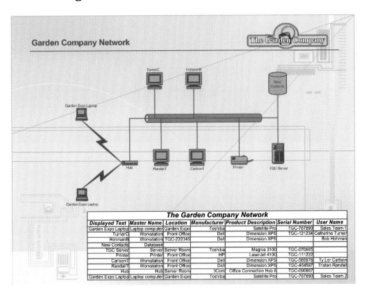

15 On the **File** menu, click **Close**, but don't save your changes.

NetwkRpt closes.

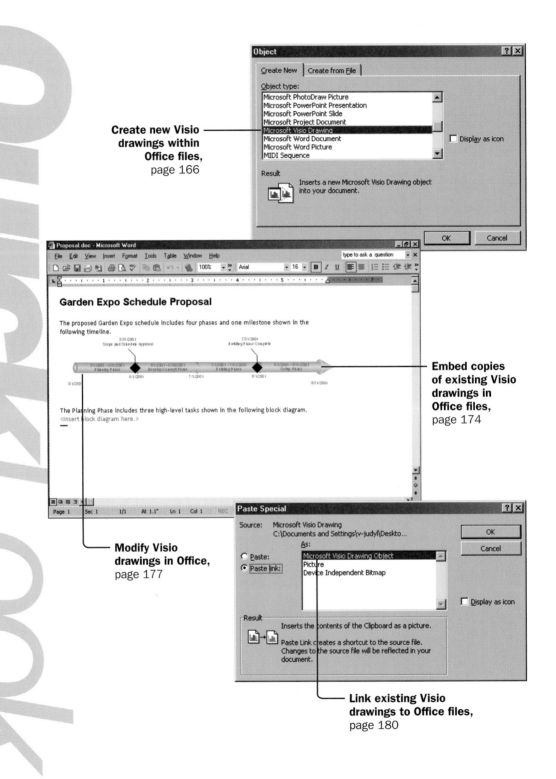

Create new Visio drawings within Office files, page 166

Embed copies of existing Visio drawings in Office files, page 174

Modify Visio drawings in Office, page 177

Link existing Visio drawings to Office files, page 180

Chapter 9
Using Visio with Office XP

After completing this chapter, you will be able to:

✔ Create new Visio drawings within Office XP files.

✔ Embed copies of existing Visio drawings in Office XP files.

✔ Link existing Visio drawings to Office XP files.

Microsoft Visio drawings can support, strengthen, and clarify the information in Microsoft Office XP files, such as Microsoft Word documents, Microsoft PowerPoint presentations, and Microsoft Excel spreadsheets. For example, you can incorporate Visio drawings to enhance the text in Word documents, illustrate the points on PowerPoint slides, support the calculations in Excel spreadsheets, and so forth. The results clearly have more impact than words or numbers alone.

You can use any of the following methods to incorporate your Visio drawings into Office XP files:

■ Create a new Visio drawing from within an Office XP file when you don't have an existing drawing that illustrates the information in the Office XP file and when you don't need to save the drawing in a separate Visio file. For example, you might want to create just a quick drawing to illustrate a point on a PowerPoint slide. The drawing you create becomes part of the Office XP file.

■ **Embed** a copy of an existing Visio drawing in an Office XP file when you already have a drawing that illustrates the information in the Office XP file and you don't want any changes you make to the copy of the drawing to appear in the original Visio drawing, and vice versa. For example, you might want to copy part of a Visio drawing and paste it into a Word document. The drawing you embed becomes part of the Office XP file.

■ **Link** an existing Visio drawing to an Office XP file when you want to synchronize an original drawing and a copy of the drawing in an Office XP file. For example, you might want to link an entire drawing to a Word document and keep the copy of it in the Word document up-to-date. Any changes you make to the original Visio drawing are reflected in the copy in the Office XP file. The drawing you link to the Office XP file doesn't become part of the file, so the size of the Office XP file stays at a minimum.

You can modify Visio drawings you created within, embedded in, or linked to Office XP files by double-clicking the drawing in the file. Visio starts and replaces many of the other Office XP program's menus and toolbars with Visio menus and toolbars so that you can modify the drawing using Visio shapes, menus, and drawing tools. Then when you're finished, you click anywhere outside the drawing in the Office XP file to return to the other Office XP program.

Important

This chapter demonstrates incorporating Visio drawings into Microsoft Word documents; however, you can use the methods in this chapter to incorporate Visio drawings into any Microsoft Office XP file or the document of any application that supports linking and embedding, including those in Office 97 and Office 2000. The menus and toolbars in other programs might vary slightly from those illustrated in this chapter.

In this chapter, you'll learn how to create a new Visio drawing within a Word document, embed a copy of an existing Visio drawing in a Word document, and link an existing Visio drawing to a Word document. You'll also learn how to modify the Visio drawings in the Word document.

This chapter uses the practice files Proposal, TimelinePrelim, and PlanPhase. For details about installing the practice files, see "Using the Book's CD-ROM" at the beginning of this book.

Creating New Visio Drawings Within Office XP Files

When you're working in an Office XP file, such as a Word document, and you think of a quick little drawing that could enhance or clarify the text, you can create a Visio drawing in the file. When you create a new drawing, you use the **Object** command on the **Insert** menu to insert a blank Visio drawing into the file. Then you create the drawing from scratch right in the file. The drawing you create becomes part of the file; that is, there isn't a separate Visio drawing file. To modify the drawing, open the Office XP file that contains the drawing, and then double-click the drawing to open it in Visio. Then use the Visio shapes, menus, and drawing tools to make your changes.

Use the **Object** dialog box to create new
Visio drawings within Office XP files.

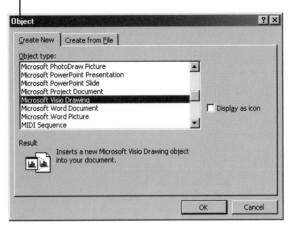

Proposal

In this exercise, you create a new block diagram in a Garden Expo Schedule Proposal
document, and then you modify the drawing in the document.

Important

You need Microsoft Word to complete this procedure; however, you can use the steps
in this procedure to create new Visio drawings in any Microsoft Office XP file. The
menus and toolbars in other programs might vary slightly from those illustrated in
this chapter.

1   Start Word.

Open

2   On the Standard toolbar, click the **Open** button.

The **Open** dialog box appears.

3   Navigate to the **SBS\Visio\OfficeXP** folder, and then double-click **Proposal**.

Word opens the document.

4   Select the blue text *<Insert block diagram here.>*, and then press Del.

Word deletes the text and places the insertion point at the beginning of the
line. If you see the insertion point at the end of the previous line, press the
Enter key to start a new line.

5 On the **Insert** menu, click **Object**.

The **Object** dialog box appears.

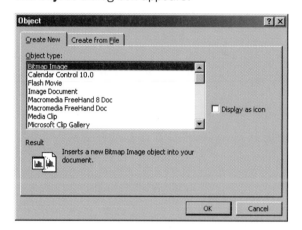

6 On the **Create New** tab, in the **Object type** list, click **Microsoft Visio Drawing**.

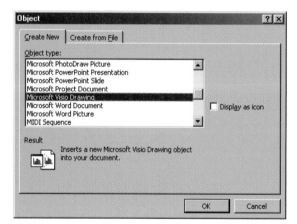

Tip

When you want a Visio icon for the drawing to appear in the document instead of the drawing itself, select the **Display as icon** check box in the **Object** dialog box. To then modify the drawing, you double-click the Visio icon.

7 Click **OK**.

Visio starts, adds a blank drawing to your document, replaces many of the Word menus and toolbars with Visio menus and toolbars, and then opens the **Choose Drawing Type** dialog box.

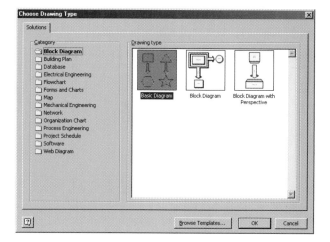

8 In the **Category** area, click **Block Diagram**, and then in the **Drawing Type** area, double-click **Block Diagram**.

In your Word document, Visio opens the **Block Diagram** template, which opens the following four stencils: **Blocks**, **Blocks Raised**, **Borders and Titles**, and **Backgrounds**.

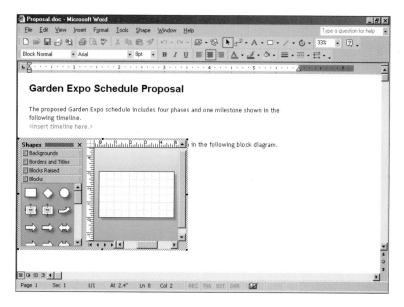

Stencil icon

9 Click the stencil icon on the title bar of the **Blocks** stencil, and then, on the menu that appears, click **Icons and Names**.

Visio displays the names and icons for the shapes on the stencils.

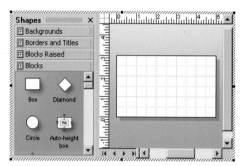

10 From the **Blocks** stencil, drag the **Arrow box** shape into the upper middle portion of the drawing page.

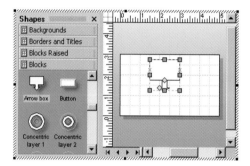

11 Drag another **Arrow box** shape to the drawing page right below the first **Arrow box** shape.

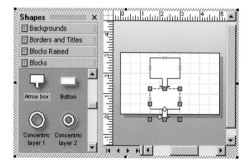

12 On the **Shape** menu, click **Center Drawing**.

Visio centers the shapes on the drawing page.

13 Select the first **Arrow box** shape, and then type **Determine Scope**.

Visio zooms in on the shape so that you can see the text better.

14 Select the second **Arrow box** shape, and then type **Create Schedule**.

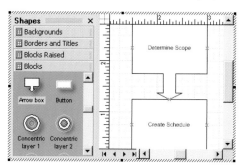

15 To lengthen the drawing area so that both shapes fit on the drawing page, drag the middle black selection handle on the black dashed drawing frame (below the page buttons) down far enough to include both shapes in your drawing.

The length of the drawing area increases.

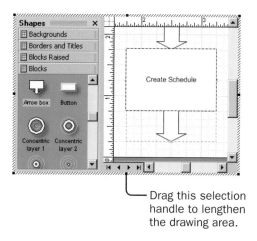

Drag this selection handle to lengthen the drawing area.

16 To quit Visio and continue working in Word, click anywhere outside the Visio drawing in the Word document.

Visio closes, and Word becomes the active application again.

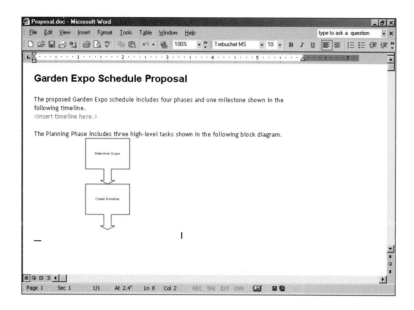

Troubleshooting

If you see a gray box behind the Visio shapes when you return to Word, don't worry about it. Some systems add a gray background to embedded objects. However, the gray box will not appear when you print the Word document.

17 To modify the Visio drawing, double-click it. Visio opens the drawing and stencils again.

18 To lengthen the drawing area to fit a third shape under the other two on the drawing page, drag the middle black selection handle on the black dashed drawing frame (below the page buttons) down far enough to include one more shape in your drawing.

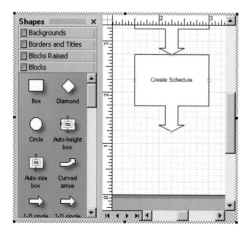

19 From the **Blocks** stencil, drag the **Box** shape below the second **Arrow box** shape on the drawing page.

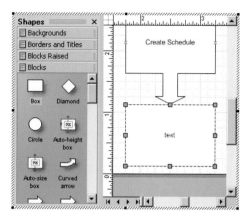

20 With the **Box** shape selected, type **Get Approval for Scope and Schedule**.

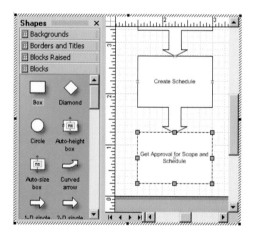

21 On the **Shape** menu, click **Center Drawing**.

Visio centers the shapes on the drawing page.

22 To quit Visio and continue working in Word, click anywhere outside the Visio drawing in the Word document.

Visio closes, and Word becomes the active application again.

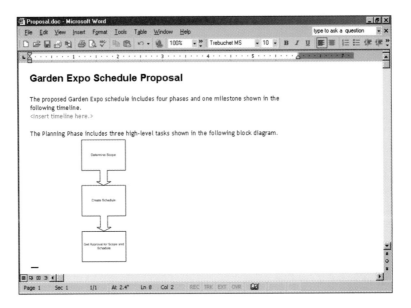

23 On the **File** menu, click **Save As**.

The **Save As** dialog box appears.

24 In the **Places** bar on the left, click **My Documents**.

25 In the **File name** box, replace **Proposal.doc** with **Proposal1**.

26 Click **Save**.

Word saves the document.

27 On the **File** menu, click **Exit**.

Word and the document close.

Embedding Copies of Existing Visio Drawings in Office XP Files

If you already have a Visio drawing that helps clarify the information in an Office XP file, you can **embed** a copy of the drawing in the file. When you embed a drawing in a file, you copy the entire drawing or pieces of it, and then you paste the copy into the Office XP file; the copy of the drawing becomes part of the Office XP file. When you modify the embedded drawing in the Office XP file, you modify the copy only. Any changes you make to the copy of the drawing won't appear in the original drawing because there's no link between the Office XP file and the Visio drawing.

Embed a Visio drawing into an Office XP file when you already
have a drawing that clarifies the information in the file.

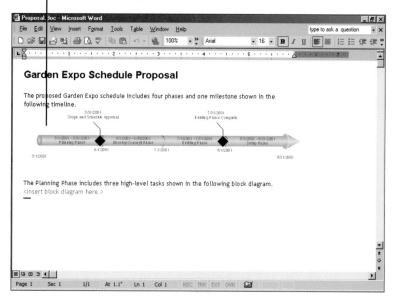

TimelinePrelim
Proposal

In this exercise, you open a preliminary Garden Expo timeline, copy it, open a
schedule proposal document, and then embed the copy of the timeline in the proposal by pasting it into the document. Finally, you modify the copy of the timeline
in the Word document.

Important

You need Microsoft Word to complete this procedure; however, you can use the
steps in this procedure to embed copies of existing Visio drawings in any
Microsoft Office XP file. The menus and toolbars in other programs might vary
slightly from those illustrated in this chapter.

1 Start Visio.

Open

2 On the Standard toolbar, click the **Open** button.

The **Open** dialog box appears.

3 Navigate to the **SBS\Visio\OfficeXP** folder, and then double-click
TimelinePrelim.

Visio opens the timeline drawing and the **Timeline Shapes** stencil, **Borders
and Titles** stencil, and **Backgrounds** stencil.

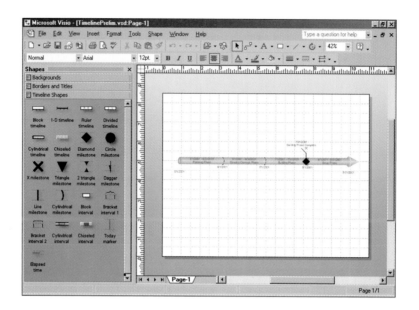

4 On the **Edit** menu, click **Select All**.

Visio selects the timeline and all the shapes on it.

Copy

5 Click the **Copy** button.

Visio copies the selected shapes.

6 Start Word.

Open

7 On the Standard toolbar, click the **Open** button.

The **Open** dialog box appears.

8 Navigate to **SBS\Visio\OfficeXP**, and then double-click **Proposal**.

Word opens the document.

9 Select the blue text *<Insert timeline here.>*, and then press `Del`.

Word deletes the text and places the insertion point at the beginning of the line. If you see the insertion point at the end of the previous line, press `Enter` to start a new line.

Paste

10 Click the **Paste** button.

Word pastes the Visio drawing in the Word document and sizes it to fit on the page.

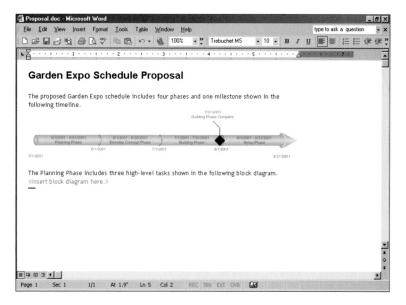

11 To modify the Visio drawing, double-click it.

Visio opens the timeline drawing and replaces many of the Word menus and toolbars with Visio menus and toolbars.

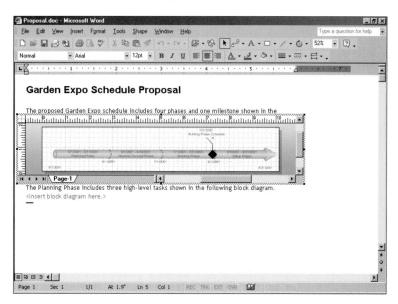

12 On the **File** menu, point to **Stencils**, point to **Project Schedule**, and then click **Timeline Shapes**.

Visio opens the **Timeline Shapes** stencil.

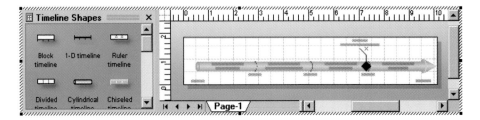

13 From the **Timeline Shapes** stencil, drag the **Diamond milestone** shape anywhere on the timeline. The **Configure Milestone** dialog box appears.

14 In the **Milestone date** box, click the down arrow to display a monthly calendar. In the calendar, click the left or right arrow to display the month of May, and then select the milestone date by clicking **31**.

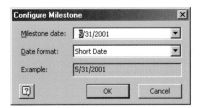

15 Click **OK** to correctly position the milestone shape on the timeline.

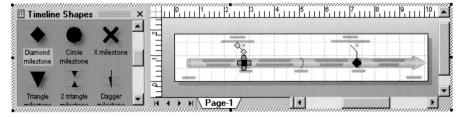

16 With the milestone selected, press the [F2] key to select and zoom in on the text.

17 Select the text *Milestone Description*, and then type a new label, **Scope and Schedule Approval**.

18 Press the [Esc] key.

Visio closes the text block and zooms back out again so that you can see the entire timeline.

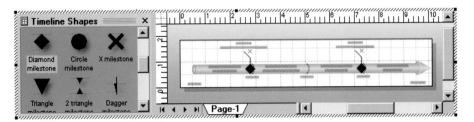

19 To quit Visio and continue working in Word, click anywhere outside the Visio drawing in the Word document.

Visio closes, and Word becomes the active application again.

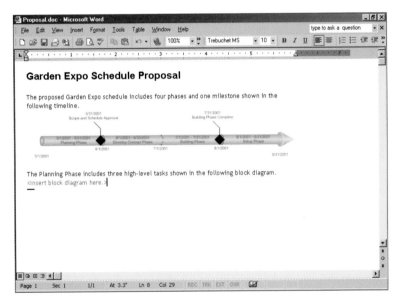

20 On the **File** menu, click **Save As**.

The **Save As** dialog box appears.

21 In the **Places** bar, click **My Documents**.

22 In the **File name** box, replace **Proposal.doc** with Proposal2.

23 Click **Save** to save the document.

24 On the **File** menu, click **Exit** to close Word and the document.

25 On the taskbar, click **Microsoft Visio - [TimelinePrelim.vsd:Page-1]** to switch to Visio.

Notice the changes you made to the copy of the drawing in your proposal don't appear in the original Visio drawing.

26 In Visio, on the **File** menu, click **Exit**.

Visio and the timeline drawing close.

179

Linking Existing Visio Drawings to Office XP Files

The main difference between linking an existing Visio drawing to an Office XP file and embedding a copy of an existing Visio drawing in an Office XP file is that a linked drawing doesn't become part of the Office XP file. You link an existing Visio drawing to an Office XP file when you want to include a copy of the drawing in the Office XP file and synchronize the original drawing with the copy in the Office XP file. For example, you might link an unfinished Visio block diagram to a Word document. Then when you make changes to the Visio drawing file, those changes are reflected in the Office XP file, so it's always up-to-date.

Use the **Paste Link** option in the **Paste Special** dialog box to link Visio drawings to Office XP files

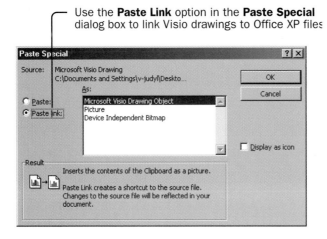

There is another difference between linking and embedding: when you link to a Visio drawing, you link to the entire drawing, including the background. However, when you embed a copy of a Visio drawing, you can copy one page of a drawing file or only specific pieces of a drawing.

Proposal
PlanPhase

In this exercise, you open a block diagram that shows the Garden Expo's preliminary planning phase, copy the entire drawing, open a Garden Expo schedule proposal document, and then link the diagram to the Word document. Finally, you modify the Visio drawing, which also updates the copy of the drawing in the Word document.

Important

You need Microsoft Word to complete this procedure; however, you can use the steps in this procedure to link existing Visio drawings to any Microsoft Office XP file. The menus and toolbars in other programs might vary slightly from those illustrated in this chapter.

1 Start Visio.

2 On the Standard toolbar, click the **Open** button.

The **Open** dialog box appears.

3 Navigate to the **SBS\Visio\OfficeXP** folder, and then double-click **PlanPhase**.

Visio opens the **Block** diagram and the following four stencils: **Blocks**, **Blocks Raised**, **Borders and Titles**, and **Backgrounds**.

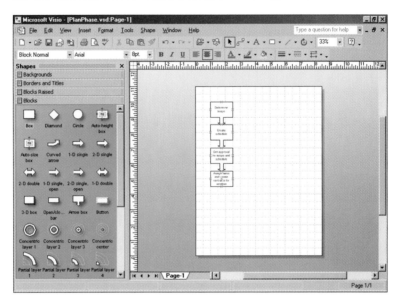

4 On the **Edit** menu, click **Copy Drawing**.

Visio copies the entire drawing.

Troubleshooting

If the **Copy** command appears instead of the **Copy Drawing** command, something on the drawing page is selected, and you will not be able to link the drawing. To get the **Copy Drawing** command to appear on the **Edit** menu, return to the drawing and press the Esc key to cancel the shape selection.

5 Start Word.

6 On the Standard toolbar, click the **Open** button.

The **Open** dialog box appears.

7 Navigate to **SBS\Visio\OfficeXP**, and then double-click **Proposal**.

Word opens the document.

8 Select the blue text *<Insert block diagram here.>*, and then press `Del`.

Word deletes the text and places the insertion point at the beginning of the line. If you see the insertion point at the end of the previous line, press `Enter` to start a new line.

9 On the **Edit** menu, click **Paste Special**. The **Paste Special** dialog box appears.

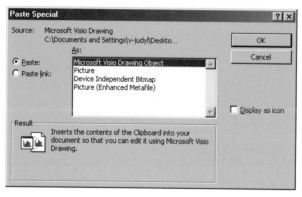

10 Click **Paste link**.

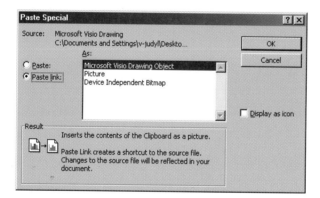

Troubleshooting

To link to a drawing, you must save it first, and then link to the entire drawing. If the **Paste link** option appears dimmed, make sure the drawing is saved, and then use the **Copy Drawing** command.

When you link a Visio drawing to an Office XP file, you link to a drawing with a specific name in a specific location. If you rename or move the Visio drawing, you must update the link. To update the link, select the linked drawing within the Office XP file, and on the **Edit** menu, click **Update Link**. If you don't update the link and you later double-click the drawing in the Office XP file, you'll receive an error message, because Office XP won't be able to find the drawing.

11 In the **As** list, make sure **Microsoft Visio Drawing Object** is selected, and then click **OK**.

Word links to the Visio file and pastes the drawing in the Word document.

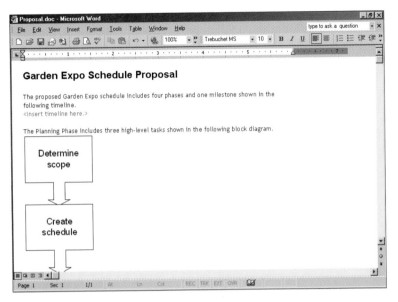

12 To modify the Visio drawing, double-click it.

The original drawing, PlanPhase, opens in a separate Visio window.

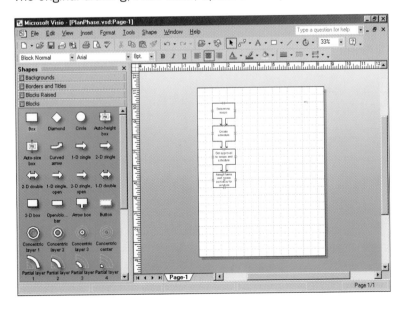

13 On the **Edit** menu, click **Select All**.

Visio selects all the shapes on the drawing page.

14 On the **Format** menu, click **Text**.

The **Text** dialog box appears.

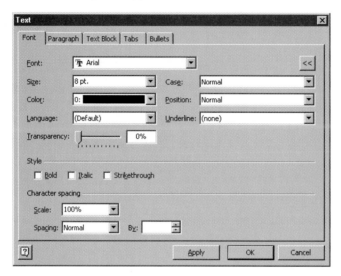

15 On the **Font** tab, in the **Color** box, select color **2** (red), and then click **OK**.

Visio changes the text color in all the shapes to red.

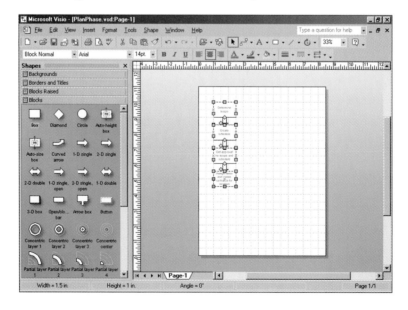

Save

16 On the Standard toolbar, click the **Save** button.

Visio saves the changes to the **PlanPhase** drawing.

17 On the **File** menu, click **Exit**.

Visio and the diagram close, and Word becomes the active application. The Word document reflects the changes to the linked diagram.

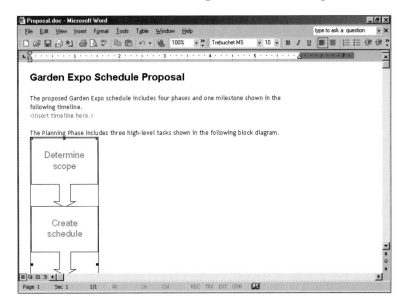

Tip

Linked drawings can be updated either automatically or manually. To specify how you want your linked drawings in a particular Office XP file to be updated, open the Office XP file, and then on the **Edit** menu, click **Links**.

18 In Word, on the **File** menu, click **Save As**.

The **Save As** dialog box appears.

19 In the **Places** bar, click **My Documents**.

20 In the **File name** box, replace **Proposal.doc** with Proposal3.

21 Click **Save**.

Word saves the document.

22 On the **File** menu, click **Exit**.

Word and the document close.

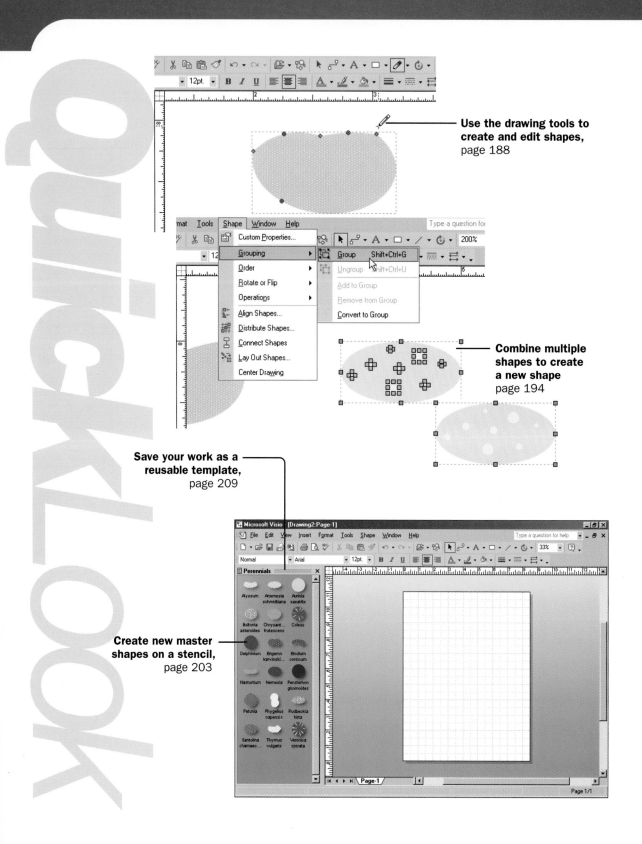

Use the drawing tools to create and edit shapes, page 188

Combine multiple shapes to create a new shape page 194

Save your work as a reusable template, page 209

Create new master shapes on a stencil, page 203

Chapter 10
Customizing Shapes and Templates

After completing this chapter, you will be able to:

✔ **Draw shapes from scratch.**
✔ **Create complex shapes by grouping and merging.**
✔ **Customize shapes.**
✔ **Save shapes as reusable master shapes on a new stencil.**
✔ **Create a new template.**

Microsoft Visio includes thousands of shapes, but sometimes you might need a special shape. If you require a shape that Visio doesn't already have, you can easily create it. For example, perhaps you want to show special equipment or furniture in an office layout. With the drawing tools, you can design a shape from scratch or take an existing shape and edit it, which means to customize it to look the way you want. After investing the effort to customize shapes, you'll want to save them for reuse. One way to do this is to create your own stencils, which you can use to store frequently used and customized shapes. Stencils keep shapes organized and also provide a convenient package for distributing your shapes to other Visio users.

Another way to customize Visio to better serve the way you work is to create your own templates. That way, you can choose the page settings you prefer and include the stencils you use most. In fact, most everything about Visio can be customized.

In this chapter, a master gardener at The Garden Company wants to plan the landscape of the demonstration perennial garden in the small space of the company's booth at the gardening expo. The gardener wants to design his own simple perennial shapes to use in landscape planning and then save the shapes in a custom stencil as part of a new template that he can reuse.

This chapter uses the practice files EditShapes, CreateStencil, GroupShapes, and Perennials that you installed from this book's CD-ROM. For details about installing the practice files, see "Using the Book's CD-ROM" at the beginning of this book.

Drawing Shapes from Scratch

Visio comes with a variety of drawing tools, most of which are not immediately visible on the Standard toolbar—you must use the drop-down menus to see all of the available buttons. When you choose a tool, it appears at the top of the toolbar. Anything you draw with one of the drawing tools is a shape. Perhaps the most frequently used drawing tool is the Pencil tool, which you can use to draw both lines and arcs. As you begin to draw with the Pencil tool, Visio quickly calculates the path the mouse is traveling and draws a line if the path is straight or an arc if the path curves.

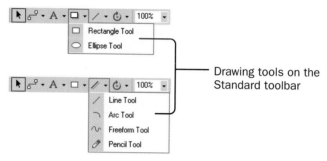

Drawing tools on the Standard toolbar

You can use the Line tool, Arc tool, and Freeform tool to draw different types of lines. In geometric terms, the Arc tool creates elliptical quarter-arc segments, while the Pencil tool draws circular arc segments. When you want to draw a continuous wavy line, you can use the Freeform tool.

Tip

The Freeform tool, to be precise, creates a **spline**, which is a type of curve that passes through specific points. In some types of technical illustrations, it's important to know that the Freeform tool creates a non-uniform rational B-spline (or NURBS for short). For most business diagrams, however, it's sufficient to think of the Freeform tool as the quick way to draw rolling hills or other curving lines.

With the Line, Arc, Freeform, and Pencil tools, you can create either one-dimensional (1-D) or two-dimensional (2-D) shapes. The Ellipse and Rectangle tools, on the other hand, create only 2-D shapes. With the Ellipse tool, you can create both ovals and circles, just as the Rectangle tool creates both rectangles and squares. By holding down [Shift] while drawing with the Ellipse or Rectangle tool, you create a symmetrical shape; that is, a circle or a square.

When you draw a shape, it can be either **closed** or **open**. Shapes like rectangles or circles are closed shapes. You can fill closed shapes with colors and patterns. Lines, half-circles, and zigzag shapes are open shapes. You can format the ends of open shapes. For example, any open shape can have an arrowhead at each end.

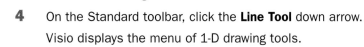

In this exercise, you use the drawing tools to create circles and ellipses that represent different plants in a landscape plan. To differentiate the plant species, you add fill color to the shapes.

1   Start Visio.

2   On the **File** menu, point to **New**, and then click **New Drawing**.

Visio opens a new, blank drawing page.

Zoom

33% ▼

3   On the Standard toolbar, click the **Zoom** down arrow, and then click **100%**.

The view is enlarged.

Line Tool

4   On the Standard toolbar, click the **Line Tool** down arrow.

Visio displays the menu of 1-D drawing tools.

5   Click **Pencil Tool**.

The pointer changes to a pencil with a crosshair.

6   Point to where you want to start the shape.

Visio displays a blue crosshair to show where the shape will start.

7   Drag in a curving motion from left to right to create an arc about 1 inch long, and then release the mouse.

As you drag, the pointer displays a crosshair and an arc. Visio creates an arc segment.

┌─── The arc icon on the pointer shows
       you're creating an arc, not a line.

Troubleshooting

If the pointer displays a line instead of an arc while you are dragging with the Pencil tool, try exaggerating your movements with the mouse—that is, move the mouse in a very circular motion.

8 Point to the endpoint of the arc segment, drag in a downward, curving motion to draw another arc segment approximately ¾ inch long, and then release the mouse button.

Visio creates a second arc segment connected to the first.

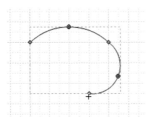

Troubleshooting

Be careful not to *select* the endpoint of the first segment. If you select an endpoint, it turns magenta. If you drag a selected endpoint, Visio resizes the existing segment instead of starting a new one. If you accidentally resize a segment rather than draw a new one, press the Ctrl+Z keys to undo the action.

9 Point to the endpoint of the second segment, drag another arc segment to the beginning point of the first arc segment you drew, and then release the mouse button.

Visio creates an irregular closed shape that looks something like the following. Don't worry if your results aren't exactly the same.

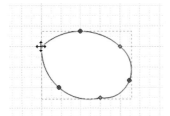

Rectangle Tool

10 On the Standard toolbar, click the **Rectangle Tool** down arrow to display the menu of 2-D drawing tools.

11 Click **Ellipse Tool**.

The pointer changes to an ellipse and crosshair.

12 Drag to create a shape approximately 1 inch wide and ½ inch tall to the right of the irregular shape.

Tip

When drawing, use the grid lines and rulers to help you position a shape.

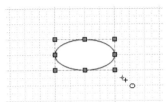

13 Click the drawing page to deselect the ellipse.

14 Hold down ⎡shift⎤ as you drag with the Ellipse tool to create a circle approximately ¾ inch in diameter beside the ellipse.

A diagonal dotted line shows you the circle's diameter. When you finish dragging, the circle is selected.

Tip

Watch the status bar as you drag to see the shape's dimensions.

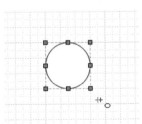

15 Hold down ⎡Ctrl⎤, and then drag down to create a copy of the circle shape that overlaps the first circle.

The copy of the circle is selected.

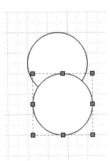

Troubleshooting

Pointer Tool

You can select and work with shapes using the drawing tools—that is, you don't have to click the **Pointer Tool** button first. However, if you accidentally draw a new shape instead of selecting or copying an existing shape, press [Ctrl]+[Z] to undo the action. Then click the **Pointer Tool** button and try again.

Fill Color

16 On the **Formatting** toolbar, click the **Fill Color** down arrow to display the color palette.

17 Click **Light Yellow**.

Visio fills the circle with the chosen color. The circle remains selected.

Important

Depending on the capabilities of your monitor and video driver, your colors might vary from those shown in this exercise. If you don't see the same color, choose something similar.

18 Click the other circle to select it.

Visio displays the shape's selection handles.

19 On the Formatting toolbar, click the **Fill Color** down arrow, and then click **More Fill Colors**.

The **Colors** dialog box appears.

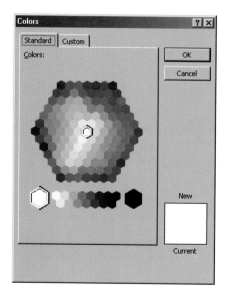

20 In the color wheel, click pink, and then click **OK**.

Visio closes the **Color** dialog box and fills the shape with the selected color. The circle remains selected.

21 Select the ellipse, click the **Fill Color** down arrow, and then click **Light Green**.

Visio fills the ellipse with the new color. The ellipse remains selected.

22 Select the irregular shape, click the **Fill Color** down arrow, and then click **Pale Blue**.

Visio fills the shape with the new color. The shape remains selected.

Pointer Tool

23 On the Standard toolbar, click the **Pointer Tool** button, and then drag a selection box around all four shapes.

The shapes are selected.

Line Color

24 On the Formatting toolbar, click the **Line Color** down arrow, and then click **No Line**.

Visio removes the black border from around the four shapes.

25 Press [Esc] to cancel the selection.

Your screen should look similar to the following.

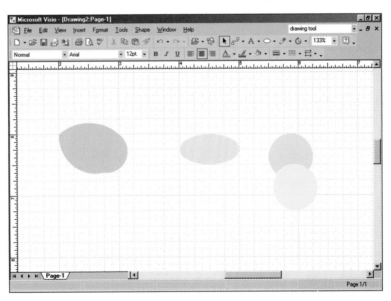

26 On the **File** menu, click **Close**.

Visio prompts you to save changes.

27 Click **No**.

The drawing is closed without saving the changes.

Grouping and Merging Shapes

You can create a variety of simple shapes with the drawing tools. The easiest way to create more complex shapes is to **group** or **merge** simpler components. These two techniques are different:

- When you group shapes, you create a new object, the group, that contains all the original shapes, each of which you can still select and edit.

- When you merge shapes, you combine or break up existing shapes to create new shapes. The original shapes are discarded.

Grouping is a great way to keep together shapes that you want to work with as a unit. For example, the conference table shapes used in office layouts are groups that include table and chair shapes. You can select a group to edit it, which affects all the shapes in the group. When you resize a group, for instance, you resize the shapes that make up the group. In addition, you can subselect each shape in the group to edit or format it individually. To subselect a shape, select the group, and then click a shape in the group. Using a group is often the best way to create a complex shape that has more than one type of formatting, which is why so many Visio master shapes are created as groups. For example, most of the title and border shapes on the **Borders and Titles** stencil are actually groups. With the **Grouping** commands on the **Shape** menu, you can create a group as well as ungroup a group to restore the original shapes.

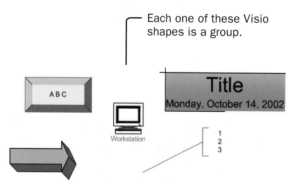

Each one of these Visio shapes is a group.

By contrast, merging shapes is a very different process, although some of the merging operations result in shapes that look like groups. You use the **Operations** commands on the **Shape** menu to merge or break up two or more shapes, creating entirely new shapes. For example, you can create two circles, one inside of the other, and then merge them to create a single doughnut shape. Some merge operations actually merge multiple shapes into one new shape. Other operations split shapes apart and discard the originals.

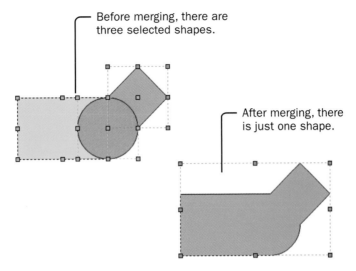

Before merging, there are three selected shapes.

After merging, there is just one shape.

The following table describes each merge command in the order it appears on the **Operations** submenu.

Merge Operation	What It Does
Union	Unites two or more overlapping closed shapes to create one shape from the perimeters of other shapes.
Combine	Create a shape with holes in it, such as a picture frame or a doughnut shape.
Fragment	Breaks a 2-D shape into smaller parts where the shapes overlap. For example, you can draw a line through a circle and then use the **Fragment** command to create two half circles.
Intersect	Creates a new shape from area enclosed by overlapping shapes. The overlapping area becomes a new shape.
Subtract	Cuts one shape out of another shape like a cookie cutter.
Join	Joins lines and arcs into a single 2-D shape.
Trim	Breaks a 1-D shape (except lines) into smaller parts.
Offset	Duplicates a shape (usually 1-D) at precise intervals. For example, you can offset lines to create regular stripes.

Important

When merging shapes, selection order is very important. The format of the first shape you select will be applied to the resulting shape. For example, if you select a red shape and a green shape, in that order, and then click **Intersect**, the resulting shape will be red. Selection order does not affect groups in the same way. Each shape retains its format when you create a group.

GroupShapes

In this exercise, you merge and group simple shapes to create more complex shapes that represent different plants for a landscape plan that The Garden Company wants to create. You start by opening a sample drawing, GroupShapes.

Open

1 On the Standard toolbar, click the **Open** button to display the **Open** dialog box.

2 Click the **Look in** down arrow, navigate to the **SBS\Visio\Customizing** folder, and then double-click **GroupShapes.**

Visio opens a diagram at 150% zoom that includes three shapes on the drawing page.

Ellipse Tool

3 On the Standard toolbar, click the **Ellipse Tool** button.

Troubleshooting

If you don't see the **Ellipse Tool** button, click the **Rectangle Tool** down arrow to display all the 2-D drawing tools, and then click **Ellipse Tool**.

4 Hold down [shift] as you drag with the Ellipse tool to create a small circle approximately ¼ inch in diameter on top of the green ellipse.

The circle remains selected.

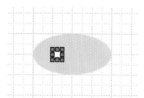

5 Press the [Ctrl]+[D] keys three times to duplicate the dot.

Visio creates three new circles at even intervals, leaving the last circle selected.

Tip

You can also duplicate shapes by clicking **Duplicate** on the **Edit** menu.

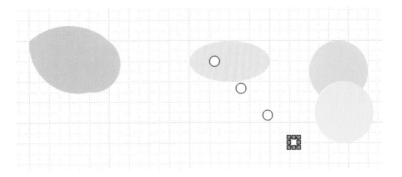

Pointer Tool

6 On the Standard toolbar, click the **Pointer Tool** button.

7 Drag the circles on top of the ellipse, arranging them in polka-dot fashion.

The shapes should look similar to the following.

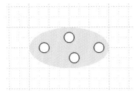

Troubleshooting

If you resize a dot accidentally when you try to drag it, press [Ctrl]+[Z] to cancel the action. It's often easier to move a small shape when it is not selected. Click the drawing page to deselect all shapes, and then point to a dot—the pointer changes to a four-headed arrow. Now drag the shape. If the pointer changes to a two-headed arrow, you will resize the shape instead. When moving small shapes, you also might want to zoom in closer first.

8 Drag a selection box around the green ellipse and dots.

Visio selects all the shapes.

9 On the **Shape** menu, point to **Grouping**, and then click **Group**.

Visio creates a group and displays the group's selection handles.

10 Click a dot in the ellipse group.

Visio subselects the shape and displays group selection handles, which appear as green squares, each containing an x.

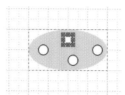

Fill Color

11 Click the **Fill Color** down arrow, and then click **Light Yellow**.

Visio fills only the subselected dot with the new color.

12 Subselect each dot in turn, and then click the **Fill Color** button to make each one yellow.

13 Click the large yellow circle to the right of the ellipse group.

14 Hold down [Shift], and then click the pink circle.

Visio selects both circles. The selection handles on the second shape you click appear light blue.

15 On the **Shape** menu, point to **Operations**, and then click **Union**.

Visio joins the two circles to create a single new shape with the same formatting as the first circle you selected.

16 Click the blue shape to select it.

17 On the **Format** menu, click **Fill** to display the **Fill** dialog box.

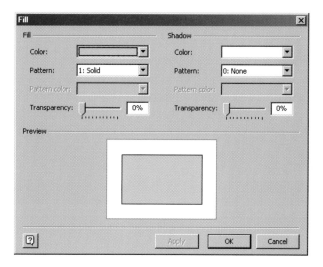

18 In the **Fill** area, click the **Pattern** down arrow to display a list of patterns, and then click pattern **12**.

In the **Preview** area, black dots fill the blue shape. The **Pattern color** option becomes available.

19 Click the **Pattern color** down arrow to display a list of colors, and then click color **1** (white).

In the **Preview** area, the dots become white.

20 Click **OK** to close the **Fill** dialog box and apply the pattern to the shape.

The shapes should now look similar to the following.

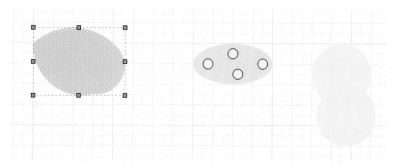

Save

21 On the Standard toolbar, click the **Save** button.

Visio saves your changes.

22 On the **File** menu, click **Close**.

Visio closes the drawing file.

Customizing Shapes

If you never thought of yourself as much of an artist, you might wonder how you can draw shapes from scratch. The key to getting the results you want is to sketch a rough version with the drawing tools, and then customize the results. Built into the lines and arcs that make up shapes are special handles that you can use to reshape, add, move, and delete line segments. So, for example, if you draw a crooked line with the Pencil tool, you can edit the line segment to straighten it out and even change it to an arc. Where line segments join, a diamond-shaped **vertex** appears, which is visible when you select a shape with the Pencil tool. In addition, in the middle of a line segment, a circular **control point** appears, which you use to change the curvature of a segment. For example, a triangle becomes a square when you add a vertex, a curving hill becomes a valley when you move the control point, and so on. So even if you can't draw a straight line, you can make a line straight after the fact by editing a shape's vertices.

Vertex

Control point

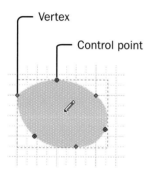

Arc segments have additional handles that you use to adjust their **symmetry**—that is, the direction in which the arc leans. An arc's control point has **eccentricity handles** that you can stretch and rotate to change the line's symmetry. To display an arc's eccentricity handles, you must first select a control point with the Pencil tool, and then you hold down [Ctrl] as you drag slightly away.

Eccentricity handles
Selected control point

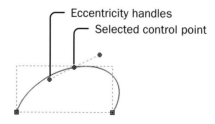

EditShapes

In this exercise, you use the Pencil tool to edit line and arc segments to refine the look of a shape that represents a plant in a landscape plan for The Garden Company. You start by opening a sample drawing, EditShapes.

Open

1 On the Standard toolbar, click the **Open** button to display the **Open** dialog box.

2 Click the **Look In** down arrow, navigate to **SBS\Visio\Customizing**, and then double-click **EditShapes.**

Visio opens a diagram that contains three shapes.

Zoom

3 On the Standard toolbar, click the **Zoom** down arrow, and then click **200%**.

Visio magnifies the view.

Pencil Tool

4 On the Standard toolbar, click the **Pencil Tool** button.

5 Click the blue shape to select it.

Visio display the shape's vertices and control points.

6 Point to the left most vertex.

The pointer changes to a four-headed arrow.

7 Click the vertex.

The vertex turns magenta.

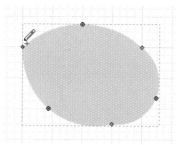

8 Drag the vertex down approximately ¼ inch.

Visio adjusts the outline of the shape.

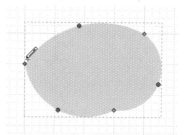

9 Click the lower right vertex to select it.

The vertex turns magenta.

10 Press `Del`.

Visio removes the vertex and redraws the shape.

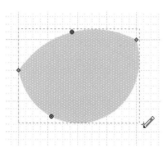

11 Click the lowest control point to select it.

The control point turns magenta.

12 Hold down `Ctrl` as you drag from the control point slightly to the right.

Visio displays the arc's eccentricity handles and changes the curvature of the arc segment.

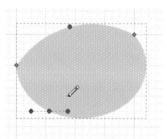

13 Drag the left eccentricity handle to the left approximately to the shape's green dotted selection border.

Visio adjusts the curvature of the arc segment.

14 Hold down `Ctrl` as you click the top edge of the shape.

Visio adds a vertex, which is selected.

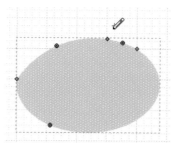

15 Drag the new vertex down and to the left approximately ¼ inch.

Visio indents the shape.

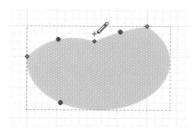

Save

16 On the Standard toolbar, click the **Save** button.

Visio saves your changes.

17 On the **File** menu, click **Close**.

Visio closes the drawing file.

Creating Master Shapes and Stencils

Just as you drag a master shape from a stencil to create a shape on the drawing page, you can drag a shape from the drawing page into a stencil to create a master shape. It's that easy. Why save shapes as master shapes? A good reason is that your shapes then become reusable. For example, let's say you customized a title shape that includes your company's logo. You can save the shape on a stencil so that you can drag it into new drawings as needed. Or maybe you always use the same shapes from several different Visio stencils. By adding those shapes to a new stencil, you create a personalized shape library that's easier to work with.

Another benefit to creating stencils is that they make it easy to distribute your shapes to other Visio users. When you create a new stencil, Visio saves it on your computer only. However, you can share a stencil just as you share drawing files by saving the stencil in a network folder that others have access to or by sending the stencil in an e-mail message. For protection, stencils are **read-only**—that is, a stencil can't be changed unless you specifically open it for editing. When you drag a shape into a read-only stencil, Visio prompts you to open the stencil for editing so that you can create a master shape. When you create a new stencil, Visio opens it as an editable file that has the file extension .vss. All Visio templates open one or more stencils for you, which are docked alongside the drawing page.

A master shape is represented by the icon that you see on a stencil. When you create a new master shape, Visio makes the master shape icon for you based on the appearance of the shape. Visio also provides a default name, which is the word *Master* followed by a period and a number, such as *Master.1*. However, you can supply the name you want by editing the master shape's properties. That's how Visio master shapes get their names; for example, the **Office Furniture** stencil contains master shapes named **Desk** and **Chair**. Besides the name, a master shape's properties include the size and alignment of the icon, the prompt that appears when you point to the master shape on the stencil, and keywords that you can use to locate the shape later.

Tip

When you save a custom stencil in the same folder that Visio uses for storing stencils on your computer (C:\Program Files\Microsoft Office\Visio10\1033\Solutions), the stencil will appear in the stencil lists you see when you use Visio.

CreateStencil

In this exercise, you open a new stencil and then create master shapes so that you can reuse customized shapes that represent plants for a landscape plan. You start by opening a sample drawing, CreateStencil, that you installed from the CD.

Open

1 On the Standard toolbar, click the **Open** button to display the **Open** dialog box.

2 Click the **Look in** down arrow, navigate to the **SBS\Visio\Customizing** folder, and then double-click **CreateStencil**.

Visio opens a diagram that contains three shapes.

3 On the **File** menu, point to **Stencils**, and then click **New Stencil**.

Visio opens a new, empty stencil named **Stencil1** and docks it alongside the drawing page.

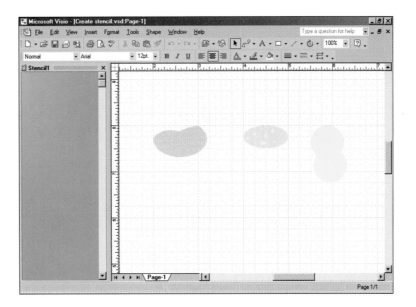

Tip

Stencil icon

When a stencil is open for editing, a red asterisk appears on the stencil icon on the stencil's title bar.

4 Drag the blue shape into the stencil window.

Visio creates a new master shape called **Master.0** with a gray icon and removes the blue shape from the drawing page.

Troubleshooting

If you're wondering why the master icon is gray when the shape is blue, understand that Visio sometimes substitutes colors when you create a master shape. If the shape on the drawing page is formatted with a fill color that is not one of Visio's default 16 colors, Visio substitutes the closest color from that 16-color palette when it creates the icon for the master shape (often gray). That way, stencils take up less disk space—a consideration when you have hundreds of stencils, as Visio does.

5 Drag the green shape and the yellow shape into the stencil window.

Visio creates two additional master shapes, **Master.1** and **Master.2**, and removes the shapes from the drawing page.

6 Right-click **Master.0** to display a shortcut menu, and then click **Master Properties**.

The **Master Properties** dialog box appears. The master name is selected.

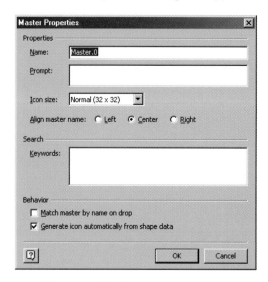

7 Type **Thymus vulgaris**, and then click **OK**.

Visio changes the name of the master shape to *Thymus vulgaris*.

8 Right-click **Master.1**, and then click **Master Properties** to display the **Master Properties** dialog box.

9 Type **Rudbeckia hirta**, and then click **OK**.

Visio changes the name of the master shape to *Rudbeckia hirta*.

10 Right-click **Master.2**, and then click **Master Properties** to display the **Master Properties** dialog box.

11 Type Phygelius capensis, and then click **OK**.

Visio changes the name of the master shape to *Phygelius capensis*.

Stencil icon

12 On the **Stencil1** title bar, click the stencil icon.

Visio displays a menu with options for working with the stencil.

13 Click **Save**.

The **Save As** dialog box appears.

14 Click the **Save In** down arrow, and then browse to and open the **C:\Program Files\Microsoft Office\Visio10\1033\Solutions** folder.

The contents of the Solutions folder are displayed.

Troubleshooting

If your version of Visio is installed in a different location, select that file path instead to locate the Solutions folder.

15 In the **File name** box, type Demo Perennials, and then click **Save**.

The **Demo Perennials.vss Properties** dialog box appears.

16 Click **OK**.

Visio saves the stencil. The new stencil name, **Demo Perennials**, appears in the stencil title bar.

Open Stencil

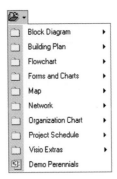

17 On the Standard toolbar, click the **Open Stencil** down arrow.

At the bottom of the list of folders, the **Demo Perennials** stencil appears.

Troubleshooting

If the **Demo Perennials** stencil doesn't appear in the stencil list, you saved it in a folder other than the Solutions folder, which is where Visio looks for all stencils by default. Click the **Open Stencil** button (not the down arrow) to display the **Open Stencil** dialog box, and then navigate to the folder in which you saved the **Demo Perennials.vss** file.

18 On the **File** menu, click **Close**.

Visio prompts you to save changes to the stencil.

19 Click **No**.

Visio closes the drawing and stencil.

Creating a New Template

If you frequently create a particular type of drawing that uses a unique page size or always includes the same information, such as a corporate logo or a title bar containing file information, consider creating a new template. A template opens a drawing page and stencils. For example, if you create landscape plans frequently, you can create a template that opens an appropriately sized drawing page and stencils containing landscaping symbols. If you've worked through the exercises in this book, you've seen how opening a template gives you a head start on a drawing, because all the tools and shapes you need are opened by the template.

You can actually save any drawing as a Visio template (a file with the extension .vst), which you can then open to start a new drawing that uses the same settings. For example, perhaps you always use the same four stencils, but no existing Visio template opens those stencils for you. You can start a new drawing, open the stencils you want, and then save the file—drawing, stencils, and all—as a template.

In addition to stencils, templates can also include the following:

- One or more drawing pages, including background pages. Each page can contain shapes, pictures, and other objects.
- Print settings that you enter in the **Print Setup** dialog box, such as a landscape-oriented page, a custom size, or a drawing scale.
- Styles for lines, text, and fills.
- Snap and glue options set in the **Snap & Glue** dialog box.
- A color palette from the **Color Palette** dialog box.
- Window sizes and positions.

In effect, you can save all the settings you work with most as a template so that you don't have to set them each time you start a new drawing.

Perennials

In this exercise, you start a blank drawing that will be the basis for a new template. You change the drawing page orientation for the template, and then you open a custom stencil, Perennials. Then you save the file as a template.

1 On the **File** menu, point to **New**, and then click **New Drawing** to open a new, blank drawing.

2 On the **File** menu, click **Page Setup**.

The **Page Setup** dialog box appears and displays the **Print Setup** tab.

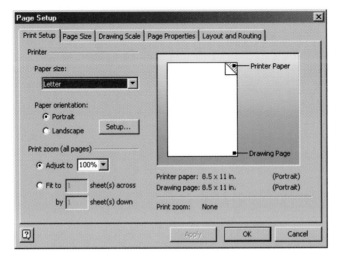

3 In the **Paper orientation** area, click the **Landscape** option.

Visio updates the preview in the dialog box to show a landscape-oriented drawing page.

4 To close the **Page Setup** dialog box, click **OK**.

Visio changes the drawing page orientation so that the page is wider than tall.

Open Stencil

5 On the Standard toolbar, click **Open Stencil**.

The **Open Stencil** dialog box appears.

Troubleshooting

Make sure to click the **Open Stencil** button, not the button's down arrow. If you click the **Open Stencil** down arrow, a list of folders appears. If you click the button itself, the **Open Stencil** dialog box appears.

6 Click the **Look in** down arrow, navigate to the **SBS\Visio\Customizing** folder, and then double-click **Perennials**.

Visio opens the **Perennials** stencil and docks it to the left of the drawing page.

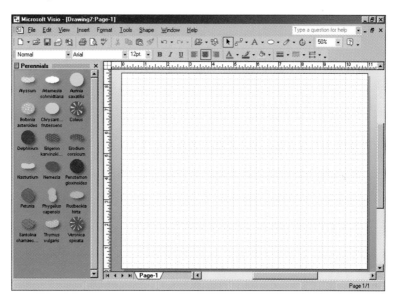

Save

7 On the Standard toolbar, click the **Save** button to open the **Save As** dialog box.

8 Click the **Save As Type** down arrow.

Visio displays a list of file types.

9 **Click Template (*.vst)**.

10 Click the **Save in** down arrow, and then navigate to and open the **C:\Program Files\Microsoft Office\Visio10\1033\Solutions** folder.

The contents of the Solutions folder are displayed.

Troubleshooting

If your version of Visio is installed in a different location, select that file path instead to locate the Solutions folder.

11 In the **File name** box, select the existing text and type Perennial Garden Plan.

12 Click the **Save** button.

The **Perennial Garden Plan.vst Properties** dialog box appears.

13 Click **OK**.

Visio creates a new template, **Perennial Garden Plan.vst**, in the Solutions folder.

14 On the **File** menu, click **Close**.

Visio closes the template file.

15 On the **File** menu, point to **New**.

At the bottom of the menu, the **Perennial Garden Plan** template appears.

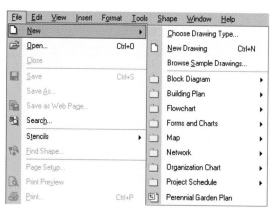

Troubleshooting

If the **Perennial Garden Plan** template doesn't appear on the menu, you saved it in a folder other than the Solutions folder, which is where Visio looks for all templates by default. Click the **Open Stencil** button (not the down arrow) to display the **Open Stencil** dialog box, and then navigate to the folder in which you saved the **Perennial Garden Plan.vst** file.

16 Click **Perennial Garden Plan**.

Visio starts a new, blank drawing file based on the **Perennial Garden Plan** template and opens the **Perennials** stencil.

17 On the **File** menu, click **Exit**.

Visio closes the drawing.

18 If Visio prompts you to save changes, click **No**.

Appendix A
Visio Stencils and Templates

Microsoft Visio Standard 2002 includes all the templates and stencils listed in the following table. These files are installed by default in C:\Program Files\Microsoft Office\Visio 10 \1033\Solutions. However, you can start a drawing with a template or open a stencil at any time using these methods:

New

- To open a template, on the Standard toolbar, click the **New** down arrow, point to a category, and then click the template you want.

Open Stencil

- To open a stencil, on the Standard toolbar, click the **Open Stencil** down arrow, point to a category, and then click the stencil you want.

Category	Template	Stencils Opened by the Template
Block Diagram	Basic Diagram	Backgrounds, Basic Shapes, Borders and Titles
	Block Diagram	Backgrounds, Blocks, Blocks Raised, Borders and Titles
	Block Diagram with Perspective	Backgrounds, Blocks with Perspective, Borders and Titles
Building Plan	Office Layout	Cubicles, Office Accessories, Office Equipment, Office Furniture, Walls, Doors and Windows
Flowchart	Audit Diagram	Audit Diagram Shapes, Backgrounds, Borders and Titles
	Basic Flowchart	Backgrounds, Basic Flowchart Shapes, Borders and Titles
	Cause and Effect Diagram	Cause and Effect Diagram Shapes, Backgrounds, Borders and Titles
	Cross-Functional Flowchart	Basic Flowchart Shapes, Cross-Functional Flowchart Shapes Horizontal or Cross-Functional Flowchart Shapes Vertical
	Mind Mapping Diagram	Backgrounds, Borders and Titles, Mind Mapping Diagram Shapes

Category	Template	Stencils Opened by the Template
Flowchart	TQM Diagram	Backgrounds, Borders and Titles, TQM Diagram Shapes
	Work Flow Diagram	Backgrounds, Borders and Titles, Work Flow Diagram Shapes, Miscellaneous Flowchart Shapes
Forms and Charts	Charts and Graphs	Backgrounds, Borders and Titles, Charting Shapes
	Form Design	Form Shapes
	Marketing Charts and Diagrams	Backgrounds, Borders and Titles, Charting Shapes, Marketing Diagrams, Marketing Shapes
Map	Directional Map	Landmark Shapes, Metro Shapes, Recreation Shapes, Road Shapes, Transportation Shapes
	Directional Map 3D	Directional Map Shapes 3D
Network	Basic Network	Backgrounds, Basic Network Shapes, Basic Network Shapes 2, Basic Network Shapes 3D, Borders and Titles
Organization Chart	Organization Chart	Backgrounds, Borders and Titles, Organization Chart Shapes
	Organization Chart Wizard	Backgrounds, Borders and Titles, Organization Chart Shapes
Project Schedule	Calendar	Calendar Shapes
	Gantt Chart	Backgrounds, Borders and Titles, Gantt Chart Shapes
	PERT Chart	Backgrounds, Borders and Titles, PERT Chart Shapes
	Timeline	Backgrounds, Borders and Titles, Timeline Shapes
Visio Extras		Backgrounds, Borders and Titles, Callouts, Connectors, Embellishments, Symbols

Appendix B
Visio Shapes

Each stencil in Microsoft Visio Standard 2002 includes a variety of shapes that you can use to create a particular type of drawing. To help you locate the shapes at a glance, this reference shows each stencil's shapes organized by category.

Open Stencil

At any time while working in Visio, you can open a stencil to make its shapes available to your drawing. On the Standard toolbar, click the **Open Stencil** down arrow, point to a category, and then click the stencil you want.

Find Shape

If you still can't locate the shape you want after browsing through the following reference, click the **Find Shape** button on the Standard toolbar. Then you can type keywords associated with the shape you want.

Block Diagram Shapes

With the shapes on the **Basic Shapes**, **Blocks**, **Blocks Raised**, and **Blocks with Perspective** stencils, you can create simple diagrams that communicate business relationships and processes to annotate reports, presentations, proposals, and so on.

Building Plan Shapes

With the shapes on the **Cubicles**, **Office Accessories**, **Office Equipment**, **Office Furniture**, and **Walls, Doors and Windows** stencils, you can create scaled buildings, home plans, and office layouts.

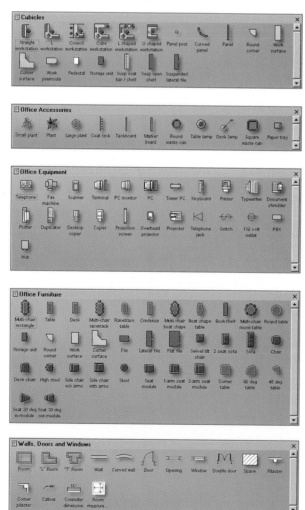

Flowchart Shapes

With the shapes on the flowchart stencils, you can create both general-purpose and specialized flowcharts; and data flow, work flow, and planning diagrams. Visio includes the following flowchart stencils: **Audit Diagram Shapes** stencil, **Basic Flowchart Shapes** stencil, **Cause and Effect Diagram Shape** stencil, **Cross-Functional Flowchart Shapes Horizontal** stencil, **Cross-Functional Flowchart Shapes Vertical** stencil, **Mind Mapping Diagram Shapes** stencil, **Miscellaneous Flowchart Shapes** stencil, **TQM Diagram Shapes** stencil, and **Work Flow Diagram Shapes** stencil.

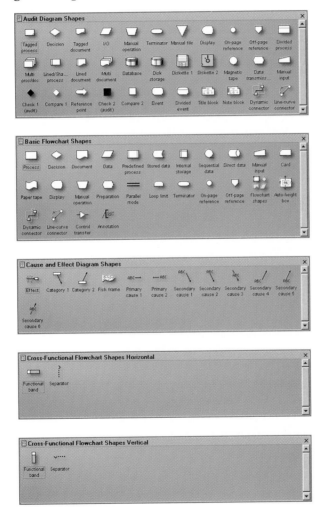

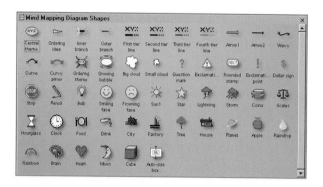

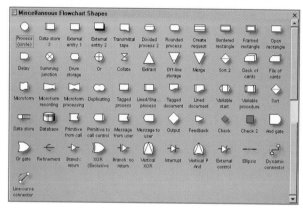

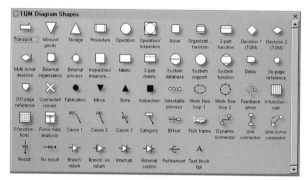

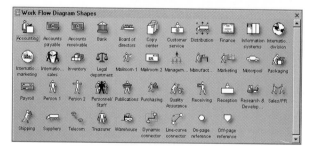

Forms and Charts Shapes

With the shapes on the **Charting Shapes**, **Form Shapes**, **Marketing Diagrams**, and **Marketing Shapes** stencils, you can create charts and graphs, order and inventory forms, sales target diagrams, market share figures, and so on.

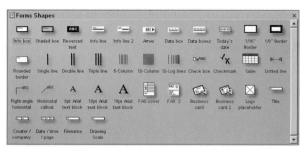

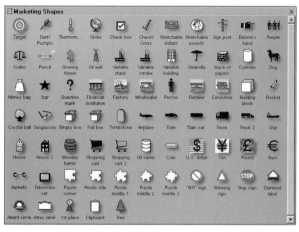

Map Shapes

With the map shapes, you can create simple and attractive maps for invitations, Web sites, brochures, and presentations. Visio includes the following map stencils: **Directional Map Shapes 3D** stencil, **Landmark Shapes** stencil, **Metro Shapes** stencil, **Recreation Shapes** stencil, **Road Shapes** stencil, and **Transportation Shapes** stencil.

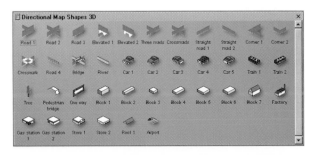

Network Shapes

With the shapes on the **Basic Network Shapes**, **Basic Network Shapes 2**, and **Basic Network Shapes 3D** stencils, you can create high-level network diagrams for presentations and proposals.

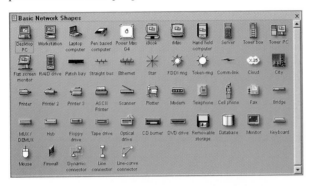

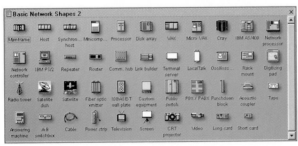

Organization Chart Shapes

With the shapes on the **Organization Chart Shapes** stencil, you can show an organization's reporting hierarchy and employee-manager relationships.

Project Schedule Shapes

With the **Calendar Shapes** stencil, you can create monthly and yearly calendars. With the **Gantt Chart Shapes** stencil, you can show the sequence of tasks necessary for completing a project. With the **PERT Chart Shapes** stencil, you can use shapes that conform to the Program Evaluation and Review Technique (PERT), a project management method developed in the 1950s by the U.S. Navy and used today to diagram project details. With the **Timeline Shapes** stencil, you can show the lifespan of a project or process in a linear format that includes tasks, milestones, and intervals.

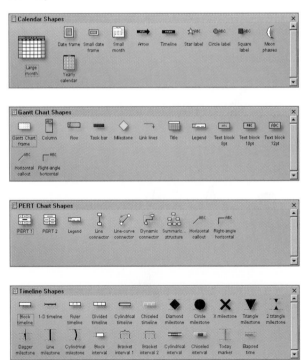

Visio Extras Shapes

Visio Extras are shapes that you can use to annotate or decorate any diagram. The shapes on the **Backgrounds** and **Borders and Titles** stencils are described throughout this book. The **Callouts** stencil includes lines, arrows, and text shapes for notes. The **Connectors** stencil includes straight, curving, and angled connectors. The **Embellishments** and **Symbols** stencils contain ornamental shapes.

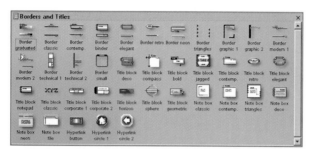

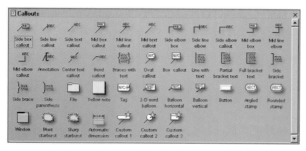

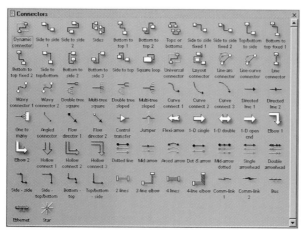

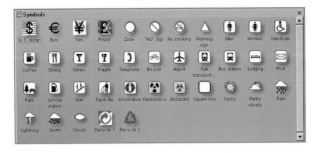

Quick Reference

15 **To change how master shapes appear on a stencil**

1 On a stencil title bar, click the stencil icon in the top left corner.

2 Click **Icons and Names**, **Icons Only**, **Names Only**, or **Icons and Details**.

10 **To move a stencil**

● Drag the stencil by its title bar or drag the **Shapes** title bar to another side of the Visio window.

14 **To close a stencil**

1 On the stencil title bar, click the stencil icon in the top left corner.

2 Click **Close**.

16 **To display help for a topic**

1 Type a keyword in the Ask A Question box on the menu bar, and then press ⏎ Enter .

2 In the list of topics, click a topic.

16 **To display help about a particular drawing type**

1 On the **Help** menu, click **Microsoft Visio Help**.

2 On the **Contents** tab, click **Drawing Types**, click a category, click a diagram type, and then click the topic you want.

16 **To display the Contents pane in online Help**

Show

1 On the **Microsoft Visio Help** toolbar, click the **Show** button.

2 Click the **Contents** tab.

Chapter **2** **Adding Shapes to Diagrams**

Page 21 **To create a block diagram**

1 On the **File** menu, point to **New**, point to **Block Diagram**, and then click **Block Diagram**.

2 Drag shapes from the **Blocks** and **Blocks Raised** stencils onto the drawing page.

24 **To select a shape**

Pointer Tool

● Click the **Pointer Tool** button on the Standard toolbar, and then click a shape.

28 **To select multiple shapes**

1 Click the **Pointer Tool** button on the Standard toolbar.

2 Hold down `shift`, and then click the shapes.

28 **To select multiple shapes that are close together**

1 Click the **Pointer Tool** button on the Standard toolbar

2 Drag a rectangle around the shapes you want.

25 **To add text to a shape**

● Select a shape, type, then click `Esc`.

30 **To format text**

1 Select the shape containing the text to be formatted.

2 On the **Format** menu, click **Text**.

3 Choose the formats you want, and then click **OK**.

29 **To size a shape**

● Select the shape, and then drag a selection handle in the direction you want.

31 **To find out what a control handle does**

● Point to the control handle until a ScreenTip appears.

33 **To duplicate a shape**

● Select the shape, and then press `Ctrl`+`D`.

36 **To find a particular shape on a stencil**

Find Shape

1 On the Standard toolbar, click the **Find Shape** button.

2 In the **Search For** box, type one or more keywords.

3 Click **Go**.

38 **To save a drawing file for the first time**

Save

1 On the Standard toolbar, click the **Save** button.

2 In the **Save In** box, navigate to the folder in which you want to save the drawing.

3 In the **File name** box, type a name for the drawing file.

4 Click **Save**.

38 **To save changes to a drawing file**
- On the Standard toolbar, click the **Save** button.

38 **To enter properties about a drawing file**

1   On the **File** menu, click **Properties**.

2   Type the information you want, and then click **OK**.

Chapter   3   Formatting Shapes and Diagrams

Page   42   **To change a shape's line color**

1   Select the shape.

Line Color   2   On the Formatting toolbar, click the **Line Color** down arrow, and then click a color.

45   **To change a shape's line thickness**

1   Select the shape.

Line Weight   2   On the Formatting toolbar, click the **Line Weight** down arrow, and then click an option.

44   **To change a shape's fill color**

1   Select the shape.

Fill Color   2   On the Formatting toolbar, click the **Fill Color** down arrow, and then click a color.

46   **To change text size**

1   Select the shape that contains the text you want to change.

Font Size   2   On the Formatting toolbar, click the **Font Size** down arrow, and then click a size.

8pt.

43   **To change text font**

Font   1   Select the shape that contains the text you want to change.

Arial   2   On the Formatting toolbar, click the **Font** down arrow, and then click a font.

47   **To change text color**

1   Select the shape that contains the text you want to change.

Text Color   2   On the Formatting toolbar, click the **Text Color** down arrow, and then click a color.

42   **To add end patterns to a line**

    1   Select the line or other 1-D shape.

Line Ends

    2   On the Formatting toolbar, click the **Line Ends** down arrow, and then click a pattern.

45   **To copy a shape's format to another shape**

    1   Select the shape that has the formatting you want to copy.

Format Painter

    2   On the Standard toolbar, click the **Format Painter** button.

    3   Click the shape to which you want to copy the formatting.

45   **To copy a shape's format to multiple shapes**

    1   Select the shape that has the formatting you want to copy.

    2   On the Standard toolbar, double-click the **Format Painter** button.

    3   Click each shape in succession to which you want to copy the formatting.

    4   When you are finished, click the **Format Painter** button.

49   **To add a border to a diagram**

    ●   Drag a border shape from the **Borders and Titles** stencil to the drawing page.

51   **To add a background to a diagram**

    1   Drag a background shape from the **Backgrounds** stencil to the drawing page.

    2   In the **Make a Background** dialog box, click **Yes**.

50   **To add a title shape to a diagram**

    ●   Drag a title shape from the **Borders and Titles** stencil to the drawing page.

53   **To format a diagram with a color scheme**

    1   On the **Tools** menu, click **Color Schemes**.

    2   In the **Choose a color scheme** list, click the scheme you want.

    3   Click **OK**.

54   **To remove a color scheme**

    1   On the **Tools** menu, click **Color Schemes**.

    2   In the **Choose a color scheme** list, click **Black & White**.

    3   Click **OK**.

57 **To change page size**

1 On the **File** menu, click **Page Setup**.

2 On the **Page Size** tab, click **Pre-defined size**, and then select an option. Or click **Custom size**, and then type the size you want.

3 Click **OK**.

57 **To change page orientation**

1 On the **File** menu, click **Page Setup**.

2 On the **Print Setup** tab, click **Portrait** or **Landscape**.

3 On the **Page Size** tab, make sure **Same as printer paper size** is selected.

4 If **Same as printer paper size** is not selected, click an option under **Page orientation** that matches the option you selected on the **Print Setup** tab.

5 Click **OK**.

56 **To preview a diagram before printing**

● On the **File** menu, click **Print Preview**.

56 **To display page breaks**

● On the **View** menu, click **Page Breaks**.

58 **To print the current page**

● On the Standard toolbar, click the **Print Page** button.

58 **To print a diagram**

1 On the **File** menu, click **Print**.

2 Choose the options you want, and then click **OK**.

Chapter 4 **Connecting Shapes**

Page 63 **To create a flowchart**

1 On the **File** menu, point to **New**, point to **Flowchart**, and then click **Basic Flowchart**.

2 On the Standard toolbar, click the **Connector Tool** button.

3 Drag shapes from the **Basic Flowchart Shapes** stencil onto the drawing page.

63 **To draw a connector**

Connector Tool

1 On the Standard toolbar, click the **Connector Tool** button.

2 Draw a line from one shape to the next (that is, from step one to step two, and so on.)

232

70 **To create a shape-to-shape connection**

1 With the Connector tool, point to the first shape until a red border appears around the entire shape.

2 Drag to the second shape until a red border appears around the shape, and then release the mouse.

70 **To create a point-to-point connection**

1 With the Connector tool, point to the first shape until a red border appears around a connection point.

2 Drag to a connection point on the second shape, and then release the mouse.

65 **To add text to a connector**

● Select the connector, type, and then press Esc.

69 **To insert a shape in a connected diagram**

1 Select the connector between the two shapes where you want to insert a new shape.

2 Press Del.

3 Drag the new shape into position.

4 With the Connector tool, reconnect the shapes.

69 **To remove a connector**

● Select the connector, and then press Del.

74 **To change the layout style of a connected diagram**

1 On the **Shape** menu, click **Lay Out Shapes**.

2 In the **Placement** area, click an option in the **Style** list.

3 Click an option in the **Direction** list.

4 Click **OK**.

76 **To distribute shapes evenly**

1 Select three or more shapes.

2 On the **Shape** menu, click **Distribute Shapes**.

3 In the **Distribute Shapes** dialog box, click the option you want.

4 Click **OK**.

78 **To subselect shapes in a group**

1 Click to select a group.

2 Click a shape in the group to subselect that shape.

78 **To type in a group**

● Subselect a shape in the group, and then type.

78 **To replace text in a title shape**

Text Tool

A

1 Click the **Text Tool** button on the Standard toolbar.

2 Select the text you want to replace, and then type.

Chapter 5 Creating Project Schedules

Page 83 **To create a timeline**

1 On the **File** menu, point to **New**, point to **Project Schedule**, and then click **Timeline**.

2 Drag a timeline shape from the **Timeline Shapes** stencil onto the drawing page.

3 In the **Configure Timeline** dialog box, set the date range, scale, and format, and then click **OK**.

4 Drag milestone and interval shapes from the **Timeline Shapes** stencil onto the timeline.

87 **To add milestones to a timeline**

1 Drag a milestone shape from the **Timeline Shapes** stencil onto the timeline.

2 In the **Configure Milestone** dialog box, enter the milestone date, select a date format, and then click **OK**.

88 **To change the milestone description**

1 Double-click the placeholder text to select the text block.

2 Select the text you want to replace, and then type. Press Esc.

86 **To add interval markers to a timeline**

1 From the **Timeline Shapes** stencil, drag an interval shape onto the timeline.

2 In the **Configure Interval** dialog box, choose the interval start date, finish date, and date format, and then click **OK**.

91 **To modify a milestone shape in a timeline**

1 Right-click the milestone, and then click **Set Milestone Type**.

2 In the **Milestone Shape** list, click an option, and then click **OK**.

92 **To export a timeline**

1 Click the border of the timeline to select it.

2 On the **Tools** menu, point to **Macros**, point to **Project Schedule**, and then click **Export Project Data Wizard**.

3 On the first wizard page, choose an export file format, and then click **Next**.

4 On the second wizard page, type a name for the file.

5 Click **Browse**, and then locate the folder where you want to save your project data. Select the folder, and then click **Save**.

6 Click **Next**, and then click **Finish**.

94 **To create a Gantt chart**

1 On the **File** menu, point to **New**, point to **Project Schedule**, and then click **Gantt Chart**.

2 On the **Date** tab, type a number in the **Number of tasks** box.

3 Choose options for **Time units**, **Duration options**, and **Timescale range**, and then click **OK**.

4 Type task names, start dates, finish dates, and durations.

5 Add tasks and milestones, and then link tasks.

99 **To modify duration information in a Gantt chart**

1 Click the cell that contains the duration you want to change.

2 Type the new duration using the following abbreviations: *m* for minutes, *h* for hours, *d* for days, and *w* for weeks.

97 **To add a column for resource names to a Gantt chart**

1 Right-click a column in the Gantt chart, and then click **Insert Column**.

2 In the **Column Type** list, click **Resource Names**.

3 Click **OK**.

99 **To add a new task to a Gantt chart**

● Right-click a cell in the row below the task you want to insert, and then click **New Task**.

100 **To change the milestone format**

1 On the **Gantt Chart** menu, click **Options**.

2 On the **Format** tab, click a milestone in the **Shapes** list.

3 Click **OK**.

Chapter 6 Creating an Organization Chart

Page 107 **To create an organization chart**

    1 On the **File** menu, point to **New**, point to **Organization Chart**, and then click **Organization Chart**.

    2 Drag the **Executive** shape from the **Organization Chart Shapes** stencil onto the drawing page, and then type a name and title for the shape.

    3 Drag a **Manager** shape from the **Organization Chart Shapes** stencil directly onto the **Executive** shape, and then type a name and title of the manager. Repeat until you've added all the managers.

    4 Drag a **Position** shape from the **Organization Chart Shapes** stencil onto a manager shape, and then type the name and title of the employee. Repeat until you've added all the employees.

108 **To import Microsoft Excel data for an organization chart**

    1 On the **File** menu, point to **New**, point to **Organization Chart**, and then click **Organization Chart Wizard**.

    2 On the first wizard page, click **Information that's already stored in a file or database**, and then click **Next**.

    3 Click **A text, Org Plus (*.txt), or Microsoft Excel file**, and then click **Next**.

    4 Click **Browse**, locate and select the file you want, click **Open**, and then click **Next**.

    5 Identify the columns in your Excel file that contain employee names and managers, and then click **Next**.

    6 Click **Next**, and then choose additional columns from your Excel file that you want to include. Click **Next**, and then click **Finish**.

108 **To add shapes to an organization chart**

    1 Drag a shape from the **Organization Chart Shapes** stencil onto a manager shape, and then type the name and title of the employee.

    2 Repeat until you've added all the employees you want.

108 **To add names to an organization chart**

    1 Select an organization chart shape.

    2 Type a person's name, press `Enter`, and then type the person's title.

    3 Press `Esc` or click outside the shape.

111   To add employee information to an organization chart

1   Right-click the organization chart shape that represents the employee you want to add information about.

2   Click **Properties**.

3   Type the information you want, and then click **OK**.

113   To change the information shown in employee shapes

1   On the **Organization Chart** menu, click **Options**.

2   Click **Set Display Fields**.

3   Use the **Add** and **Remove** buttons to move fields to the **Displayed fields** list, and then click **OK**.

4   In the **Options** dialog box, click **OK**.

112   To display the Custom Properties window

●   On the **View** menu, click **Custom Properties Window**.

115   To change the layout of organization chart shapes

1   Select a top-level shape, such as a manager.

2   On the **Organization Chart** toolbar, click a layout option.

116   To move a department to a new page

1   Right-click a manager shape, and then click **Create Synchronized Copy**.

2   In the **Create Synchronized Copy** dialog box, choose the page you want to move the shapes to, and then click **OK**.

117   To add a hyperlink to another page

1   Select a shape, and then click **Hyperlinks** on the **Insert** menu.

2   Click **Browse** next to the **Sub-address** box.

3   In the **Page** list, click a page, and then click **OK**.

4   In the **Description** box, type a name for the hyperlink, and then click **OK**.

120   To apply a design theme to an organization chart

1   On the **Organization Chart** menu, click **Options**.

2   In the **Org chart theme** list, click a theme, and then click **OK**.

122 **To save a diagram as a Web page**

1 On the **File** menu, click **Save as Web Page**.

2 In the **File name** box, type a name for the Web page file.

3 Click **Change Title**, type a name for the Web page, and then click **OK**.

4 Click **Publish**.

5 Choose the options you want, and then click **OK**.

Chapter 7 Laying Out Office Space

Page 129 **To create an office layout diagram**

1 On the **File** menu, point to **New**, point to **Building Plan**, and then click **Office Layout**.

2 Drag room or wall shapes from the **Walls, Doors and Windows** stencil onto the drawing page to create the building structure.

3 Drag door and window shapes from the **Walls, Doors and Windows** stencil onto the wall shapes.

4 Add furniture and office equipment by dragging shapes from the stencils to the drawing page.

129 **To change the drawing scale**

1 On the **File** menu, click **Page Setup**.

2 On the **Drawing Scale** tab, click options in the **Pre-defined scale** lists, and then click **OK**.

132 **To create walls from space shapes**

1 Drag the **Space** shape from the **Walls, Doors and Windows** stencil onto the drawing page.

2 With the space shape selected, click **Convert to Walls** on the **Plan** menu.

3 Select the options you want, and then click **OK**.

135 **To add a door to an office layout**

● Drag the **Door** or **Double door** shape from the **Walls, Doors and Windows** stencil onto a wall shape.

136 **To change door size**

1 Right-click the door shape, and then click **Properties**.

2 In the **Door Width** list, click a size, and then click **OK**.

136 **To reverse the direction in which a door opens**

● Right-click the door shape, and then click **Reverse In/Out Opening**.

136 **To change the direction of the door swing**

● Right-click the door shape, and then click **Reverse Left/Right Opening**.

137 **To add a window to an office layout**

● Drag the **Window** shape from the **Walls, Doors and Windows** stencil onto a wall shape.

140 **To see which layers a shape is assigned to**

● Select a shape, and then click **Layer** on the **Format** menu.

141 **To lock the shapes on a layer**

1 On the **View** menu, click **Layer Properties**.

2 Click to place a check mark in the **Lock** column for the layers you want to lock, and then click **OK**.

142 **To change the color of shapes on a layer**

1 On the **View** menu, click **Layer Properties**.

2 Click to place a check mark in the **Color** column for a layer.

3 In the **Layer Color** list, click a color, and then click **OK**.

142 **To hide the shapes on a layer**

1 On the **View** menu, click **Layer Properties**.

2 Click to clear the check mark in the **Visible** column for the layers you want to hide, and then click **OK**.

145 **To import a picture**

1 On the **Insert** menu, point to **Picture**, and then click **From File**.

2 Locate the folder that contains the picture you want to insert, click the picture file, and then click **Open**.

143 **To crop a picture**

Rotation Tool

1 Select the picture, click the **Rotation Tool** down arrow on the Standard toolbar, and then click **Crop Tool**.

2 Drag a selection handle to crop the picture.

3 Point to the picture until the pointer changes to a hand icon, and then drag to adjust the portion of the picture that appears.

197 **To group shapes**

1 Select the shapes you want.

2 On the **Shape** menu, point to **Grouping**, and then click **Group**.

194 **To ungroup shapes**

1 Select a group.

2 On the **Shape** menu, point to **Grouping**, and then click **Ungroup**.

198 **To merge shapes**

1 Select two or more shapes.

2 On the **Shape** menu, point to **Operations**, and then click the merge operation you want.

201 **To edit a line**

Pencil Tool

1 Click the **Pencil Tool** button on the Standard toolbar.

2 Click the line, and then move or delete vertices.

202 **To add a vertex to a line or arc**

1 Click the **Pencil Tool** button on the Standard toolbar.

2 Click the shape.

3 Hold down Ctrl, and then click where you want to add the vertex.

202 **To edit an arc**

1 Click the **Pencil Tool** button on the Standard toolbar.

2 Click the arc, and then drag a control point.

202 **To change the way an arc leans**

1 Click the **Pencil Tool** button on the Standard toolbar.

2 Click the arc to display its control point.

3 Hold down Ctrl, and then drag slightly away from the control point to display the eccentricity handles.

4 Drag an eccentricity handle to a new position.

205 **To create a master shape**

1 Drag a shape from the drawing page into a stencil.

2 If Visio prompts you to open the stencil for editing, click **Yes**.

206 **To edit master shape properties**

1   Right-click a master shape on a stencil that's open for editing, and then click **Master Properties**.

2   Make changes, and then click **OK**.

204 **To create a stencil**

●   On the **File** menu, point to **Stencils**, and then click **New Stencil**.

207 **To save a stencil**

1   Click the icon in the top left corner of the stencil title bar, and then click **Save As**.

2   Navigate to a folder, type a file name, and then click **Save**.

210 **To create a template**

1   On the **File** menu, point to **New**, and then click **New Drawing**.

Open Stencil

2   Click the **Open Stencil** button, and then locate and select the stencil you want to include in the template.

3   On the **File** menu, click **Page Setup**, select the page settings you want to use, and then click **OK**.

4   If desired, add shapes or a background to the page.

5   On the **File** menu, click **Save As**.

6   In the **Save as type** list, click **Template (*.vst)**. Navigate to a folder, type a file name, and then click **Save**.

Glossary

1-D shape A shape, such as a line, that has endpoints you can connect to other shapes. The terms *connector* and *1-D shape* are sometimes used interchangeably. See also *2-D shape; connector; endpoint.*

2-D shape A shape, such as a rectangle or ellipse, that has up to eight selection handles that you can use for resizing. To connect 2-D shapes to each other, you must use a 1-D shape. See also *1-D shape.*

alignment box The rectangle that appears around shapes as you move them, which you use to align shapes and objects with guides, the grid, and other shapes. See also *selection box.*

attributes Qualities of a shape that you can format, including text font and color; line color, ends, weight, and pattern; and fill color, pattern, and shadow.

backbone The physical network configuration, or topology, that you can depict in a network diagram by using a shape such as the **Ethernet** shape on the **Basic Networks Shapes** stencil. See also *network ring.*

background A shape from the **Backgrounds** stencil that applies a decorative background to a drawing.

begin point The selection handle that appears at the start of a selected 1-D shape and is marked by an ×. See also *endpoint; end point.*

building shell The outline of a room or building that includes walls, windows, doors, and other structural elements. You can create a building shell with the **Office Layout** template.

closed shape A 2-D shape, such as a box, with a solid border. You can apply a fill color and pattern to a closed shape. See also *2-D shape; open shape.*

color scheme A set of coordinated colors that you can apply to an entire diagram and its shapes by clicking the **Color Schemes** command on the **Tools** menu. Not all diagram types support the use of a color scheme. When that is the case, the command does not appear on the **Tools** menu.

connected drawing Any Visio diagram type that shows shapes connected by connectors, such as flowcharts, network diagrams, and organization charts.

Glossary

Connection
point

connection point A point on a shape where you can attach a connector or 1-D shape. Each connection point appears as a blue mark on a shape when the **Connection Points** command is selected on the **View** menu.

connector A 1-D shape designed to connect other shapes. The **Connectors** stencil in the **Visio Extras** folder contains a variety of connector shapes for use in any drawing type. See also *1-D shape.*

Control handle

control handle A yellow diamond-shaped handle that controls a shape's behavior in special ways. Depending on the shape, a control handle might adjust the position of a line, reshape an arrow, or connect to other shapes. To find out what a control handle does, point to the handle to display a ScreenTip.

Control point

control point The circular handle that appears on a line, arc, or spline when you select it with the Pencil tool. You can drag a control point to change the curve of an arc or ellipse.

Crop tool

crop To reduce the size of an imported picture. You use the Crop tool to drag one of the picture's selection handles to the desired size, and then you drag the picture to frame the portion of it you want to see.

custom property Information about a shape, which appears in the **Custom Properties** window. For example, a shape that represents office furniture can have custom properties that identify its inventory number, owner, and location. You can enter values for a custom property and define your own custom properties for a shape.

docked window A window that is attached to a side of the drawing page window. For example, stencils are docked by default on the left side of the Visio window. See also *floating window; stencil.*

drag and drop To use the mouse to move a shape from a stencil to a drawing page. When you release the mouse, you drop the shape on the page, creating an instance of the master shape. See also *instance; master shape; stencil.*

drawing file A file that stores one or more Visio drawings. By default, drawing files have the file extension .vsd.

drawing page The printable area in the Visio window that contains a drawing. Each drawing page has a size, which usually corresponds to a standard printer paper size, and other properties that you can change with the **Page Setup** command on the **File** menu.

drawing scale A measure of the relationship between real-world sizes or distances and the sizes represented in a Visio drawing. For example, an office layout might have a drawing scale of one foot of actual distance to one inch in the drawing. To set a drawing scale, click the **Page Setup** command on the **File** menu.

dynamic grid A dotted line that appears on the screen when you drag a shape near another shape. The dynamic grid shows the optimal alignment. To turn on the dynamic grid, click the **Snap & Glue** command on the **Tools** menu.

Eccentricity handles

eccentricity handle The circle that appears at each end of a dotted line when a control point of an arc is selected with the Pencil tool. You can change the way an arc leans by dragging an eccentricity handle.

embed To paste or insert an object, such as text or a group of shapes, from one program into a file created in another program. The embedded object becomes part of the file, but you can double-click it to edit it in its original program. See also *link*.

end point The selection handle that appears at the end of a selected 1-D shape and is marked by a +. See also *begin point; endpoint*.

Endpoints

endpoint Either of the selection handles that appears at the beginning or end of a selected 1-D shape. The endpoint at the beginning of the shape (begin point) is marked by an ×. The endpoint at the end of the shape (end point) is marked by a +.

field Placeholder text that Visio uses to display dates or other information that is in a shape. You can insert a field into text with the **Field** command on the **Insert** menu.

fill The color and pattern inside a shape. The default fill is solid white.

floating window A window that you can display and move anywhere within the Visio window. For example, you can drag a stencil into the drawing page to display it in a floating window. See also *docked window*.

format To apply a style or attribute that changes the look of a shape or text. For example, you can format a shape to change the thickness and color of its lines, the color and pattern inside the shape, and its font.

Gantt bar A bar in a Gantt chart that represents the duration of a task.

Gantt chart A diagram type you create in Visio with the **Gantt Chart** template that describes the discrete tasks associated with a project. In a Gantt chart, bars represent the duration of each task within a timescale that is displayed in the chart.

247

glue Shape behavior that causes one shape to stay connected to another, even if the shape to which it is glued moves.

grid Nonprinting horizontal and vertical lines displayed at regular intervals on the drawing page. The grid makes it easier to align shapes and position them precisely.

group A shape composed of one or more shapes. A group can also include other groups and objects from other programs. You can move and size a group as a single shape, but its members retain their original appearance and attributes. You can also subselect individual shapes in the group to edit them. See also *subselect*.

guide A visual reference line that you can drag from the horizontal or vertical ruler onto the drawing page to help position and align shapes precisely. Guides do not appear on the printed page.

instance A copy of a master shape that Visio adds to your drawing when you drag a shape from a stencil onto the page.

interval marker A shape used to designate a period of time in a diagram created with the **Timeline** template.

landscape orientation A setting that creates a printed page or drawing page that is wider than it is tall. You can change page orientation in Visio with the **Page Setup** command on the **File** menu. The orientation of the printed page and drawing page can differ. See also *portrait orientation*.

layer A named category to which shapes are assigned in some diagram types, such as office layouts and network diagrams. You can organize shapes in your drawing by selectively viewing, editing, printing, or locking layers, and you can control whether you can snap and glue shapes on a layer.

line The border that surrounds a shape. The default line is solid black.

line end A pattern, such as an arrowhead, that can appear on the ends of 1-D shapes.

link To create a dynamic link from one file to another so that the contents of the original file appear in the linked file. When changes are made to the original file, you can update the link so that the most recent version of the object appears in the linked file. See also *embed*.

lock A setting that limits the ways you can change a shape. For example, a lock can prevent you from resizing a shape using the selection handle. When you select a locked shape, padlocks often appear on the handles. See also *padlock*.

master shape A predefined shape stored on a stencil. You drag a master shape from a stencil onto a drawing to create an instance of the master.

measurement units The measurement system used in a drawing and displayed on the rulers. You specify the measurement units (inches, centimeters, points, miles, and so on) with the **Page Setup** command on the **File** menu.

merge shapes To create a new shape by combining or splitting apart existing shapes using an **Operations** command on the **Shape** menu.

merge windows To combine windows by dragging a window, such as the **Pan & Zoom** window, into another, such as the **Shapes** window. Merging consolidates windows to save space on the screen.

milestone A shape from the **Timeline Shapes** stencil that shows a significant date in a timeline.

network ring The physical configuration or topology of a network that shows the configuration of cables, computers, and other peripherals. To create a network diagram, start with the **Basic Network** template.

object linking and embedding See *OLE*.

OLE In Microsoft Windows, the ability to link or embed a shape or other object created in one program, such as Visio, into a document created in a different program, such as Microsoft Word.

open shape A shape that does not have a continuous border, such as a line or arc. You cannot apply fill color or patterns to open shapes. See also *closed shape*.

padlock A type of selection handle that appears when you select a shape that is locked to prevent certain types of actions. See also *lock*.

page breaks Gray lines that appear on the drawing page when you click the **Page Breaks** command on the **View** menu. Page breaks show you where the page will break when you print a large diagram.

pan To change the view by moving the drawing page. You can use the horizontal and vertical scroll bars in the Visio window to pan a drawing, or you can use the keyboard shortcut: Hold down the Shift and Ctrl keys as you drag with the right mouse button.

pasteboard The blue area around the drawing page, which you can use as a temporary holding area for shapes. Shapes on the pasteboard are saved with a drawing but not printed.

picture A graphic file created in another program or clip art that you can add to a Visio diagram. To insert a picture, click the **Picture** command on the **Insert** menu.

point-to-point connection A connection between shapes in which the endpoint of a connector stays attached to a particular point on a shape, even when the shape is moved.

portrait orientation A setting that creates a printed page or drawing page that is taller than it is wide. You can change page orientation in Visio with the **Page Setup** command on the **File** menu. The orientation of the printed page and drawing page can differ. See also *landscape orientation*.

primary shape The first shape you select in a multiple selection, which can affect the outcome of a command, including the **Distribute Shapes** and **Operations** commands on the **Shape** menu.

report A collection of information about a drawing based on the properties stored with the drawing's shapes. To create a report, you click the **Report** command on the **Tools** menu. When you run a report, you can generate the output as a shape, a Microsoft Excel file, or an HTML file.

report definition The settings and shape properties included in a report, which you can customize with the **Report** command on the **Tools** menu.

rulers The horizontal and vertical rulers that appear on the top and side of the drawing page, which you can hide and show by clicking **Rulers** on the **View** menu. The rulers display the units of measurement specified by the **Page Setup** command on the **File** menu.

ScreenTip Descriptive text that appears in a box when you point to an item on the toolbar, a master shape on a stencil, or a control handle on a shape.

select To click a shape so that it becomes the focus of the next action. Selected shapes display handles. Selected text is highlighted.

Selection handle

selection handle One of the handles that appear on a selected shape. Visio displays different types of selection handles depending on the tool you used to select the shape.

selection box The dotted line that surrounds a shape and shows that it is selected.

shape An object that is created using the Visio drawing tools or commands, or an instance of a master shape on a drawing page.

shape-to-shape connection A connection between shapes in which the endpoint of a connector stays attached to a shape at the closest point, even when you move the shape.

shortcut menu The menu that appears when you right-click a shape. Many Visio shapes have special commands that appear only on a shortcut menu.

snap The way a shape aligns itself automatically with the nearest grid line or guide.

Freeform Tool

spline A curve that you create with the Freeform tool, which technically creates a non-uniform rational B-spline (NURBS).

stacking order The order in which shapes overlap other shapes on the page. You can change stacking order with the **Order** commands on the **Shape** menu.

stencil A Visio file that stores a collection of master shapes that you can drag into a drawing. Stencil files have the file extension .vss.

subselect To select an individual shape within a group.

Pencil Tool

symmetry The direction in which an arc leans, which you can change by adjusting an arc's eccentricity handles with the Pencil tool.

synchronized copy In a drawing created by the **Organization Chart** template or wizard, a copy of a shape or several shapes that remain synchronized with the originals as changes are made. For example, you can make a synchronized copy of a company's department on a new page and then change an employee's title. The title change will be reflected on the original page as well.

template A Visio file that starts a new drawing and opens one or more stencils. A template can also contain settings for a particular drawing type, for example, the appropriate drawing scale and grid. Template files have the file extension .vst.

Text Block

text block The text area associated with a shape that appears when you click the shape with the Text Block tool or select the shape and start typing. You can size a text block and move a text block in relation to its shape.

theme An option available in a drawing created by the **Organization Chart** template or wizard that applies decorative formatting to all of the organization chart shapes.

tile *1.* To arrange windows side by side; for example, by using the **Tile** command on the **Window** menu. *2.* To print oversized drawing pages on multiple sheets of paper so that they can be assembled into a complete drawing.

timeline A linear graphic that represents a specific period of time and the events that occur during that time. You create a timeline in Visio using the **Timeline** template.

units of measure See *measurement units*.

Vertex

vertex A diamond-shaped handle that appears when you select a shape with the Pencil tool. Each vertex defines a point at the beginning or end of a line segment.

Visio table shape A type of shape that Visio can create when you run a report using the **Report** command on the **Tools** menu. Visio displays the report information in a table shape.

zoom The degree of magnification of a drawing. A zoom of 100% displays the drawing page at the same size it will be when it is printed.

Index

N

naming
master shapes, 205–7
name fields in organization charts, 106–7
tasks in Gantt charts, 99

network diagrams
aligning shapes in, 154–56
backbones added to, 150, 151
backgrounds added to, 156
color schemes added to, 156–57
creating, 150–54
hardware shapes in, 157
network rings added to, 150
network shapes in, 157
remote connections added to, 153
templates for, 149, 150–54
workstation shapes in, 151, 157

New down arrow, 9
New Drawing task pane, 4–5, *4–5*, 6
non-uniform rational B-spline (NURBS), 188
nudging (moving) shapes in flowcharts, 67–68
NURBS (non-uniform rational B-spline), 188

O

Object dialog box (Microsoft Office), 167–68, *167, 168*
ODBC-compliant database applications, 106
office layout
creating, *128,* 128–34
layers in, 139–42
pictures imported into, 143–47
shapes in
doors, 135–36
furniture shapes, 138
wall shapes, 129–32
window shapes, 136–37
templates for, 127–28, 129–33, 143

Office Layout template, 127–28, 129–33, 143
Office, Microsoft. *See* Microsoft Office
one-dimensional shapes. *See* 1-D (one-dimensional) and 2-D (two-dimensional) shapes
Open Database Connectivity (ODBC)-compliant database applications, 106
Open dialog box, 11, *11*
open shapes, 188
Open Stencil dialog box, 14, 210–11
Options dialog box, 15, 113, 120, *120*
Options tab in Customize Dialog box, 12, *12*
Organization Chart template, 2, 105, 107–10, 118–21
organization charts
backgrounds added to, 118–20, 120–21
color schemes added to, 119–20
creating, 106–10
custom properties, 111–14
customizing, 118–21
described, 105
design themes added to, 118, 120
employee name fields, 106–7
hyperlinks in, 114, 117–18
importing data into, 106–10
layout, 114–18
multi-paged, 114
opening, 119
pictures in backgrounds, 120–21
position shapes in, 105, 157
Reports to fields, 106–7
synchronized copies of, 114, 116, 117

zooming in and out in Web browsers, 124
orientation of pages before printing, 56

P

padlock handles, 77, 77
page breaks, previewing, 55, 56
Page Setup dialog box
backgrounds applied to specific pages in, 119–20
drawing scale set in, 130, *130*
orientation of pages set in, 75, 210, *210*
page size set in, 55, *55,* 57–58, *58*
page tabs, 6, 7
pages. *See also specific page types*
previewing, *55,* 56–59, *57*
setting size, 55, 56, 57–58
Pan & Zoom window, 10, *10,* 13–14
panning drawing pages, 7, 10. *See also* Pan & Zoom window
Paste Special dialog box (Microsoft Office), *180,* 182–83, *182*
pasteboard, 6, 7
patterns, filling shapes with, 198–99
Pencil tool, 188, 189–90, 200, 201
Picture dialog box, 146–47, *146*
pictures
formatting (editing), 143, 146–47
importing, 143–47
inserting, 145-46
inserting into backgrounds, 120–21
previewing, 145
resizing, 146
transparent, 146–47

About the Authors

Jennifer Angier has fifteen years' experience writing and editing for training, technical, marketing, and employee communications purposes. For six of those years, she has specialized in creating online and print materials about technical subjects for non-technical audiences. Ms. Angier was editor for *Microsoft Outlook 2000 Step by Step*.

Nanette J. Eaton is an award-winning software writer and author of *Microsoft Visio 2002 Inside Out* and *Microsoft Works 2001 Step by Step*, published by Microsoft Press. Formerly a managing Web editor and senior technical writer at Visio, she has written more than 20 user manuals and programmer guides.

Lori Schultz Goff is a Seattle-based technical writer with more than ten years of software industry experience. She began her career writing training manuals for Microsoft developers. A former senior online help developer at Visio, she has written award-winning documentation about Visio products for eight years.

Judy Lemke has more than seven years' experience writing about and working with Microsoft Visio products. During this time, she has written Visio end-user documentation, developer documentation, and award-winning training materials.

The manuscript for this book was prepared using Microsoft Word 2000. Pages were composed by Resources Online using Adobe FrameMaker+SGML 6.0 for Windows, with text in Garamond and display type in Franklin Gothic. Composed pages were delivered to the printer as electronic prepress files.

Writing, editing, production, and graphic services were provided by Resources Online. The project team included:

Project Manager:	Sharon Evans
Editorial Team:	Janice Bultmann
	Jill Carlsen
	Norreen Holmes
Graphics & Production:	April Richards
	Pamela MacFetridge
	Sharon Evans
Index:	Katrina Lemke

Resources Online produces top-quality instructional products that help business professionals master new technologies. Its team of content and instructional design experts deliver authoritative learning resources in print, CD, DVD, Web, and video formats.

Contact Resources Online at:

- ■ E-mail: info@ronline.com
- ■ Web site: *www.ronline.com*

Work smarter
as you experience
Office XP
inside out!

You know your way around the Office suite. Now dig into Microsoft Office XP applications and *really* put your PC to work! These supremely organized references pack hundreds of timesaving solutions, troubleshooting tips and tricks, and handy workarounds in concise, fast-answer format. All of this comprehensive information goes deep into the nooks and crannies of each Office application and accessory. Discover the best and fastest ways to perform everyday tasks, and challenge yourself to new levels of Office mastery with INSIDE OUT titles!

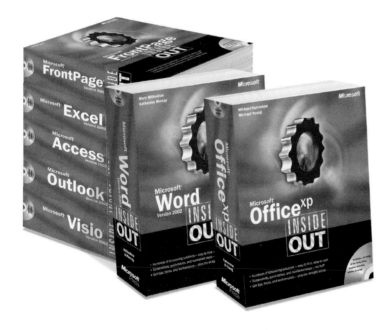

- MICROSOFT® OFFICE XP INSIDE OUT
- MICROSOFT WORD VERSION 2002 INSIDE OUT
- MICROSOFT EXCEL VERSION 2002 INSIDE OUT
- MICROSOFT OUTLOOK® VERSION 2002 INSIDE OUT
- MICROSOFT ACCESS VERSION 2002 INSIDE OUT
- MICROSOFT FRONTPAGE® VERSION 2002 INSIDE OUT
- MICROSOFT VISIO® VERSION 2002 INSIDE OUT

Microsoft®

mspress.microsoft.com

Self-paced
training
that works
as hard as you do!

Information-packed STEP BY STEP courses are the most effective way to teach yourself how to complete tasks with Microsoft® Office XP. Numbered steps and scenario-based lessons with practice files on CD-ROM make it easy to find your way while learning tasks and procedures. Work through every lesson or choose your own starting point—with STEP BY STEP modular design and straightforward writing style, *you* drive the instruction. And the books are constructed with lay-flat binding so you can follow the text with both hands at the keyboard. Select STEP BY STEP titles also provide complete, cost-effective preparation for the Microsoft Office User Specialist (MOUS) credential. It's an excellent way for you or your organization to take a giant step toward workplace productivity.

- **Microsoft Office XP Step by Step**
  ISBN 0-7356-1294-3

- **Microsoft Word Version 2002 Step by Step**
  ISBN 0-7356-1295-1

- **Microsoft Excel Version 2002 Step by Step**
  ISBN 0-7356-1296-X

- **Microsoft PowerPoint® Version 2002 Step by Step**
  ISBN 0-7356-1297-8

- **Microsoft Outlook® Version 2002 Step by Step**
  ISBN 0-7356-1298-6

- **Microsoft FrontPage® Version 2002 Step by Step**
  ISBN 0-7356-1300-1

- **Microsoft Access Version 2002 Step by Step**
  ISBN 0-7356-1299-4

- **Microsoft Project Version 2002 Step by Step**
  ISBN 0-7356-1301-X

- **Microsoft Visio® Version 2002 Step by Step**
  ISBN 0-7356-1302-8

Microsoft®

mspress.microsoft.com

Target your
solution *and fix it*
yourself—*fast!*

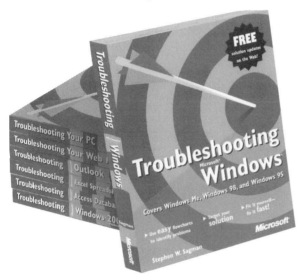

When you're stuck with a computer problem, you need answers right now. *Troubleshooting* books can help. They'll guide you to the source of the problem and show you how to solve it right away. Use easy diagnostic flowcharts to identify problems. Get ready solutions with clear, step-by-step instructions. Go to quick-access charts with *Top 20 Problems* and *Prevention Tips*. Find even more solutions with handy *Tips* and *Quick Fixes*. Walk through the remedy with plenty of screen shots to keep you on track. Find what you need fast with the extensive, easy-reference index. And keep trouble at bay with the Troubleshooting Web site—updated every month with new FREE problem-solving information. Get the answers you need to get back to business fast with *Troubleshooting* books.

Get a **Free**
e-mail newsletter, updates,
special offers, links to related books,
and more when you

register on line!

Register your Microsoft Press® title on our Web site and you'll get a FREE subscription to our e-mail newsletter, *Microsoft Press Book Connections.* You'll find out about newly released and upcoming books and learning tools, online events, software downloads, special offers and coupons for Microsoft Press customers, and information about major Microsoft® product releases. You can also read useful additional information about all the titles we publish, such as detailed book descriptions, tables of contents and indexes, sample chapters, links to related books and book series, author biographies, and reviews by other customers.

Registration is easy. Just visit this Web page and fill in your information:

http://www.microsoft.com/mspress/register

Microsoft®

Proof of Purchase

Use this page as proof of purchase if participating in a promotion or rebate offer on this title. Proof of purchase must be used in conjunction with other proof(s) of payment such as your dated sales receipt—see offer details.

Microsoft® Visio® Version 2002 Step by Step
0-7356-1302-8

CUSTOMER NAME

Microsoft Press, PO Box 97017, Redmond, WA 98073-9830

MICROSOFT LICENSE AGREEMENT
Book Companion CD

IMPORTANT—READ CAREFULLY: This Microsoft End-User License Agreement ("EULA") is a legal agreement between you (either an individual or an entity) and Microsoft Corporation for the Microsoft product identified above, which includes computer software and may include associated media, printed materials, and "online" or electronic documentation ("SOFTWARE PRODUCT"). Any component included within the SOFTWARE PRODUCT that is accompanied by a separate End-User License Agreement shall be governed by such agreement and not the terms set forth below. By installing, copying, or otherwise using the SOFTWARE PRODUCT, you agree to be bound by the terms of this EULA. If you do not agree to the terms of this EULA, you are not authorized to install, copy, or otherwise use the SOFTWARE PRODUCT; you may, however, return the SOFTWARE PRODUCT, along with all printed materials and other items that form a part of the Microsoft product that includes the SOFTWARE PRODUCT, to the place you obtained them for a full refund.

SOFTWARE PRODUCT LICENSE

The SOFTWARE PRODUCT is protected by United States copyright laws and international copyright treaties, as well as other intellectual property laws and treaties. The SOFTWARE PRODUCT is licensed, not sold.

1. **GRANT OF LICENSE.** This EULA grants you the following rights:

   a. **Software Product.** You may install and use one copy of the SOFTWARE PRODUCT on a single computer. The primary user of the computer on which the SOFTWARE PRODUCT is installed may make a second copy for his or her exclusive use on a portable computer.

   b. **Storage/Network Use.** You may also store or install a copy of the SOFTWARE PRODUCT on a storage device, such as a network server, used only to install or run the SOFTWARE PRODUCT on your other computers over an internal network; however, you must acquire and dedicate a license for each separate computer on which the SOFTWARE PRODUCT is installed or run from the storage device. A license for the SOFTWARE PRODUCT may not be shared or used concurrently on different computers.

   c. **License Pak.** If you have acquired this EULA in a Microsoft License Pak, you may make the number of additional copies of the computer software portion of the SOFTWARE PRODUCT authorized on the printed copy of this EULA, and you may use each copy in the manner specified above. You are also entitled to make a corresponding number of secondary copies for portable computer use as specified above.

   d. **Sample Code.** Solely with respect to portions, if any, of the SOFTWARE PRODUCT that are identified within the SOFTWARE PRODUCT as sample code (the "SAMPLE CODE"):

      i. **Use and Modification.** Microsoft grants you the right to use and modify the source code version of the SAMPLE CODE, *provided* you comply with subsection (d)(iii) below. You may not distribute the SAMPLE CODE, or any modified version of the SAMPLE CODE, in source code form.

      ii. **Redistributable Files.** Provided you comply with subsection (d)(iii) below, Microsoft grants you a nonexclusive, royalty-free right to reproduce and distribute the object code version of the SAMPLE CODE and of any modified SAMPLE CODE, other than SAMPLE CODE, or any modified version thereof, designated as not redistributable in the Readme file that forms a part of the SOFTWARE PRODUCT (the "Non-Redistributable Sample Code"). All SAMPLE CODE other than the Non-Redistributable Sample Code is collectively referred to as the "REDISTRIBUTABLES."

      iii. **Redistribution Requirements.** If you redistribute the REDISTRIBUTABLES, you agree to: (i) distribute the REDISTRIBUTABLES in object code form only in conjunction with and as a part of your software application product; (ii) not use Microsoft's name, logo, or trademarks to market your software application product; (iii) include a valid copyright notice on your software application product; (iv) indemnify, hold harmless, and defend Microsoft from and against any claims or lawsuits, including attorney's fees, that arise or result from the use or distribution of your software application product; and (v) not permit further distribution of the REDISTRIBUTABLES by your end user. Contact Microsoft for the applicable royalties due and other licensing terms for all other uses and/or distribution of the REDISTRIBUTABLES.

2. **DESCRIPTION OF OTHER RIGHTS AND LIMITATIONS.**

   • **Limitations on Reverse Engineering, Decompilation, and Disassembly.** You may not reverse engineer, decompile, or disassemble the SOFTWARE PRODUCT, except and only to the extent that such activity is expressly permitted by applicable law notwithstanding this limitation.

   • **Separation of Components.** The SOFTWARE PRODUCT is licensed as a single product. Its component parts may not be separated for use on more than one computer.

   • **Rental.** You may not rent, lease, or lend the SOFTWARE PRODUCT.

   • **Support Services.** Microsoft may, but is not obligated to, provide you with support services related to the SOFTWARE PRODUCT ("Support Services"). Use of Support Services is governed by the Microsoft policies and programs described in the user manual, in "online" documentation, and/or in other Microsoft-provided materials. Any supplemental software code provided to you as part of the Support Services shall be considered part of the SOFTWARE PRODUCT and subject to the terms and conditions of this EULA. With respect to technical information you provide to Microsoft as part of the Support Services, Microsoft may use such information for its business purposes, including for product support and development. Microsoft will not utilize such technical information in a form that personally identifies you.

- **Software Transfer.** You may permanently transfer all of your rights under this EULA, provided you retain no copies, you transfer all of the SOFTWARE PRODUCT (including all component parts, the media and printed materials, any upgrades, this EULA, and, if applicable, the Certificate of Authenticity), **and** the recipient agrees to the terms of this EULA.

- **Termination.** Without prejudice to any other rights, Microsoft may terminate this EULA if you fail to comply with the terms and conditions of this EULA. In such event, you must destroy all copies of the SOFTWARE PRODUCT and all of its component parts.

3. **COPYRIGHT.** All title and copyrights in and to the SOFTWARE PRODUCT (including but not limited to any images, photographs, animations, video, audio, music, text, SAMPLE CODE, REDISTRIBUTABLES, and "applets" incorporated into the SOFTWARE PRODUCT) and any copies of the SOFTWARE PRODUCT are owned by Microsoft or its suppliers. The SOFTWARE PRODUCT is protected by copyright laws and international treaty provisions. Therefore, you must treat the SOFTWARE PRODUCT like any other copyrighted material **except** that you may install the SOFTWARE PRODUCT on a single computer provided you keep the original solely for backup or archival purposes. You may not copy the printed materials accompanying the SOFTWARE PRODUCT.

4. **U.S. GOVERNMENT RESTRICTED RIGHTS.** The SOFTWARE PRODUCT and documentation are provided with RESTRICTED RIGHTS. Use, duplication, or disclosure by the Government is subject to restrictions as set forth in subparagraph (c)(1)(ii) of the Rights in Technical Data and Computer Software clause at DFARS 252.227-7013 or subparagraphs (c)(1) and (2) of the Commercial Computer Software—Restricted Rights at 48 CFR 52.227-19, as applicable. Manufacturer is Microsoft Corporation/One Microsoft Way/Redmond, WA 98052-6399.

5. **EXPORT RESTRICTIONS.** You agree that you will not export or re-export the SOFTWARE PRODUCT, any part thereof, or any process or service that is the direct product of the SOFTWARE PRODUCT (the foregoing collectively referred to as the "Restricted Components"), to any country, person, entity, or end user subject to U.S. export restrictions. You specifically agree not to export or re-export any of the Restricted Components (i) to any country to which the U.S. has embargoed or restricted the export of goods or services, which currently include, but are not necessarily limited to, Cuba, Iran, Iraq, Libya, North Korea, Sudan, and Syria, or to any national of any such country, wherever located, who intends to transmit or transport the Restricted Components back to such country; (ii) to any end user who you know or have reason to know will utilize the Restricted Components in the design, development, or production of nuclear, chemical, or biological weapons; or (iii) to any end user who has been prohibited from participating in U.S. export transactions by any federal agency of the U.S. government. You warrant and represent that neither the BXA nor any other U.S. federal agency has suspended, revoked, or denied your export privileges.

DISCLAIMER OF WARRANTY

NO WARRANTIES OR CONDITIONS. MICROSOFT EXPRESSLY DISCLAIMS ANY WARRANTY OR CONDITION FOR THE SOFTWARE PRODUCT. THE SOFTWARE PRODUCT AND ANY RELATED DOCUMENTATION ARE PROVIDED "AS IS" WITHOUT WARRANTY OR CONDITION OF ANY KIND, EITHER EXPRESS OR IMPLIED, INCLUDING, WITHOUT LIMITATION, THE IMPLIED WARRANTIES OF MERCHANTABILITY, FITNESS FOR A PARTICULAR PURPOSE, OR NONINFRINGEMENT. THE ENTIRE RISK ARISING OUT OF USE OR PERFORMANCE OF THE SOFTWARE PRODUCT REMAINS WITH YOU.

LIMITATION OF LIABILITY. TO THE MAXIMUM EXTENT PERMITTED BY APPLICABLE LAW, IN NO EVENT SHALL MICROSOFT OR ITS SUPPLIERS BE LIABLE FOR ANY SPECIAL, INCIDENTAL, INDIRECT, OR CONSEQUENTIAL DAMAGES WHATSOEVER (INCLUDING, WITHOUT LIMITATION, DAMAGES FOR LOSS OF BUSINESS PROFITS, BUSINESS INTERRUPTION, LOSS OF BUSINESS INFORMATION, OR ANY OTHER PECUNIARY LOSS) ARISING OUT OF THE USE OF OR INABILITY TO USE THE SOFTWARE PRODUCT OR THE PROVISION OF OR FAILURE TO PROVIDE SUPPORT SERVICES, EVEN IF MICROSOFT HAS BEEN ADVISED OF THE POSSIBILITY OF SUCH DAMAGES. IN ANY CASE, MICROSOFT'S ENTIRE LIABILITY UNDER ANY PROVISION OF THIS EULA SHALL BE LIMITED TO THE GREATER OF THE AMOUNT ACTUALLY PAID BY YOU FOR THE SOFTWARE PRODUCT OR US$5.00; PROVIDED, HOWEVER, IF YOU HAVE ENTERED INTO A MICROSOFT SUPPORT SERVICES AGREEMENT, MICROSOFT'S ENTIRE LIABILITY REGARDING SUPPORT SERVICES SHALL BE GOVERNED BY THE TERMS OF THAT AGREEMENT. BECAUSE SOME STATES AND JURISDICTIONS DO NOT ALLOW THE EXCLUSION OR LIMITATION OF LIABILITY, THE ABOVE LIMITATION MAY NOT APPLY TO YOU.

MISCELLANEOUS

This EULA is governed by the laws of the State of Washington USA, except and only to the extent that applicable law mandates governing law of a different jurisdiction.

Should you have any questions concerning this EULA, or if you desire to contact Microsoft for any reason, please contact the Microsoft subsidiary serving your country, or write: Microsoft Sales Information Center/One Microsoft Way/Redmond, WA 98052-6399.

New Features in Visio 2002

The same AutoCorrect, AutoUpdate, AutoSave, and AutoRecovery features in Microsoft Office XP

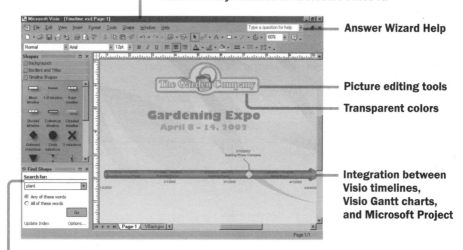

Answer Wizard Help

Picture editing tools

Transparent colors

Integration between Visio timelines, Visio Gantt charts, and Microsoft Project

Find Shape command

Common Keyboard Shortcuts

Ctrl + Shift + click	Zoom in
Ctrl + Shift + right-click	Zoom out
Ctrl + Shift + drag a rectangle	Zoom in on a selected area
Ctrl + Shift + right-drag the page	Pan
Ctrl + drag a shape	Duplicate the shape
← ↓ ↑ →	Nudge the selected shape
Ctrl + Z	Undo the last action
Ctrl + Y	Redo the last action
Ctrl + V	Find text in the diagram
Ctrl + L	Rotate the selected shape left
Ctrl + R	Rotate the selected shape right
Ctrl + O	Open a document
Ctrl + S	Save the open document
Ctrl + A	Select all shapes on the drawing page
Ctrl + Shift + B	Send the selected shape to the back
Ctrl + Shift + F	Bring the selected shape to the front
Shift + F4	Go to page
F7	Check spelling

To create a new drawing based on a template

1. On the **File** menu, point to **New**, and then click **Choose Drawing Type**.
2. In the **Category** list, click a category.
3. In the **Template** area, click the template you want.

To open a stencil containing more shapes

1. On the Standard toolbar, click the **Open Stencil** down arrow.
2. In the list of categories, point to a folder, and then click a stencil.

To display long menus instead of personalized menus

1. On the **Tools** menu, click **Customize**.
2. On the **Options** tab, select the **Always show full menus** check box, and then click **OK**.

To insert a page

1. On the **Insert** menu, click **New Page**.
2. In the **Page Setup** dialog box, click **OK** to insert a new page with the same settings as the current page.

To remove a page and everything on it

- Right-click the page tab for the page you want to remove, and then click **Delete Page**.

To find a particular shape

1. On the **File** menu, click **Find Shape** to display the **Find Shape** window.
2. In the **Search for** box, type one or more keywords associated with the shape you want, and then click **Go**.

To connect shapes

1. On the Standard toolbar, click the **Connector Tool** button.
2. Point to the shape until a red border appears around the entire shape (or a point on the shape).
3. Drag to the next shape until a red border appears around the shape (or a point on the shape), and then release the mouse.

To change a shape's fill color

1. Select a shape.
2. On the **Formatting** toolbar, click the **Fill Color** down arrow.
3. Click the color you want.

To apply a color scheme to an entire diagram

1. In a diagram that supports color schemes (such as a flowchart, organization chart, or block diagram), on the **Tools** menu, click **Color Schemes**.
2. In the **Choose a color scheme** list, click an option, and then click **Apply**.

To add text to a shape

- Select a shape, and then type the text you want.

To close a shape's text box after typing

- Click outside the shape or press Esc.

To edit text

1. On the Standard toolbar, click the **Text Tool** button.
2. Click in the text, and then make changes.

To embed a Visio drawing in a Microsoft Office document

1. In Visio, click **Copy Drawing** on the **Edit** menu.
2. Open the Microsoft Office document and display the page you want to add the Visio drawing to.
3. Press Ctrl+V to paste the drawing.

To revise an embedded Visio drawing

- Double-click the drawing to open it for editing in Visio.